Contents

Note from the Editor

Joseph H. Prouser

The current issue of this journal has been prepared and published at a critical and painful time, a watershed moment in the history of the Jewish People and the Jewish State. Israel is at war, defending itself against an existential, genocidal threat in the wake of the attacks and depredations perpetrated by Hamas on October 7, 2023. Those in Israel are living a transformed reality. Those of us in the diaspora cite with conviction the famous epigram of Yehuda Halevi: "My heart is in the East, though I am in the farthest reaches of the West."

In the pages of this journal, Rabbi Chaya Rowen Baker, Dean of the Schechter Rabbinical Seminary in Jerusalem, shares a deeply moving and thoughtful personal account of the Israeli home front and the experience of Israeli civilians since October 7. We are in her debt for her "Letter from Israel." Rabbi Rowen Baker previously served as rabbi of Congregation Ramot Zion in the French Hill neighborhood of Jerusalem, leading that flagship congregation for sixteen years. Ramot Zion's sanctuary is called "Ohel Tuvia"—in memory of Rabbi Theodore Friedman, a past president of the Rabbinical Assembly and pioneer of the Masorti movement in Israel and beyond.

In this issue is reprinted another "Letter from Israel"—this one by Rabbi Friedman—written in the wake of the 1973 Yom Kippur War. The parallels are striking and agonizing. Rabbi Rowen Baker points out that the congregation she would come to lead held its first public services in observance of the High Holy Days of 1973. In personal correspondence, she wrote to me of Rabbi Friedman: "I am honored to follow in his footsteps in this way. And pained that it is necessary." I know this journal's readership joins me in responding: The honor is ours, and even "in the farthest reaches of the West," we share your pain.

We are also privileged to include in this issue JTS Chancellor Emeritus Ismar Schorsch's admiring and inspiring remembrance of his father, Emil Schorsch, and his rabbinate. In an essay rich in history, we read of the Schorsch family, including young Ismar, escaping Nazi Germany in December of 1938: "Relatives in London had secured for us visas to England from its chief rabbi, Joseph H. Hertz, who had been given authority to

MASORTI
The New Journal of Conservative Judaism

VOLUME 68   NUMBER 1   WINTER 2024

A publication of the Rabbinical Assembly, the Jewish Theological Seminary of America,
the Schechter Institutes, Inc., the Seminario Rabínico Latinoamericano,
the Zacharias Frankel College, and the Ziegler School of Rabbinic Studies

Masorti: The New Journal of Conservative Judaism, Volume 68, Number 1, Winter 2023-2024

Masorti: The New Journal of Conservative Judaism is published semiannually under the sponsorship of the Rabbinical Assembly, the Jewish Theological Seminary of America, the Schechter Institutes, Inc., the Seminario Rabínico Latinoamericano, the Zacharias Frankel College, and the Ziegler School of Rabbinic Studies. Members of the Rabbinical Assembly and Cantors Assembly receive an online subscription *gratis*. The annual price for an online subscription is US$18.00. Individual print issues are available for US$18.00 and can be ordered from Ben Yehudah Press.

Article manuscripts, as well as announcements of books for review, are welcome and should be sent to the editor at masortijournal@gmail.com. Books for review can be sent to

Masorti Book Reviews
CSAIR
475 West 250th Street
Bronx, NY 10471

Manuscripts are subject to double-blind peer review by at least two outside readers as well as the editor. Guidelines for submissions are available at https://masortijournal.org/call-for-submissions/.

Published by Ben Yehuda Press
122 Ayers Court #1B
Teaneck, NJ 07666

http://www.BenYehudaPress.com

To subscribe to our monthly book club and support independent Jewish publishing, visit https://www.patreon.com/BenYehudaPress

Ben Yehuda Press books may be purchased at a discount by synagogues, book clubs, and other institutions buying in bulk. For information, please email markets@BenYehudaPress.com

ISBN13 978-1-953829-72-6

24 25 26 / 10 9 8 7 6 5 4 3 3   20240321

rescue rabbis from Germany. Years later I would quip that the first rabbi to be ordained by the Jewish Theological Seminary in New York in 1894 was destined to rescue the child who had just turned three and would eventually become the institution's sixth chancellor in 1986." Chancellor Schorsch writes of his father's depth of determination to become a rabbi: "A deeply religious personality, he believed that surviving the chaos of war destined him to join the forces of those committed to preventing its recurrence."

Alas, we have not been spared the tragedy of recurrent war.

As Purim and Pesach approach, with their own foundation in genocidal attacks upon the Jewish People, may we be privileged to receive, as Rabbi Rowen Baker explains is now the customary formulation in the Jewish State, *besorot tovot*: only good news.

Joseph H. Prouser is rabbi of Temple Emanuel of North Jersey in Franklin Lakes, New Jersey, and editor of this journal.

The Place

Rachel Barenblat

Wherever two gather to learn
is the gateway of heaven.
Have the courage of your convictions
but remember when Mashiach comes
our lenses might change.

When Mashiach comes
all of our old arguments
will become mulch
sustaining the Tree of Life
in the center of the *beit midrash.*

Every soul has a cubby there
to hold siddur, kippah clips, tefillin.
Supernal light always shines—
there's no need for sunrise, so
they rest in velvet sleeping bags.

We'll feel their imprint anyway—
like the wedding ring in a coffee cup
behind the sink for safekeeping
while we're doing dishes
for our beloved without being asked.

We'll always be holding hands
with the Holy Blessed One.
In *'olam haba* our debates
won't sharpen our wits like swords
but sweeten us like dates.

Eden will be everywhere.
Torah's beauty will twine
through our words
like the sapphire of the firmament,
like the heavens, like the sea.

Rabbi Rachel Barenblat, the Velveteen Rabbi, is author of several poetry collections including 70 Faces: Torah Poems (Phoenicia Publishing) and Texts to the Holy (Ben Yehuda Press). A co-founder of Bayit: Building Jewish, she serves Congregation Beth Israel of the Berkshires.

A Rabbi For All Seasons: In Two Registers

Ismar Schorsch

Since stepping down as chancellor of the Jewish Theological Seminary in 2006, I have lived much of my life in reverse, seeking to understand the nature of my roots. On each visit back to Esslingen (where my mother was born) and Hanover (where my fathr served as rabbi from 1927 to 1938), I was asked to speak, and each time I chose to explore an aspect of my father's rabbinate associated with the place. To my surprise, although written separately, the individual pieces added up to a memorable portrait of a rabbi whose deep faith was wrapped in integrity and hard work. Despite the infrequent overlaps, I offer it as if, in retrospect, inspired by a singular vision of the whole. To complete the portrait, I added over the past summer a chapter on my father's twenty-four-year rabbinic career in Pottstown, Pennsylvania, for which I could serve as a primary source. Sometimes our most precious treasure lies buried in our own heirlooms.
— October 13, 2023, Erev Shabbat Bereshit 5784

My Father and the Great War

I wish to express my admiration to Esslingen for its bold and enlightened decision to turn the one hundredthh anniversary of World War I into an ongoing teaching experience for the entire community. At this point, after more than three years of commemoration, instruction, and reflection, I need not rehearse for you the destructive chain reaction set off by the world's first global conflict, rightly called the Great War because it spanned and wrecked the twentieth century. Yet this was a war that was hardly inevitable. In 1931, when Kathé Kollwitz dedicated a memorial to her son Peter, who had been killed in battle on October 30, 1914, she surely spoke for millions when she declared: "there is in our lives a wound that will never heal." Two years earlier, in 1929, Erwin Piscator, the brilliant founder of political theater, who in 1963 would produce in Berlin the explosive drama *The Deputy* (*Der Stellvertreter*) by Rolf Hochhuth, wrote in his book, *Das politische Theater*:

> I reckon time from August 4, 1914. From that day the barometer began to climb: 13 million dead; 11 million

crippled; 50 million soldiers who marched; 6 billion guns; 50 billion cubic meters of gas. What is "personal growth" in the face of that? No one can develop "personally" here. Something else develops him. The war arose before the 20-year old. Destiny. It made every other teacher superfluous.

The most poignant war poem I know was written by Wilfred Owen, destined to die at twenty-five as a British infantryman in 1918, one week before the armistice of November 11. Called "The Parable of the Old Man and the Young," it resonates so deeply because it transforms and magnifies a well-known biblical tale into a nightmare without end. God tests Abraham's faith by instructing him to offer his one and only beloved son as a sacrifice. But, in Owen's bitter poem, Abraham ignores God's last-minute intervention:

> When lo! An angel called him out of heaven,
> Saying, Lay not thy hand upon the lad,
> Neither do anything to him.
> Behold, A ram, caught in a thicket by its horns;
> Offer the ram of Pride instead of him.
> But the old man would not so, but slew his son,
> And half the seed of Europe, one by one.

What stirs me in this lament is that Owen turns the biblical tale on its head. Meant to instruct Abraham that God is no longer to be worshipped by the sacrifice of what we most cherish—our children—the tale is read to prove the very opposite. In the Great War, parents slaughtered their children to false gods on a scale beyond numbers. Although masters of science and technology, European nations were led by moral midgets. Sacrificing our children was still a valid path to national glory and salvation.

In the final line, however, Owen's voice shifts from outrage to compassion. Casualty statistics are comprised of identifiable human beings, born of loving parents, raised in caring communities, and prizing their own individual names. We are incapable of mourning the loss of an aggregate of individuals, only of single human beings created in the image of God.

My father, Emil Schorsch, was such a distinctive individual, a product of Esslingen forever altered by his experience as a *Frontkämpfer*, a veteran of the Western front in the final year of Germany's defeat. He came to Esslingen at the age of seven to take up residence in the *Wilhelmspflege*, the Jewish boarding school named after the king of Württemberg, which was headed by my grandfather Theodor Rothschild. His two older brothers, Joseph and Hugo, had preceded him. The family lived in the small Baden village of Hüngheim where my father, born in 1899, had attended a Catholic *Volksschule* for the first few years of his education. It was in that rural setting that he developed a lifelong love for nature, at the cost of being handicapped by a lack of educational options.

When my father arrived at the *Wilhelmspflege* in 1906, there were about thirty-five youngsters in its school, divided into a lower and upper class, the latter of which was taught by my grandfather. The children no longer wore uniforms and enjoyed a good deal of freedom, although required to take responsibility for a specific daily household chore. Teachers, staff, and children ate together as an extended family, while the Jewish calendar and ritual governed their daily and weekly lives.

My grandfather Theodor, like my father, was a rural Jew. Born in 1876 in Buttenhausen, a village in the eastern part of Württemberg with a substantial Jewish population, Theodor had graduated from the Esslingen teachers' seminary (Protestant) in 1896. That year he came to teach at the *Wilhelmspflege* and four years later married Anna, the daughter of the *Hausvater* Leopold Stern, who unfortunately died suddenly in 1899. By 1901, Theodor was selected to succeed him as *Hausvater* and would remain at the helm until August 1939, when the *Wihelmspflege* was shut down by the Nazi regime. It was Theodor who presided over the two-year construction of the *Wilhelmspflege*'s stately new building atop a prominent hill near the landmark Esslingen castle, which was dedicated on November 11, 1913 in the presence of the king of Württemberg and a host of official dignitaries. On the land surrounding the building Theodor introduced a component of farming to teach his fledglings to work with their hands as well as their minds.

Theodor was a robust outdoorsman with an impressive command of the Latin names of all the trees and plants that grew in southwest Germany. He was also a sensitive and inspiring educator who would counsel his teachers when confronted by the misbehavior of an unruly child to focus on the turmoil in his personal life rather than on the disruption caused by his behavior. Above all, he was devoted to the children in his care and refused to apply for a visa to the United States prior to the *Reichspogromnacht*, in order to forestall the threatened closure of the *Wilhelmspflege* by the Nazis should he do so.

Theodor soon became a surrogate father to Emil. In 1913, when he finished the eighth and final year of the *Volksschule* in the *Wilhelmspflege*, Theodor advised him to apply to the *Lehrerseminar* in Esslingen to become a teacher. My father heeded the advice. Out of the 235 applicants that year, my father was one of the thirty who were accepted. During the next few years, he was the only Jewish student out of a student body of two hundred. But the seminary minimized the friction caused by Saturday classes. At 9:00 in the morning my father was excused until 10:30 to attend religious services in the local synagogue. He did not write on Saturdays, and, if an exam fell on that day, he would stand next to the instructor to give him the answer to write down. In addition to the curriculum of the seminary, my father was required to take twelve hours a week of Hebrew grammar, Bible, Jewish history, Mishnah, and halakhah in order to eventually pass the state exam for a Jewish teacher's license. Not surprisingly, his instructor for Hebrew grammar, Bible, and Jewish history was my grandfather. At the seminary, my father excelled at mathematics and music.

In the summer of 1917, the war finally halted his studies. Having turned eighteen in January, he was drafted into the infantry as a reservist but was soon transferred to a field artillery unit that served directly behind the front line. By June 1918 his unit was shipped to the western front. My father's assignment was to lay the phone lines connecting the artillery to the infantry, a precarious job that carried with it the prospect of a quick promotion. That prospect, though, saved his life, because the son of a general soon displaced him only to be killed on his first time out. Until then his unit had not lost a man.

In the final months of the war his unit beat a steady but orderly retreat along the Aisne River deep inside France, south of Soissons. Before the start of the armistice on November 11, a final air raid subjected his unit to one last drubbing. With no place to hide, my father sat out in the open with his head buried between his knees, awaiting what looked like his inexorable end. The trauma of the moment left him with an insight that would shape his philosophy of life. Imagination should enable us to live our lives from the end. As our candle flickers, what will our life's decisions amount to—a source of meaning and satisfaction or of self-incrimination and regret? On that forsaken battlefield, my father found a measure of skill at music and mathematics to be insufficient to give his life a sense of ultimate purpose. Our final reckoning in the face of death ought to be the compass for mastering life.

My father credited his commanding officer for maintaining the discipline of his troops during the four-hundred-kilometer march back to Marburg and long cherished his personal good wishes to him when their paths parted. In commenting on his life in Germany in later years, my father tended to recall the spontaneous acts of humanity of ordinary Germans toward Jews rather than symptoms of the systemic antisemitism that intensified as the war effort faltered and Weimar replaced the Second Reich.

Thus in my father's occasional recollections there is no trace of the infamous survey of Jewish soldiers initiated by the Prussian war ministry in October 1916, ostensibly to lay to rest the ever louder denunciation that Jews were evading military service. The ministry's unilateral decision signaled the end of the emperor's celebrated declaration of reconciliation as Germany went to war: "I know no parties any longer; I know only Germans." And indeed many barriers fell that defined the second-class citizenship of Germany's Jews. Now, for the first time since their emancipation in 1869, Jews became army officers and entered the upper echelons of the government's bureaucracy. Worse than the hurt and fury aroused among Jews by the intent to do the survey was the inexcusable refusal by the war ministry to ever publish its results, which would have laid the unwarranted charge to rest. In the wake of the bitter acrimony that would swirl around the issue after the war, my father's military service slipped into a contested statistic, one of ten young Jewish men from Esslingen to have served in the army.

Upon his return to Esslingen my father resumed his studies at the *Lehrerseminar* to receive his teaching certification in 1919. Thereafter he taught for eleven months in two different Jewish schools. But the war experience had pushed him to consider the rabbinate for a career, and, on August 19, 1920, he wrote to Professor Markus Brann at the Jewish Theological Seminary in Breslau inquiring what he needed to do to qualify for admission. Breslau had opened in 1854 as the first German modern rabbinical seminary. As a haven for critical Jewish scholarship, Breslau required of its applicants the vaunted *Abitur* diploma of a *Gymnasium*, and of its graduates in addition to ordination from Breslau a doctorate from a German university. For my father the *Abitur* with its heavy dosage of Latin and Greek constituted a formidable barrier. At the *Lehrerseminar* he had studied neither. Brann responded immediately, in part, I suspect, because few young German Jews were applying in the turmoil of the postwar years. An age of rampant secularization also diminished interest in religion. His message, however, offered little consolation: "In truth even today no one can become a well-educated theologian [i.e., rabbi], if he does not have a thorough grounding in Latin and Greek."

But my father was not to be deterred. The hurdles he had to overcome to switch educational tracks, in a society structurally not amenable to switching, attested the depth of his determination to become a rabbi. A deeply religious personality, he believed that surviving the chaos of war destined him to join the forces of those committed to preventing its recurrence. For two years he withdrew to the solitude of the home of his aunt and uncle in Lehrensteinsfeld in Baden to strive to achieve the equivalence of seven years of Greek and nine years of Latin. By March 22, 1924 he had secured a document from the department of higher education in Stuttgart certifying his accomplishment in both languages. In those same years he began his doctoral studies in Tübingen, which he completed in 1925 with a dissertation on *The Teachability of Religion* (*Die Lehrbarkeit der Religion*) published in 1929.

In 1928 my father was ordained by the Breslau seminary and to this day I have the large handwritten Hebrew ordination document on parchment signed by Professor Michael Guttman, the seminary's official ordaining authority, hanging in my office. In a graduating class of three that year, my father was the only student from Germany. While at the seminary he took additional courses at the University of Breslau, among them two years of Arabic, a Semitic language still *de rigueur* for students entering the rabbinate. In his retirement he could still proudly recite for me by heart the opening lines of the first sura of the Quran. In short, a fine memory, a prodigious ability to concentrate, and an iron will combined to help my father scale an intellectual mountain in turbulent weather.

In 1927, already a year before he graduated from Breslau, my father received an invitation from the Jewish community in Hanover to become its junior rabbi (*Ortsrabbiner*). With some 5500 Jews, Hanover was one of the larger Jewish communities in Germany. Its senior rabbi (*Landesrabbiner*), Samuel Freund, had also studied at Breslau. Adding to its attractiveness was the fact that relatives of my father owned a plywood factory nearby and were active members of the community. Both his brothers worked for the firm. Decisive for him, however, was the absence of an organ in the grand sanctuary of its Romanesque synagogue. My father had learned to play the organ in the *Lehrerseminar* and felt strongly that it Christianized the synagogue service. The presence of an organ in the synagogue in Munich prompted him to turn down its invitation to him just prior to accepting Hanover. By the twentieth century the organ had become the most prominent ritual demarcation between Reform and Conservative synagogues in Germany and the United States. In 1935 my father had an opportunity to return to Württemberg when the Jewish community of Stuttgart invited him to fill its pulpit. My mother, the older daughter of Theodor, very much wanted him to accept the offer. As the status of Jews in Germany deteriorated, she desperately wanted to be nearer my grandfather. My father tried to oblige her and asked Stuttgart to remove the organ. But the community refused to accommodate his wishes.

My father and mother married in December 1926. My father did not want to come to Hanover alone. In truth, they never left Esslingen. They would come down from Hanover for vacations, and as my sister, born in 1929, grew older she would take the train to Stuttgart alone, armed with a sign hung around her neck indicating her destination. After the *Wilhemspflege* was plundered in broad daylight on November 10, 1938 and shuttered that summer, Theodor finally did apply at the American consulate in Stuttgart for a United States visa, but by then the waiting list was long and his number distressingly high. With the meager resources available to them, my parents and aunt and uncle (Bertel was Fanny's younger sister) did their utmost to expedite his flight. In the correspondence between them up to December 7, 1941, which survives, one can follow the tortuous decline of his number. But he never came close to being granted a visa and died on July 10, 1944 in Theresienstadt. I still feel the pall that settled over our house in Pottstown when the news of his death arrived.

Not long after my father settled in Hanover he wrote a valuable description of the rural Judaism of Baden-Württemberg in which he grew up and published it in the leading intellectual journal of Weimar Jewry. His voice was that of an informed and engaged observer trying to capture a type of Judaism fast disappearing. Germany's Jews had for a century been in the forefront of the steady migration from the country to the city. Although a eulogy of sorts, the essay is not overly sentimental. The rural Judaism he cherished is intimate, sincere, and utterly natural. It is without pretense and affectation and conspicuously lacks intellectual superstructure or theological justification. In a world saturated with nature, God is a felt reality, a commanding presence to whom one connects through ritual. Observance springs from a sense of obligation and is enacted simply and comfortably.

There is no doubt an undertone of criticism in this depiction of rural Judaism. The positive implied animosity toward an unstated negative. My father bristled quietly at the sterility and artistry of the cathedral synagogue in which he officiated, symbolized by his clerical robe and the *Zylinderhut* ("stovepipe") of the male worshippers. A gifted cantor and decorous service accentuated the dimension of performance but minimized the power of personal prayer. Genuine piety was beyond the reach of part-time, self-conscious Jews.

Thus, on the joyous festival of Simchat Torah he did not linger in the synagogue. The festival celebrates boisterously the completion of the annual Torah reading cycle in the synagogue, even as it launches immediately into the beginning of a new cycle. Having performed his official duties, my father chose to visit the *Stieblach* ("prayer conventicles") of the eastern European Jews in Hanover. By war's end their number had risen to about 1300. He yearned to taste the authenticity and exuberance of their celebration of the festival. Intuitively he sensed the affinity between their expressive piety and the unstaged simplicity of the Judaism of his youth. Neither suffered from a surfeit of choreography.

Although members of the Jewish community by law, the Jews from Eastern Europe were not deemed fully equal because they lacked German citizenship. Accordingly, they were unwelcome in the formal services of the synagogue's main sanctuary, a policy that remained lamentably in force until 1937, when their numbers were needed to constitute the quorum for a public worship service, or minyan. The immigrants tended to be Orthodox, lived in their own neighborhoods, closed their shops on Saturdays, and prayed in one of their three small *Stieblach* run by them. Clearly the discomfort of Hanover's German Jews in the face of their less assimilated coreligionists mirrored the longstanding hostility in German society toward immigrants from the east, intensified by the war, but it also bespoke the anxiety of an insecure minority group in fear of having its own emancipation thrown into jeopardy. Nevertheless, it bears saying that such overt internal discrimination was atypical of German Jewish communal life at the time.

There was little my father could do to alter the institutionalized prejudice in Hanover. Power lay in the hands of a lay board on which the rabbis did not sit. But his actions betrayed a steadfast critical stance. For a decade he enjoyed the loyal and competent secretarial service of a woman who had come from Eastern Europe. Still bolder, he had been invited to Hanover to reconnect its children with the synagogue. Toward that end, not long after his arrival, he set about to create a model community for the young (*eine Jugendgemeinde*) with just fifteen boys as founding members. Its main initial activity was to meet on Saturday afternoons for a *Minḥah* service led by students trained by him, which he always opened with a lesson based on the week's Torah portion. Attendance soon grew to thirty-five and then shot up with the decision to include girls. At the services, the girls sat behind the boys. By the celebration of their first Simchat Torah service, some six hundred children and adolescents filled the room. In due time, with better accommodations, some 150 boys and girls attended Saturday services regularly. Entirely self-governing, the *Jugendgemeinde* quickly supplemented its religious agenda by subdividing into smaller groups for social and athletic activities. By 1932, there were eleven such groups each led by an adult volunteer. The community maintained its cohesion by always praying together on Saturday afternoons.

My father made a sustained effort to include the children of Eastern European parents. The message he delivered incessantly was that Judaism is a religion without religious, partisan, or ethnic divisions. In a tribute to him on his birthday, on January 12, 1935, his young congregants gave heartening evidence that they had internalized his message: "You, Herr Doktor, gave us values that give us for life a firm, enduring stance, that we honor Jews as Jews, that we belong together as Jews…and have no need of internal turmoil."

The leitmotif of this portrait of my father has been the extent to which his life was shaped by his early years in Esslingen. Many aspects of his life in America after March 1940 continued to highlight that indebtedness, not least the love, support, and companionship from his childhood sweetheart from Esslingen, my mother. During his twenty-four years as rabbi of Congregation Mercy and Truth in Pottstown, Pennsylvania, my father also served for twenty-one of them as the civilian Jewish chaplain at the army hospital in Valley Forge. It was the second largest military hospital on the East Coast, and, in 1943, he was invited to become its only Jewish chaplain on a part-time basis. On Wednesdays he would walk its endlessly long halls to visit its wounded Jewish patients and return on Thursday evenings with a few women volunteers from Pottstown to conduct a *Ma'ariv* service, deliver a sermon, and conclude with a collation of kosher corn beef sandwiches. On occasion I would tag along on Thursday evenings. I had a weakness for cold cuts.

No part of my father's rabbinate was more deeply satisfying than his work at Valley Forge, because he, above all, was a genuine *Seelsorger*, the wonderful German word for a clergyman, a caretaker of human souls. His young congregants were the human wreckage of war, the spiritually broken and physically injured in desperate need of comfort, wisdom, and meaning. His own precarious war experience had surely given him insight into their pitiful plight. The senseless horrors of World War I had persuaded him to enter the rabbinate, not to thwart the onset of the next one but to minister to its victims and alleviate their suffering. His rock-solid faith, his love of Judaism, his unpretentious practice, and his well-stocked mind endowed him with the humanity to help fellow Jews and Christians in need.

When my wife and I settled in Riverdale, New York after my own two-year stint in the army as a chaplain, I happened upon a Jewish internist who had served at Valley Forge as an army doctor. His first words to me as we began to exchange pleasantries related to me how impressed he was with the sermons of my father that he heard there during his tour of duty. Again, as so often, I had become the beneficiary of the life lived by my father.

In one of his autobiographical fragments, my father recalls how as a twelve-year-old at the *Wilhelmspflege* he slipped into its empty prayer room on a Saturday afternoon. Inside he proceeded to take out a *sefer Torah* (the Hebrew scroll of parchment on which the Torah is handwritten) from the wooden ark that contained it and walk around the bimah (the table on which it is read) many times, imploring God to reveal Himself to him. In retrospect, the rabbinate became his calling, and his subsequent life of good deeds amply attests that God had answered his prayer.

Religion under Assault

The decision of the city of Hanover to honor the memory of my father by affixing his name to one of its parks fills me with feelings of deep gratitude. Permit me to grace this nook of real estate with a tincture of his spirit.

On January 8, 1937, the board of the Jewish community of Hanover sent my father a letter of deep appreciation for ten years of unstinting service. The tribute spelled out his enormous impact on the conduct of Jewish education. For the young he had revised and reordered the religious instruction they received in the cities' schools, created separate services conducted by them on Saturday afternoons and recreational activities during the week, and even acquired a stand-alone youth center in which to hang out. For the adults he set up a *Lehrhaus* for courses in Hebrew and Judaica and later for preparation for emigration and, above all, preached weekly in the grand Oppler synagogue. The board saluted my father's acute awareness that he needed to counter the indifference of parents to Judaism if he wanted to register any success with their children. It also singled out his determined efforts to fully integrate the children of German-Jewish parents with those of Eastern European parents in his manifold activities for the young. And, finally, the board thanked my father for the welcome funds that he had regularly secured from his relatives to implement his sundry programs.

In responding to the board's effusive praise, my father distinguished between a calling for which one can prepare and a contractual obligation that works as an inner command to which one must give evidence of being called. "I have always striven to think of my work as a holy office for which I must give account and reckoning before God and Judaism." In brief, the *Gemeinde's* words of tribute, encouragement, and assurance of continued employment bespoke its confidence that their young rabbi in his first pulpit had the competence, maturity, and faith to handle and endure tempestuous times.

Emil Schorsch had taken an arduous path to the rabbinate. As a rural Jew from southwestern Germany raised in a Jewish orphanage in Esslingen, he was a graduate not of a *Gymnasium* but of a teachers' seminary. An exposure to near-certain death as a rank non-officer in a German artillery unit in 1918 prompted him to opt for a career in the rabbinate. Facing death, he took no comfort in his expertise in mathematics. After the war he returned to Esslingen to finish its renowned *Lehrerseminar* and began teaching in a Jewish elementary school. But to gain admission to the modern rabbinical school of Breslau, founded in 1854, was no easy matter. He needed to achieve the equivalence of a vaunted *Abitur* with its seven years of Greek and nine years of Latin. Two years of solitary study eventually secured for him the certification from the Württemberg ministry of education and entrance into Breslau, the oldest modern rabbinical school in Germany, in 1922.

By 1927, in his final year in Breslau, he already had an invitation in hand from Hanover as its *Ortsrabbiner* ("city rabbi") under the supervision of Samuel Freund, its *Landrabbiner* ("state rabbi"), also a graduate of Breslau, who had originally come to Hanover in 1907. The handwritten Hebrew ordination on parchment dated 1928 with the wax seal of the Breslau seminary attached still hangs in my office at the Jewish Theological Seminary in New York. In addition to his intensive rabbinical studies, my father had earned a doctorate in Tübingen on the topic of *Die Lehrbarkeit der Religion* (To What Extent Can Religion Be Taught?) plus two years of Arabic at the University of Breslau.

In 1925, the Jewish community (*Gemeinde*) of Hanover numbered 5,521

Jews, of whom 1311 were immigrants from Eastern Europe. While all were members of the *Gemeinde* by law and paid taxes for the maintenance of its communal structure, only those who enjoyed German citizenship could vote, which meant that those from Eastern Europe, most of whom lacked citizenship, were denied the right to vote. Women received the right to vote and run for office in *Gemeinde* elections in 1930, but the *Ostjuden* in Hanover did not until 1937, partly because by then their attendance at services in the Oppler synagogue had become urgent with increasing emigration. My father observed in his memoir that on the Shabbat that coincided with the sudden massive expulsion of Polish Jews from Germany (October 29, 1938), the Oppler synagogue was nearly empty.

Generally, the Eastern Jews of Hanover lived in the poorer neighborhoods of the city, closed their stores on Friday afternoon at 3:00 for Shabbat and prayed in one of their own small *Stieblach* (*Bethäuser*). They also maintained separate religious schools for their children, religious judges for their internal disputes, and slaughterers for kosher meat. Notwithstanding their insularity and far slower pace of assimilation, my father recalled that the *Ostjuden* mixed more freely and intimately with their Christian neighbors than did their German-Jewish coreligionists. In 1931 the centralized welfare budget of the *Gemeinde* approximated some 200,000 Reichsmarks, with some 60 percent of it going to the Jews from Eastern Europe. Yet, despite its deep internal fissures, the Jewish community of Hanover with an annual budget of 350,000 Reichsmarks remained organizationally a viable *Einheitsgemeinde* (i.e., a united Jewish community).

Several local features drew my father to Hanover. First, the religious services in its stunning freestanding Romanesque synagogue designed by Edwin Oppler, its Jewish architect, were conducted without benefit of an organ or German prayers. The stentorian tenor of its celebrated cantor, Israel Alter, filled the dome-covered sanctuary with an authentic blend of traditional and contemporary music. Twice my father turned down invitations to come to Stuttgart, which was but a few kilometers from Esslingen, my mother's birthplace and the orphanage run by her well-known father, Theodor Rothschild, because the synagogue had an organ, the hallmark of radical religious Reform.

But my father also had close relatives in Hanover, who owned the largest plywood factory in Germany in Wiedenbruck, Westphalia. His older brother Joseph was its bureau chief, and when my parents came to Hanover they took an apartment in the building where Joseph and his family resided. In

July 1933, when my father traveled to Palestine to determine how best to prepare young Jews to live there, the trip was paid for by his relatives. Similarly, they funded the renovation of the old abandoned synagogue of the *Gemeinde* to turn it into an attractive youth center (*Jugendheim*) and refuge. These special gifts, repeated annually with contributions to the *Gemeinde*'s welfare and maintenance budgets, gave my father a cherished sense that he was not a mere employee of the *Gemeinde*.

Of the many duties my father was expected to fulfill upon his arrival, none was as demanding as preaching in the Oppler synagogue. To those who sat behind one of the fancy pillars that held up the lofty dome, his sermons were barely audible. With strenuous effort, he soon acquired the forensic power and self-confidence to turn his words into a balm of comfort and meaning. On the last Yom Kippur in the Oppler synagogue, on October 4–5, 1938, the printed schedule still has my father preaching three times. When we were about to leave after his release from Buchenwald, the board, in its testimonial letter of December 6, 1938, singled out his exceptional preaching.

> In particular we must mention the impact and effectiveness of his sermons on all the members of the *Gemeinde*. His sermons were marked by his ability to transmit to his audience gems of the tradition clothed in modern garb. In the best and worst of times they truly offered edification to all those still yearning for it. The words which emanated from the depth of his heart penetrated the hearts of all, even those but mildly open for religious meaning.

Indeed, many came to hear. According to the recollections of my father, some one hundred men usually attended on Friday evenings to welcome the onset of Shabbat. Women customarily stayed at home for this service. On Shabbat morning attendance rose to about five hundred worshippers, with women seated in the galleries. For holiday services that number tripled to about 1500. For the High Holy Days of Rosh Hashanah and Yom Kippur, the synagogue typically filled to overflowing, which required that admission tickets be withheld from the *Ostjuden*, who were not yet full members. Irrespective of the service, men came attired in a *Zylinderhut* ("stovepipe") to underline the formality of the worship. Although services always abounded with dignity and decorum, the excessive emphasis on performance tended to minimize congregational participation and displays of exuberance.

Fanny Dessau frequented the services at which my father preached. She lived in Hanover with her sister and mother. Often his sermons caught hold of Fanny's artistic imagination, and she would return home to execute a visual representation of the text, thought, or ritual that my father had embedded in his sermon. The expressiveness of Fanny's images, their muted crayon colors and bold Hebrew lettering touched my father deeply, and he treasured the more than fifty drawings that Fanny gave him over the few years of their mutual admiration. Obviously upon request, Fanny designed the bookplate for his personal library and the cover of his small notepad that he had kept to record what he saw and thought on his trip to Palestine in July 1933. I would like to think that Fanny's creativity and loyalty had everything to do with the skill, substance, and authenticity of my father's spoken words. Tragically, Fanny was deported, along with her sister and mother, by the Nazis to Riga on December 15, 1941, never to return.

As a trained teacher, Emil Schorsch was ideally suited to tackle the badly hobbled Jewish educational system for the children of the *Gemeinde*. Energetically, he organized twenty-eight different classes for some 640 children in the city's lower and upper schools, set about revising the curriculum, convened meetings for the Jewish teachers of the entire province of Hanover, and gave annual reports to the adults of the *Gemeinde*. He was not only a gifted teacher who could enthrall children of all ages with the telling of a good story but also a highly efficient administrator.

But formal education had its shortcomings. The attendance of many children was spotty, and others skipped classes entirely. Then, too, the gap between what was taught in school and what was experienced at home was growing ever wider. Secularism was steadily eviscerating the religious content of many a Jewish home.

To counter these drawbacks, Emil Schorsch seized upon a novel initiative of informal Jewish education. In 1927, he invited some fifteen young boys to meet him for a *Minḥah* religious service on a Saturday afternoon. In Germany, Saturday mornings were still the domain of public education. This was to be a service conducted entirely by them. Their number tripled quickly with the inclusion of girls, who sat behind the boys during the service. By the festival of Simchat Torah ("the joy of Torah") in the fall, when the annual public reading of the Torah was completed and immediately begun anew, the number of children in the Oppler synagogue had leap-frogged to six hundred.

To be sure, youth movements of all sorts proliferated in Weimar Germany, and Emil Schorsch's *Jugendgemeinde* ("youth congregation") soon adopted many of their distinctive features. The children were divided into small groups by gender, each with their own adult leader, with my father at first leading one group and my mother another. The groups were free to plan their activities independently. But at the core of the *Jugendgemeinde* was a religious heartbeat. Every Saturday afternoon all participating children came together for a religious service, often begun with a talk by my father about the Torah reading of the week but then led by the children for the rest of the worship. The goal was clearly to teach them synagogue skills. Annually on the three pilgrimage festivals of Passover, Shavuot, and Sukkot (concluding with Simchat Torah), the children would join the adult services in the Oppler synagogue. In 1936, despite the steady emigration, some four hundred adults and six hundred children assembled in the Oppler synagogue to celebrate Simchat Torah.

The intent of the *Jugendgemeinde* was to provide children a lived experience of Judaism to make up minimally for what was missing at home and to ready them for an adult appreciation of the synagogue. But it also quietly pursued a social agenda. From the beginning my father was determined to surmount the divide between the children of German and Eastern European parents. The *Jugendgemeinde* welcomed children of all backgrounds, often benefitting from the better synagogue skills of the latter group. To help him administer this project, my father selected a woman from Eastern Europe, and, when she unfortunately died in the first year, he recruited her sister, Bertha Schul, who stayed with him till 1937.

But mixing the backgrounds was more complicated than simply putting the children into proximity with each other. As Bertha was to learn, different standards of etiquette got in the way. As a group leader, Bertha had chosen to use the informal personal pronouns to increase the camaraderie of the group. To her dismay, she soon discovered that the young girls from German homes were utterly unaccustomed to addressing an adult with the pronoun "Du."

I, too, tasted of the gratitude engendered by my father's disruptive agenda. When I came to Jerusalem in July 1967 after the Six Day War for research on my doctoral dissertation, I had arranged to stay at a small pension called Greta Ascher. The owner greeted me personally at the door when I arrived and immediately asked me if I was the son of Rabbi Emil Schorsch. When I acknowledged the fact somewhat perplexed, she embraced me because my father had dared to include her in his *Jugendgemeinde*. Sadly, at the time I was in the dark as to the full meaning of her social redemption.

To bring along the parents on the religious journey of their children, my father founded in 1927 a *Lehrhaus* (an institute for adult education) funded at first by his relatives. Modeled after what Franz Rosenzweig and Marin Buber had created in Frankfurt am Main in 1919, it was designed to promote textual, collaborative, and nonacademic learning. I cherish the annotated copies of Rosenzweig's *Der Stern der Erlösung* and Max Picard's *Die Flucht Vor Gott* (*Fleeing in the face of God*) that my father taught more than once therein. In 1931, he gave a lengthy lecture on the subject "Hat die Religion in heutiger Zeit noch einen Sinn?" ("Does religion in our day still have any meaning?"), in which he vigorously rejected Freud's denigration of religion as an illusion. And in 1936–37 he was still scheduled to teach Talmud, Picard, and what he called a course on "Lebendige Geschichte" ("Living History").

In addition, my father, a lover of books, was from the outset assigned responsibility for the renowned synagogue library of Hanover with its large collection of Judaica and Hebraica. I suspect that its destruction on Kristallnacht pained him even more deeply than the desecration of the Oppler synagogue.

In retrospect, then, in hiring young Emil Schorsch in 1927, the Hanover *Gemeinde* gained the leadership of an exceptionally well-rounded rabbi fully dedicated to the religious essence of his profession. Despite the unfathomable turbulence of the period, his inner life was not preoccupied with either antisemitism or Zionism. When it came time to flee, he did not seek to go to Palestine, although his admiration of the Zionist accomplishments under the British mandate pervaded the notes on his trip in 1933. But neither the secular Zionists nor the ultra-Orthodox were receptive to the service of a Conservative rabbi. In a 1934 Hanukkah sermon, rich in text and ideas, he chided the Zionists in Palestine for their strident secularism. Thus, four years later his destination would be the United States, where he could be a rabbi. He did not fear the impediment of a new language. To enter Breslau, he had mastered Greek and Latin.

For my father it was religion that mattered most. He never forgot his decision to become a rabbi in the face of death, and all his life, from his doctoral dissertation in Tübingen to his reflections on his years in Hanover written in retirement, he grappled with the viability of religion in a rampantly secular age. His faith had been forged by the rural Judaism in which he had been nurtured. In a 1930 essay published in a leading German-Jewish intellectual journal, he graphically depicted the piety of that rapidly disappearing Judaism on the basis of deep personal experience and not academic research. He highlighted its intimacy, its proximity to nature, and its pervasive sense of duty. The family was the seedbed for its transmission unencumbered by the artifice of pathos and extensive book learning. Between the lines one could sense that the stress on decorum, performance, and aesthetics in Hanover may have been but a fig leaf for a faith in absentia. At the end of services in the Oppler synagogue on Simchat Torah, my father hurried to one of the *Stieblach* to taste the genuine joy of having completed yet another reading of the annual Torah cycle.

Wherever fate might place him, he was prepared to serve God to the fullest. Expulsion neither lessened his sense of duty nor caused him to fixate on what was lost. His gaze was forward. World War I and its wrenching aftermath had taught him just how imperiled were the fundaments of civilization. To his lasting credit, he worked with the same idealism and intensity in Pottstown, Pennsylvania as in Hanover, Germany. For what he ultimately cared about was not the religious accoutrements that came with power and prestige but the inner purity of his faith.

A Voice out of the Whirlwind

My indebtedness to the city of Hanover runs deep. After the passage of eighty-five years the city has seen fit to fulfill its original promise to honor the memory of my beloved father, its last *Ortsrabbiner*, by attaching his name in perpetuity to a charming public park. In preparing my remarks for this occasion, I thought of reflecting on his role as a *Seelsorger*, a pastor invited to nurture the souls of his flock. What was the content and power of the sermons that he delivered in the cathedral sanctuary of the grand Oppler synagogue during his tumultuous eleven-year tenure? To what extent were they a screen for the events that wrecked the lives of his congregants as well as his own, especially after 1933? The thoroughness of his preparation enables me to do just that. For behind each sermon lay a carefully typewritten manuscript dated and aligned to the Hebrew scriptural reading of the day.

The manuscript does not imply that he read from a text. Growing up by my father's side, I know that he valued speaking freely, never letting a written text get between him and his congregation. To communicate effectively, he was determined to make eye contact, and that meant being unhindered. Diligent preparation enabled him not only to gather and arrange his thoughts in an orderly manner, but also to commit them to memory in unencumbered language. At the age of twenty-eight, in his first full-time pulpit, and having grown up in the intimate rural synagogues of southern Germany, my father had to master the voice projection, physical gestures, and oratorical style dictated by the grandeur of the space and the number of worshipers. But in time he did and left us a sermonic legacy forged in a harsh crucible.

At first, he shared the pulpit with Rabbi Samuel Freund, Hanover's *Landesrabbiner* who had come in 1907. His presence provided my father with an admirable and sympathetic mentor and lightened his preaching load to no more than two times a month. On September 25, 1938, coinciding with the eve of the Jewish new year holiday, a much reduced and deeply grateful Jewish community commemorated his retirement after forty-nine years of unstinting service. My father delivered the *laudatio* in commensurate words of appreciation. Despite his many official duties, Rabbi Freund, no longer well, was above all a religious leader of unshakeable faith. His observance of Jewish practice never wavered in the face of internal erosion or external hostility. Like my father, he believed the institution of the synagogue to be absolutely vital, and the daily minyan (its worship service) akin to the altar in Jerusalem's ancient temple, whose fire was never allowed to go out.

Thus, in the final month and a half before Kristallnacht, my father preached a total of fourteen times, in part because of Rabbi Freund's retirement, and in part because of the many holidays that crowd the Jewish fall calendar. Each one of those sermons engendered a well-rounded, integrated text borne aloft by a singular idea and suitable vocabulary. The external intensity did not alter the unhurried pace of conception and formulation. The last sermon he delivered, on November 5, 1938, coincided with *Lekh Lekha*, the Torah portion in which God instructs Abraham to leave his homeland: "Go forth from your native land and from your father's house to the land that I will show you." My father called this "die Sidra der Auswanderung" ("the portion of emigration"). He acknowledged and enumerated the hardships that awaited going into exile but concluded with a symbol of hope:

> *Die Kerne der Früchte sind grössten Theile bitter, aber aus*
> *ihnen entfaltet sich ein lebendiger, blühender Fruchtbaum.*
> *So ist es auch mit dem Geschick der Ortsveränder. Seien wir*

überzeugt, dass das mit verbundene Leid letzten Endes die Blüte eines neues Glück aus sich herausfalten wird. — The seeds' fruit are largely bitter but eventually give rise to a flourishing and productive fruit tree. Thus it also is with the fate of a wanderer in exile. We are convinced that the pain that accompanies the final end will once again yield the good fortune of many blossoms.

Little could anyone anticipate the brutal eruption of hatred about to occur. Less than one month later the Schorsch family arrived by plane in England to light that evening the second candle of the Hanukkah festival. And ten years later, unbeknownst to me, I would celebrate my bar mitzvah in Pottstown, Pennsylvania on the Sabbath of *Lekh Lekha*, coinciding with the very Torah portion that marked the end of my father's German rabbinate. The discovery of that thrilling linkage I owe to Hanover's respect for my father, which prompted me to examine his final words of comfort from the pulpit.

The format of my father's sermons did not change over time. From the beginning he strove to derive meaning and wisdom from the Torah portion of the week. He often opened with a line of the text or even a single word that seemed to stand out. Hebrew punctuated his exposition. The events of the day did not call for description or lamentation. An ancient rabbinic comment (a midrash) or telling image of his own creation would be invoked to give the text expansion and resonance. For him the words of Scripture were not to be taken literally but as an indicator (*ein Fingerzeichen*) of deeper meaning or larger ideas. Thus, when on October 22, 1938 the annual cycle of the weekly Torah reading returned to *Bereshit* (the beginning of Genesis), he dared to make sense of the endless repetition. The ritual is to be understood in a circular rather than a linear fashion. Like the rings of a tree, the Torah constantly enriches the Jewish soul with new insight and experience. Tree-like, we grow from the inside out, in all directions simultaneously. New growth fortifies us gradually to withstand all kinds of inclement weather.

My father was not a romantic intent on touching the human soul but a rationalist of deep faith. His heroes were men like Ibn Gabirol, Pascal, and Kant, who reached out through reason to an ever-present and ubiquitous God. If we could only learn to pray again, we would find God readily accessible. Hence, in the early years of his rabbinate in Hanover, his primary mission was to persuade a secular and highly assimilated Jewish community of the beauty, power, and meaningfulness of traditional Jewish thought and practice. What did change with the rise of the Nazis to power was the intensity of his sermon. Grim circumstances suddenly ladened every one of his words with existential weight. To instruct was now to generate the willpower, faith, and language to make it through the next day. God could not be recovered without community and worship, while discipline and consistency remained the soil for a spiritual life. In short, it was the tone of his preaching rather than its format that underwent change.

What strikes me in the study of my father's sermons is the remarkable authenticity and maturity of his faith. His well-rounded words ring with conviction, a product of deep thought and sustained practice. Religion as a domain of human expression fascinated him, with Judaism his lived specialty. The clarity of his ideas, the richness of their articulation, and the urgency of his delivery amounted to an undeterred sense of calling, embodying for his distressed flock a riveting example of a true *Seelsorger*.

But the religious pathos of those sermons did not convey the depth of his inner disquiet. The tragedy of 1933 had not shattered the basic secularity of German Jews. On September 2, 1936, with Rosh Hashanah fast approaching, he recorded for himself his sense of futility. As long as Jews have money, they will pursue sports like bridge and tennis as an ersatz religion. Indeed, Shabbat was perfect for tennis tournaments, for which a Jewish community like Berlin would occasionally fund the prizes. Few Jews attended synagogue anymore or manifested a sense of religious obligation. Shabbat observance and dietary restrictions were long gone. Jews seemed to fear only the heavy hand of the law, public opinion, and impoverishment. The faith in "the angel who rescues me from all evil" was no longer operative, nor was the piety of our ancestors.

Lamentably, the status of the rabbi had been eviscerated. Religious policy was the function of a board of knowledgeless laymen. Salary, pension, and titles were designed to offset the rabbis' loss of authority. As he wrote these bitter words, my father surely must have recalled the woeful fact that, in his 1928 graduating class of three students from Breslau, only one was from Germany. Two days later my father reiterated his dark thoughts to Theodor Rothschild, his beloved father-in-law and mentor, in an uninhibited letter, concluding that "I have never felt so strongly that genuine *teshuvah* ["repentance"] is the only salvation."

In short, my father's rabbinic role was torn between compassion and contempt. His fervent words of Torah from the pulpit failed to alleviate or alter the plight of his flock. Like a biblical prophet, though, he refused to let despair bring him to abandon his mission. He would stay at his post until expelled by the furor of the Nazis.

An Unbroken Vow

The Schorsch family of four left Germany by plane on December 18, 1938, which coincided with the first day of Hanukkah. That year we lit the first candle of our *hanukkiyah* in Germany and the second in England, making the festival of Hanukkah for us ever after a celebration of personal redemption. We fled by plane because the ship on which we were booked was unexpectedly delayed. My parents, exceedingly apprehensive, spent the money they could not take with them out of Germany on plane tickets. Relatives in London had secured for us visas to England from its chief rabbi, Joseph H. Hertz, who had been given authority to rescue rabbis from Germany. Years later I would quip that the first rabbi to be ordained by the Jewish Theological Seminary in New York in 1894 was destined to rescue the child who had just turned three and would eventually become the institution's sixth chancellor in 1986.

It was those visas that my mother bravely took to the Gestapo to secure the release of my father from Buchenwald, where he had been taken along with some 250 other notables of Hanover on the night the Nazis torched hundreds of synagogues across Germany. Among their number was the renowned free-standing Romanesque synagogue of Hanover dedicated in 1870. Arrested in the early morning as he was prepared to attend daily services, my father saw the ruins of that grand edifice only upon his release ten tortured days later, which the Gestapo conditioned on his immediate departure from Germany and on his consent not to reveal to anyone what he had witnessed and experienced in Buchenwald.

The entry into England was similarly on the condition that we not stay, and that my father not work while there. To be sure, our intention had always been to move to the United States. My father had two sisters already living there, as did my mother whose sister and her husband had left Germany in 1937. The two large containers of belongings that we were still allowed to take with us were sent directly to New York. But my father put the compulsory respite to good use. During the four months that we lived with family in London, he attended an interpreters' school for English. And for the ten months we spent on the southern shore in Bexhil by the Sea, I'm sure he worked diligently to improve his skills. For, by the time we arrived in New York in March 1940, my father felt confident enough in English to seek a rabbinic post with an American congregation. To master a new language at age forty in such a short time was truly a mean feat. No doubt his solid knowledge of Latin and Greek helped him to unravel English vocabulary. A photograph of my father seated at his desk in our home in 1950 that appeared in a front page story on him in the local daily newspaper prominently displayed an English dictionary lying at his fingertips. The choice may have been serendipitous, but it resonates with symbolism. The dictionary had become his primary tool for speaking publicly and publishing professionally in a language acquired in midlife.

By August 1, 1940 my father had been installed as the rabbi of Congregation Mercy and Truth in Pottstown, Pennsylvania, in the southeastern corner of the state, not far from Philadelphia. Upon our arrival in New York he had immediately turned to the placement commission of the Rabbinical Assembly and identified himself as a Conservative graduate of the Jewish Theological Seminary in Breslau (today Wroclaw, Poland), founded in 1854 as the first modern rabbinical school and the model for the Jewish Theological Seminary in New York, which was founded in 1886. Composed in 1940 of fewer than one hundred families who largely hailed from Russia and Hungary, the congregation had been originally chartered in 1892. In 1940 it enjoyed the services of a learned and qualified cantor, who also served as its kosher slaughterer and proudly sported a handsome basilica-like synagogue near the center of town, which was finished in 1925. In short, my father had chosen to start his career in the American rabbinate in a distinctly non-German synagogue infinitely smaller in scale than Hanover.

Remarkably, the choice was utterly bereft of lament. My father concentrated his energy entirely in the present and on the tasks ahead. European history had sadly embittered the relationship between German Jews and their less fortunate coreligionists further east, and that lugubrious legacy impeded the acceptance by some congregants of their new rabbi. But setbacks never triggered remorse. I lived in my parents' home for some fifteen years and witnessed many a heated exchange between them on matters pertaining to congregational affairs, in which they were equally invested, yet I never detected a note of self-pity over what had been left behind in Hanover. Testimony to that resolve was the absence of spoken German in our household. By the time we came to Pottstown they spoke English as best they could. I have no memory of switching languages, and it was surely fractured German that I sputtered for the first three years of my life.

Incontrovertibly, it was the cumbersome furniture from Germany that darkened the décor of our home, but the language that reverberated therein was English. And twice daily an American newspaper landed at our doorstep, the *Pottstown Mercury* in the morning and the *Philadelphia Evening Bulletin* in the late afternoon. The motivation to master English, though, ran even deeper than hatred for Germany. It also sprang from the realization that to transmit Judaism one had to command the language of the locals.

In Pottstown, my father was a full-service rabbi without benefit of staff, ministering to young and old, sick and healthy, those grieving and those celebrating, Jews and Christians. As in Hanover, he attended services morning and evening because he firmly believed that the daily minyan symbolized the lived sanctity of the synagogue. Without it, the edifice stood bereft of God's presence. To salvage the minutes waiting for a minyan, my father always had in hand a sacred text to study. Given his multiple duties, he never wasted a pausal interval.

Shabbat had its special demands. In the winter, we welcomed Shabbat in prayer twice, first with a service at the proper time just a few minutes before sunset and then at 8:00 p.m. for a late Friday evening service for those who could not attend on Shabbat morning because of economic pressures. In between, my father and I would dash home for a delicious but hurried Shabbat meal. The late evening services were more formal and musical, often with a choir trained by my father and an occasional guest speaker. In general, though, my father delivered the sermon, as he did again Shabbat morning at the more traditional service at which the full Torah portion was always read from a handwritten scroll. The two sermons were never identical because the religious needs of those in attendance diverged.

The Friday evening sermon was clearly the *pièce de résistance* of the week, utterly different from the constricted sermons in Hanover that rarely strayed from an exposition of the weekly Torah portion. In Pottstown, his carefully prepared talks, typed in advanced but delivered freely, burst with religious conviction and intellectual creativity. His point of departure was usually a topic of global interest and existential significance. For example, in the early months of 1943, he discoursed on such conundrums as "A Fire which Does Not Consume," "Is Misfortune a Penalty?" "Creative Silence," "Rather Dead than Slave," "Is Civilization Declining?" and "It's the Small Things that Count." After a lucid but brief analysis of the issue that troubled him, he would deftly reformulate it in Jewish terms with a striking verse or character or episode from the Bible or rabbinic literature. For added impact, he did not hesitate to marshal illustrations from current events. The unfolding nightmare of the Nazi extermination of European Jewry intruded again and again. He celebrated the meeting of President Roosevelt and Prime Minister Churchill in Casablanca in January 1943 for their demand that Germany must surrender unconditionally and called in his own words for the world to match that declaration with a moral Casablanca. For it had been the incontrovertible erosion of religion, he believed, that had paved the way for the nihilism of the Nazis. The week before, he had waxed eloquent on the subject of creative silence as the only medium in which God's voice might become audible. Cities inundate us with noise. Among the most devout humans are farmers and astronomers who often detect God's presence in their lonely contact with the natural world. But, ultimately, my father acknowledged that God's existence could not be proven in words. It had to be experienced.

What made my father's often demanding sermons more readily accessible were telling anecdotes and illustrations. A keen eye feasted on his classical higher education in Germany and his voracious consumption of American literature. Let one gem stand for many:

> Some years ago, a Dutch Professor was ascending one of the steep mountains of Switzerland, with the assistance of a guide. Having arrived at the top the Professor stepped to the jagged summit, stood there in erect posture with outstretched arms and admired the grandiose panorama. The wind was roaring around him and would have swept him from the precipice, when he suddenly heard the voice of the guide: "Professor, go down on your knees. Here you are safe only on your knees."

For my father, some six months after Hiroshima and Nagasaki, that graphic vignette summed up the human predicament at the dawn of the atomic age. Could religion still temper our lust for power and domination?

Emil Schorsch also mentored the adults in his community in other ways. Committed to hospitalization in one of Pottstown's two hospitals, one could count on one or more visits by the rabbi. My father would always be displeased if family failed to notify him of a member's illness. If called upon,

he would readily officiate at the funeral, at the local funeral home certified
to handle end of life Jewish rituals. Like his sermons, his eulogies were
carefully prepared not only because he knew his congregants intimately, but
also because he regarded the rapt attention of those present as offering a rare
moment in the face of death to touch on Judaism's most profound thoughts
and tender practices. His collected eulogies preserved much of the raw data
for the history of a typical small-town Jewish community.

The pastoral care of my father's rabbinate grew with trust in his expertise.
At the university he had studied psychology extensively, and in this country
he was taken by its more pragmatic orientation. He enjoyed entertaining
guests in our home with his arresting ability to read hands and handwriting.
The structure of one's hands would often yield insights into character and
disposition. The young couples whom he married he would always counsel
in several sessions. The austere synagogue building in Pottstown did not
lend itself to an inviting rabbinic study, and the individuals who sought
his help would often meet with him in our living room with its large desk,
elegant sideboard, and tall bookcases. My father gave of himself willingly
and often provided succor to couples whose marital lives were beginning to
unravel or to parents with unruly children or souls tormented by life. It was
an era when counsel that arose from deep faith could still make a difference.

Prior to his decision in World War I to enter the rabbinate, Emil Schorsch
had studied to be a teacher like his future father-in-law in Esslingen, who
ran the Jewish orphanage in which he spent his formative years. Later, at
the university in Tübingen, he even wrote his Ph.D. dissertation on the
pedagogical principles and techniques by which one could make religion
accessible to young and old. Hence my father neither feared nor shunned
the teaching of children. When we arrived in Pottstown in 1940, its small
synagogue had a Hebrew school of only seven children. By 1950 the number had increased dramatically to eighty-eight by dint of sustained effort. It
was an afternoon school that met four days a week plus Sunday mornings,
although each child attended only two afternoons and Sunday mornings.
Children were especially encouraged to come to services Saturday morning.
My father administered the school, taught the more advanced classes, and
conducted the Sunday assemblies for all the children enrolled together. He
also conscientiously prepared youngsters for their bar or bat mitzvah, often
writing their synagogue address for them, always on the Torah portion, as
he did mine in 1948. In short, his English was good enough to handle their
slang, coarse humor, and instances of disrespect. What held their attention

was his mastery of the art of storytelling, whether from the Bible, Jewish history, or current events. The charts he composed on large sheets of white paper to reuse highlighted the order of the material to be covered and assembled the place-names and *dramatis personae* on whom the story turned. Above all, the consistent study of Hebrew was intended to facilitate their entry into the language of the Torah and the siddur (the Hebrew prayer-book). The practice of Judaism required literacy.

The trouble with this ambitious curriculum was finding the faculty to teach it. Being small, Pottstown lacked suitable personnel other than the cantor and, being also fairly isolated, could not rely on teachers to commute from elsewhere. With Sunday school largely devoted to biblical material in English, volunteers could be uncovered locally. It was family that filled the remaining gap. My mother, a trained and gifted teacher, taught introductory Hebrew to young children in their first year of Hebrew school. Her ebullience, musicality, and love of children would render that year for many an experience they would long cherish. By high school I, too, was drafted, although, as an adolescent in love with sports, I must admit that my heart lay elsewhere. In the spring of my senior year in college, still living at home, I finally rebelled to go out for the Ursinus tennis team. An absence of talent allowed me to attain the number-three spot on the team. The rank, however, concealed the insurmountable gap that separated me from numbers one and two. Nevertheless, the panache earned me the opportunity to serve as tennis counselor at the seminary's Poconos Ramah for my last three summers at camp.

My father's conception of the rabbinate always reached beyond the pulpit. To remain connected with his post–bar and bat mitzvah students, he created a youth group affiliated with the dynamic national organization United Synagogue Youth (USY), whose regional conferences and annual national conventions brought youngsters together from all over the country. If the unstated intent was to help adolescents meet a potential Jewish spouse, the investment paid off handsomely for his son. For it was within the framework of USY that I first met Sally Jane Korn from Norristown, some twenty-five miles east of Pottstown, who in 1960 after college would become my wife and soulmate for more than sixty-three years. To lead the youth group, my father was usually able to find a local young person to rise to the challenge.

At least once a month my father would compose a congregational bulletin to reach the many members who rarely set foot in a weekly synagogue service. Whether in Hanover or Pottstown, his lifelong adversary was the multiple forces of secularization. Modernity had triggered an ever-growing estrangement from religion. Accordingly, every issue of the bulletin, in addition to announcements of synagogue events and news about family members, would carry a pithy word of Torah. For Emil Schorsch, for whom Judaism was a living reality, no opportunity would be missed to convey its meaningfulness. And, to facilitate that agenda, he had the precious ability of treating large subjects in few words and striking images. Once back from the printer, the task of folding and stuffing the bulletins for mailing fell unhappily on the sullen shoulders of his daughter and son.

My father had the wisdom to remain in Pottstown despite the modest size. As an immigrant rabbi in middle age, his chances of advancing to a larger pulpit were indisputably slim. Stability had its rewards for his children and for him. Above all, a functioning synagogue that minimally nourished his inner life gave him the chance to fulfill his calling as a rabbi. In 1943, the United States Army opened a vast new military hospital at Valley Forge (actually Phoenixville, Pennsylvania) and invited my father to become its civilian Jewish chaplain. He would carry out these onerous but gratifying duties till his retirement from Pottstown in 1964. In retrospect, he would call the hospital his introduction to American Judaism. On a far deeper level, the wreckage of war that arrived at the hospital was in desperate need of genuine pastoral care. Twice a week my father would journey to Phoenixville, on Wednesday morning for a day of visiting wounded GIs individually and on Thursday evening for a religious service for them and Jewish medical personnel on staff. For the services, the large wooden chapel was always divested of its Christian symbols. While my father traveled alone for years by train on Wednesdays (before we acquired a car), on Thursdays a small troupe of women from the congregation accompanied him and my mother, always bringing cold cut sandwiches and sodas for the collation that followed the services. On occasion I would tag along for the cold cuts.

In truth, the soldiers came to hear my father's sermons. Given the gravity of their situation, they thirsted for thoughts that would stir their minds, for words of Torah that would hearten their faith and sparks of faith that would relieve their depression. On Wednesdays he would sometimes relate how traumatized were the patients he tried to touch in the mental wards or how immobilized were the young men in need of prosthetic limbs and months of rehabilitation. His own frightening experiences as an eighteen-year-old in World War I, his deep knowledge of psychology, and his resolute faith in God had equipped him at least partially for the intensity of this degree of pastoral care. In 1964, returning from two years of military service in the army as a Jewish chaplain, I settled in Riverdale in the Bronx with my wife and young son and unwittingly selected as our family practitioner an internist who had served as a physician during my father's tenure at Valley Forge, and who waxed eloquent about his unforgettable sermons. There is no doubt in my mind that Valley Forge profoundly deepened my father's rabbinic experience and confirmed the wisdom of his decision to stay in Pottstown. In the trenches few could afford the luxury of secularism.

One other duty Emil Schorsch assumed with conviction was representing Judaism to the Christian community. The irrationality and destructiveness of Nazism weighed heavily on his mind. Brotherhood week coinciding with George Washington's birthday temporarily came to dominate the winter calendar. Clergymen often spoke at our late Friday evening services to commemorate the event, and my father would reciprocate on a Sunday morning at their church services. Ideally suited, he had a deep understanding of religion, a firm command of Judaism, and an unimpeded manner of speaking. The Hebrew Bible was part of his native vocabulary. In small towns like Pottstown, where it was not unusual to see three or four churches on the corners of a single street crossing, the architecture bespoke the comity of brotherhood. As the only rabbi in town, my father spoke when asked in lodges and schools, as well as churches. One year he even delivered the brotherhood address at the Hill School, Pottstown's prestigious private boys' school, to which a few local Jewish boys were gradually being admitted as day students.

This year, on September 7, I received an unexpected email from the son of a Jewish student who had been in attendance the day my father spoke. He wrote:

> My father attended the Hill School in Pottstown, PA, graduating in 1954. Many times my father told the story of the visiting rabbi who gave a homily from our altar at the Episcopalian church on campus. Probably 1953. The message was that many students would require a step of faith to believe there was a creator. It might even require a leap or a long jump. There might be additional steps, leaps, leading them on a journey. The journey might lead to "there is a God!" The message resonated with my father at that age, and he can still talk about it to this day, aged

88, with Alzheimer's dementia. The message supported, no, propelled my father in his wonderful life journey, his work, raising a family, spiritual endeavors, fundraising and charitable work, and more.

In amazement I offer this serendipitous gift as singular testimony of the prowess of my father's preaching. He long believed that, if his words could connect with but one attentive congregant, his taxing preparations would not have been in vain. The honesty, intensity, and fertility of his faith in a secular age, I believe, moved many others to give Judaism a second chance.

By the time I began attending Ursinus College in the fall of 1953, I had a good smattering of knowledge about some of the Protestant denominations in Pottstown, like the Seventh Day Adventists. Ursinus was a liberal arts school affiliated with the Christian Reformed Church and still had a daily chapel requirement from which I was, ironically, exempted as a day student commuting from home.

Nourishing that far-flung and demanding range of activity was my father's rich inner life. His personal copies of the Hebrew Bible and the Horeb edition of the Mishnah are filled with underlined passages and marginalia. He would end each day before retiring seated at his desk reciting a nugget of Torah in memory of an ancestor, friend, or teacher whose life had impacted his own. His well-stocked library of classical Hebrew texts that made it to America provided him with a sacred silo in which to endure his perilous journey. Not infrequently my father and I meet on the pages of one of his books even now in my library. His voluminous papers teem with notes on ideas and topics with which he grappled, and which would often appear later in a sermon, article, or essay. Sadly, his papers are also the repository of essays that did not make it into print. But one that did on the magnificent poetic prayer *Adon Olam* (*Lord Eternal*) is a stirring testament to the vibrancy of his religious thought. In the learned and creative hand of my father, the poet confronts and resolves the daunting tension between our objective knowledge of God and our subjective experience of a personal redeemer. In truth, I believe the key to my father's rabbinical effectiveness was the power of his lived faith and the ceaselessness of his robust intellectual ferment.

But I cannot bring my father's story to a close without a crucial addendum. As much as we tried to assimilate outwardly to America, we could not sever our ties to Germany inwardly. Nor did the acquisition of citizenship obliterate the past. We were acutely aware that we had left behind my beloved grandfather, my mother's father and my father's father-in-law. An admired Jewish educator in the state of Württemberg, he was the long-time director of a Jewish orphanage in Esslingen founded in 1831 and grandly enhanced in 1913 with a stately building and a good deal of farmland. By then it had become mainly a boarding school in which Jewish children lived by the Jewish calendar and ritual; learned Hebrew, Torah, and German subjects; and worked with their hands as well as their minds. My father came as a small child, gravitated to my grandfather as a surrogate father figure, and attended the same superb Protestant teachers' seminary in Esslingen as had Theodor Rothschild, his dear director and mentor. Once the Nazis came to power in 1933, Theodor steadfastly refused to apply for an American visa, for fear that, should the Nazis discover his perfidy, they would close his school and disperse his children. Notwithstanding, Nazi vandals ransacked the premises and battered its teachers and children on *Reichspogromnacht* in 1938. Theodor trudged with faculty and students to Stuttgart on foot. For six months the Nazis allowed them to return to Esslingen and then confiscated the entire facility.

Until Pearl Harbor, letters could still be sent between Germany and America, and Theodor's carefully self-censored letters depicted the rapid deterioration of the mobility and living space allotted to him and his wife in Stuttgart. Each letter ended with the brave words "Console yourselves, we are doing okay" (*Tröstet Euch, uns geht es gut*). My parents and aunt and uncle left no stone unturned to secure some form of departure for Theodor and his third wife from Germany, to no avail. Finally, on August 22, 1942 they were sent to Theresienstadt, where he died on July 10, 1944. The day that news reached Pottstown, the Schorsch household fell into prolonged mourning, which I vividly remember. With such visceral ties to Germany we truthfully lived in two worlds, one securely focused on a present filled with hope, and one silently transfixed on a past darkened with trepidation.

It is the biblical prophet Jeremiah who comes to mind if I try to encapsulate the rabbinate of my father. He kept the vow he took in the final chaotic days of World War I to become a rabbi. No matter what obstacles loomed in his path toward ordination or awaited him in his arduous career, he was determined to serve his Maker, wherever he might be sent. Neither scale nor hardship kept him from heeding the words once uttered to Jeremiah:

Ismar Schorsch

Do not say, "I am still a boy,"
But go wherever I send you.
And speak whatever I command you.
Have no fear of them,
For I am with you to deliver you.

My father's unbroken vow was planted in the purity of that faith.

Ismar Schorsch is the Rabbi Herman Abramovitz Distinguished Service Professor of Jewish History and Chancellor Emeritus of the Jewish Theological Seminary.

Living: A Letter from Israel

Chaya Rowen Baker

I was asked to write this letter about one month into the war but was also asked to write as close as possible to publication, so that the letter would be timely. Rabbi Joe Prouser, editor of this esteemed journal, wisely knew that Israel in February would be different from Israel in November.

While there still are many similarities, looking back on the last four months feels like reflecting on four years. It's hard to recall life before October 7, and thinking about everything that has happened since makes me emotionally dizzy. We have gone from sheer horror and intense fear to unsurmountable grief and constant anxiety, to anger and disappointment, to despair and searching for hope, to appreciation of what we have and survivor guilt. With all that and more, we are trying to live. We need to go to work, make dinner, do the laundry and walk the dog—normal things… when life is anything but normal and everything is clouded by sadness and worry for our loved ones.

It's hard to describe the emotional effort necessary to encompass the dissonance between these opposing states of being. It takes a huge effort just to get out of bed each morning and live, when "living" has become such a taxing experience: listening with dread to the radio on the way to work, hearing the list of soldiers who fell the day before to see if you know any of them, breathing a sigh of relief when the anchor has finished the list because you don't know any of them but then feeling awful to be relieved while for other families the world has ended, fighting traffic and suddenly realizing that the person who cut in ahead of you might be in a hurry to see a loved one in hospital or a mother rushing to work, having left late because she is single parenting while her husband is in the army, or one of the ninety thousand displaced Israelis still living as refugees—some after losing loved ones to brutal murder or to captivity or to severe trauma—strangers in their temporary city and not knowing how to navigate life, then arriving at work and needing to function normally with mundane tasks and demands. At the end of such a work day you return home to care for your scared and worried children, who—despite your best efforts—have inevitably been exposed to human behavior which no one at any age should ever imagine possible. If you are lucky, your whole family is waiting for you at home. If not, you return to a family having to function without a father or a mother or a grown sibling because they are away at war, and even if everyone is home you might be enjoying one another's company on borrowed time. My husband, who returned home two months ago after two months of *miluim* (military reserve duty), has been drafted for another six weeks, scheduled to begin two weeks hence. Not a moment of joy goes by in our family without a dark cloud looming over us as a ticking clock.

The sense of profound sadness and intense dread in which we are all wallowing has yielded a change in how we speak to one another. It has become pretty much taboo to greet one another with any phrase using the word "good": morning, evening, afternoon, week, month. The greeting *Shabbat Shalom* is widely used and said intentionally, and the common greeting for ending a conversation has become *besorot tovot* (we should hear good news). If you make the mistake of asking someone any version of *mah shlomkha* ("How are you?") the answer will seldom be the standard "fine" or "great" or even "OK." Even though normally both the question and the answer are mere pleasantries, at this point in Israel if you ask *Mah nishma?* ("How's it going?") you will likely receive the person's explanation of how they came to develop the answer they give.

Because we are most definitely not OK.

How are we?

Agility, Solidarity, and "Showing Up"

On the morning of October 7, after a few minutes in our bomb shelter, my family and I were preparing to leave for synagogue when the president of the congregation knocked on our door. She had come to confer whether we should hold services that morning.

"Of course," I said immediately. "There is a bomb shelter at the synagogue. We will restrain the *Simḥat Torah* celebrations but this is exactly the time to pray and be together."

"I'm not sure you know how bad it is," she replied. "Terrorists are driving around the town of Sderot, and twenty people have been killed."

Twenty people murdered in a terrorist attack! The number brought back memories of suicide bombings. Indeed, it was horrid. We went to synagogue, where a small crowd gathered. Some congregants who normally wouldn't had brought their cellphones. There was fear and trepidation in everyone's eyes, yet it was comforting to be together. I announced that we were going to shorten the *hakafot* (the festive dancing around the room with the Torah) and sing one mellow song of peace, comfort, or prayer for deliverance for each *hakafah*. We ended up singing song after song in this manner.

Sirens disturbed our prayers again and again. The entire country was under attack. After running downstairs to the bomb shelter three times, we decided just to stay there and complete our prayers in the bomb shelter. We felt safe in the bomb shelter. Little did we know that the real danger was not one from which a bomb shelter could save you—that from that day on none of us would ever feel fully safe even in our locked home.

We carried down the Torah and all its paraphernalia. We sang and marched sadly around in a circular embrace, and it was surreal and powerful and awful. We wept as we prayed for Israel, for the safety of our soldiers, and for peace. As the news came in through those with relatives in southern Israel, every word in the service became ever so fraught with meaning: *'Ozi vezimrat Yah vayehi li liyshua* ("Strength of spirit and God's song shall be my salvation"), *Min hameitsar qarati Yah* ("In my distress I call out to God"), and *Ana Adonai hoshia na'* ("Please, God, save us!")

Those long hours witnessed some of Israel's most courageous battles, fought not only by soldiers on duty but also by armed civilians, off-duty police personnel, and soldiers on leave or reservists. They surged, unprompted, barefoot and in their undergarments, to the battlefield—a battlefield of homes and kibbutz paths and a music festival (!). Women's combat units fiercely repelled the barbaric enemy, saving hundreds of lives in the foe's murderous and torturous path. In minutes, units mobilized to protect the breached border and literally to reconquer entire Israeli villages, blood-drenched home by home, amidst the heavy stench of burnt flesh and climbing over dismembered bodies, some of them booby-trapped.

I will never cease being in awe of the bravery and dedication that leads a person to run toward fire. Not for love of death but for love of life.

By evening that day, we were shocked to learn that the number of people murdered was likely going to exceed the number of soldiers killed in the Second Lebanese War—121. That sounded unreal. How oblivious we were.

The horrific details of the attack—its scope and viciousness—took time to unfold. We cast doubt on the rumor of a couple dozen civilians having been abducted from their homes into Gaza—how could that be true? In reality the figure was over 240! As the days passed, reports came in of many hundreds more murdered—entire families, elderly who could not hold the saferoom door handle shut, parents slaughtered in front of their children...

and bodies that remained unidentified weeks later, despite forensic teams working full force around the clock, because they were so disfigured.

Funerals with no bodies, because the bodies had been taken to Gaza; temporary burials; *shiva* on the heel of *shiva*; staggering evidence of sexual violence.... As the proportions of this atrocity were revealed, I found it hard to fathom the blindly unchanging attitude of our critics. How could those who condoned the attack on October 7 itself not adjust their response in the slightest, in the light of what had become known by October 14? Do information and reality really carry so little weight in molding opinion?

A refreshing agility of thought is surfacing in Israel. We have lost faith in constants; while terrible and disconcerting, this is also humbling. We all know in theory that reality can change in a moment, but for us in Israel radical and instantaneous change has become part of our daily routine. As a result, many of us are reconsidering truths and cultural norms, rearranging priorities, as our values take on new proportions and perspectives. Israelis are finding renewed appreciation of one another, bringing to the fore values of devotion, dedication, selflessness, and mutual support. Classical political "Right" and "Left" are wavering. While obviously not all change is desirable, I find this reexamination of paradigms to be inspiring and liberating.

The biblical verb for changing one's mind stems from the same root as the word *nehama* ("comfort, consolation"), as in Genesis 6:7: *ki nihamti ki asitim* ("for I regret that I made them"). The rabbinic verb for reconsidering is *nimlakh*, from the same root as *melekh* ("king"). Our heritage conveys the important message that flexibility of thought and ability to change paradigms are divine traits, charged with connotations of leadership and consolation.

Toward the end of that dreadful Shabbat, my husband (47) received a call. At that point we were answering the phone, which we normally wouldn't on Shabbat, anxious to hear that our daughter, who serves in a combat unit on the Egyptian border, was okay, and dreading the ring because it might mean otherwise.

He answered the phone, and on the line was a recording demanding that he depart immediately for his unit's base in the North. He is an infantry soldier, who has continued to volunteer for *miluim* since his official discharge at age forty.

Our children broke down in tears, knowing only a fraction of the horrors that had occurred that day and of the war that lay ahead. With sobbing and fearful children and a wife lying—as it turns out—to herself and to them that it would only be for a few days until things calmed down, my husband packed his army equipment and drove off.

Later that night my daughter called to say they were being deployed to the Gaza envelope to guard the kibbutzim there and to search for terrorists who were still at large. From that moment on I stopped breathing.

With a husband serving on the Lebanese border, still under attack since October 8, and a daughter serving on the Gazan border, I needed to worry about the safety of my three children with me at home. We live in a neighborhood of Jerusalem that borders on two hostile East Jerusalem neighborhoods, home to several known Hamas terrorists. The police do not enter these villages without army accompaniment. For the first few weeks we heard shooting from the villages every night. Six days into the war our neighborhood went into lockdown because of information about shooting near our home. My nighttime routine included locking the porch doors with the small latch that separates us from the outside, and pulling down the blinds (we have no bars), thinking this might give us another ten to twenty seconds to find a place to hide when terrorists come to our porch with guns. I did not let my children sleep in rooms in the side of the house facing the other direction because they have no blinds, so a rifle could be inserted directly into the room through the bars. Such were the considerations and calculations of mothers in Israel every night: How do I protect my family while alone, afraid, and the only weapon at my disposal is my common sense?

One late, sleepless night I wrote to the listserv of women rabbis around the world about how we were doing. At 2 a.m. I described how my type-A personality had me convinced that if I was awake and aware I could protect my soldiers with my thoughts, and therefore I could not go to sleep and leave them unprotected. The outpouring of support that ensued still brings me to tears. A dear colleague wrote lovingly, from a distant time zone, "You can go to sleep, Chaya. I am awake, I will take the night shift."

As others followed suit I found myself sobbing. I realized that we are a people who cannot be defeated; a people who makes sure there is always someone awake to protect the fold. Perhaps this is another way of reading the verse *Hineih lo yanum velo yishan Shomer Yisrael* ("Behold, the Keeper of Israel shall not sleep nor slumber," Psalm 121:4).

The level of stress and distress in Israel is overwhelming. So many families are missing loved ones; 136 abductees hang between life and death; scores of thousands of children are scarred for life, some having to cope without the embrace, guidance, and protection of parents; thousands of men and women will never heal from the smells and sights they encountered as victims, relief forces, or forensic specialists; hundreds of thousands of Israelis for the next six or seven decades will carry wounds, some of them visible, others not. The list of pain and damage goes on and on.

Everyone is hurting. So, who will help whom? And yet…somehow there is an outpouring of initiative, kindness, compassion, and resilience among Israelis and from Jewish communities around the world, offering all sorts of assistance to families of victims and abductees, to evacuees, to soldiers and their families, to the families of fallen or wounded soldiers…you name the need, someone has created a situation room to help. People have opened their homes and given of their time, money, and talents with immeasurable generosity. This is a glimpse of the Israel we once knew, of the sense of peoplehood we recall sharing with diaspora Jewry—and it is refreshing and centering.

Sanctifying Life

We are still in the thick of a difficult war. At this moment 136 abductees are still being kept hostage in Gaza. Even now, four months into the war, Hamas continues to fire missiles at civilian populations in Israel. Its military power has been diminished but not annihilated. Israeli evacuees still cannot return safely to their homes. Our soldiers are fighting a battle unprecedented in its complexity, because the enemy does not distinguish between civilians and soldiers—neither among us (every male over eighteen is a potential soldier, and all civilians are a fair target) nor among their own people. They disguise themselves as, are embedded in, and hide behind civilian populations. The IDF aims to fight only against military combatants, not civilians, but sometimes it is hard to tell the difference, especially when our soldiers find a weapon stash under a baby's crib, or when missiles are launched from within a school or a hospital.

The IDF strives to hold itself to a high moral standard and to condemn any wanton malice—a difficult task when faced with such criminal warfare. I have heard firsthand from soldiers who wrote letters of apology on the walls of ruined Gazan homes, although unfortunately there are those who fall short of that standard. In what seems to be a redefining moment in the IDF ethos, its challenging mission is to save Israeli lives while upholding its commitment to morality of the highest standard, inspired by the sanctity of life.

Sanctifying life means recognizing the value of Palestinian lives, too; acknowledging them as parents, as siblings and spouses, as home owners, as people who need stability, security, and faith in the good, just like anyone else. Gazan families are suffering terribly, too, many of them also displaced from their homes, in mourning, and afraid. It is hard for some of us—even for peace activists—to summon such compassion at this point in the war. It is also hard for us, knowing that the lives of our relatives serving in the war are put at greater risk for the sake of protecting Hamas's human shield. That, too, is a part of how we are. Some Israelis are capable of such magnanimity. Others are still very much inside their shells, too fraught with pain to think about others' well-being right now.

In this entangled reality we look at our young soldiers, perhaps our children and grandchildren, in awe at their stamina, determination, and dedication—traits we were not sure this young, comfortable generation necessarily had. We pray for their safety, but we are also proud of their readiness to put their lives on the line to protect our nation, and we encourage them to do so.

Parents face a terrible conflict. No parent in their right mind would knowingly encourage their child to put their life at risk, but moments like these with existential ramifications also make you think about how "life" is not only breath and pulse, but also direction and inner strength and purpose.

On one of my many dark, late nights I made the mistake of engaging in a Facebook correspondence with an October 7 denier. After a long futile exchange, she ended with "Free Palestine," and I replied with 'Am Yisra'el ḥai ("the People of Israel lives"). I am proud that in juxtaposition to the genocidal call to rid Israel of its Jewish inhabitants, the Israeli "slogan" for this war is an expression of peoplehood and life—death only when necessary to serve the value of life, and life in spite of death.

The sentiment "We love death as you love life" has been expressed by terrorists such as Mohammad Sidique Khan and Osama bin Laden and is quoted proudly by members and supporters of Hamas. Its champions assume that since Islamic terrorists are eager to die they are untouchable by the Western world, whereas Westerners are weakened by their love of life, because at war they have everything to lose.

Israelis have a strange combination of loving life but also being willing to die for it. It is an approach deeply rooted in Jewish heritage: Life is to be protected at all cost, even at the price of transgressing all of the *mitsvot*; all but the prohibitions of murder, incest, or idol worship—representing extreme harm to others, or to our spiritual identity. We do not aspire to martyrdom, but we are willing to endure it if our spiritual existence is threatened: our loved ones, our people, and our right to live freely as Jews.

Dying for life is a paradox, and for that very reason it holds a strength and depth of meaning and purpose that neither component alone can provide. That is why we will prevail.

'*Am Yisra'el ḥai.*

Rabbi Chaya Rowen Baker is Dean of the Schechter Rabbinical Seminary (SRS) in Jerusalem. Ordained by SRS in 2007, Rabbi Rowen Baker served as the rabbi of Kehillat Ramot Zion in French Hill, Jerusalem, for sixteen years and headed practical rabbinics training at SRS for seven years. Rabbi Rowen Baker was the first Masorti rabbi—and the first female rabbi—ever to be invited to teach Torah at Beit Hanasi, the Israeli President's residence.

The Study of Heschel and Kadushin in Israel

Jonathan Matt

My father, Hershel Matt ז״ל (1922–87), used to say that he came to the Jewish Theological Seminary (JTS)—where he was ordained in 1947—because of Mordecai Kaplan and stayed because of Abraham Joshua Heschel. I came to JTS because of Heschel and discovered Max Kadushin along the way. Since my ordination and aliyah in 1975, not a week passes without my noticing how much Israeli society could benefit from the insights of these two giants of Conservative/Masorti Judaism.

Most of Heschel's writings have been translated into Hebrew, primarily by Dror Bondi, a lecturer at the Schechter Institutes of Jewish Studies, who has devoted much of his scholarly work to that enterprise and to producing and facilitating scholarship on Heschel. Bondi has also republished *Torah min hashamayim ba'aspaqlariyah shel hadorot* with chapter introductions and a revised version of volume 3 (based on newly discovered manuscripts).[1] He has been teaching Heschel in many contexts, including online courses offered by the Schechter Institute.

There have been a number of Heschel events in recent years. Three stand out among the most prominent. In December 2014, the Van Leer Institute and Schechter sponsored a three-day conference on Heschel. Speakers included Susannah Heschel, Eli Schweid, Arnold Eisen, Arthur Green, David Golinkin, Alex Even-Chen, Gordon Tucker, Michael Graetz, and Bondi. In June 2022, the World Zionist Organization organized a well-attended "Heschel Conference on Jewish Peoplehood" at the ANU Museum of the Jewish People (formerly *beit hatefutsot*). President Yizhak Herzog was among the speakers, as were Green, Bondi, and others. And, in December 2022, there were a number of events commemorating Heschel's fiftieth *yahrzeit*. There is also an active Facebook group, *Avraham Yehoshu'a Heshel beYisra'el*.

Over fifty years ago, Avraham Holtz spent several summers teaching Kadushin's writings to the central figures in the *Shdemot/Oranim* group, including Avraham Shapira. They encouraged Holtz to write *Be'olam*

---

[1] In this article, *Torah min hashamayim* cites Bondi's edition: Abraham Joshua Heschel, תורה מן השמים באספקלריה של הדורות, ed. Dror Bondi (Jerusalem: Sifrei Magid, Qoren, 2021).

hamahshavah shel hazal, which was published by Sifriat Poalim and JTS in 1978.[2] Holtz's book has been out of print for several years, with no plans to republish it. As far as I know, in Israel there have been no conferences on Kadushin, and there is no Facebook group.

Teaching Heschel and Kadushin in Israel

The study of Heschel and Kadushin is gradually emerging in Israel. For the past six years, I have been a participant and teacher in *Ma'agalim*, an Upper Galilee study group that includes Orthodox and non-Orthodox Israelis. In *Ma'agalim*, I taught a session on Heschel, followed by two sessions on Kadushin. The first part of this article is my report on these sessions, through which I discovered potential synergies between Heschel and Kadushin and a modest hope for the future of a healthy Israeli Judaism.

In the first session, I taught selections from *The Prophets* and from *Torah min hashamayim*. From the introduction to *The Prophets*: "By insisting on the absolutely objective and supernatural nature of prophecy, dogmatic theology has disregarded the prophet's part in the prophetic act. Stressing revelation, it has ignored the response; isolating inspiration, it has lost sight of the human situation."[3] We discussed the connection between Heschel's take on the prophets and his devotion to social action. Participants who had heard of Heschel had also encountered the iconic photo of Heschel marching in Selma with Martin Luther King., Jr.

From *Torah min hashamayim*, I taught the section on *Shibber et haluhot*: The school of R. Ishmael follows the *peshat* of Exodus 32:18, with Moses shattering the tablets on his own initiative. R. Akiva contends that God commanded him to do so:

כתוב בתורה: וַיְהִי כַּאֲשֶׁר קָרַב אֶל הַמַּחֲנֶה וַיַּרְא אֶת הָעֵגֶל
וּמְחֹלֹת וַיִּחַר אַף מֹשֶׁה וַיַּשְׁלֵךְ מִידוֹ [מִיָּדָיו] אֶת הַלֻּחֹת וַיְשַׁבֵּר
אֹתָם תַּחַת הָהָר (שמות לב, יט). לְפִי הברייתא שהזכרנו
למעלה, שיבר משה את הלוחות מדעתו. ואילו על פי רבי
עקיבא, "לא שיבר משה את הלוחות, אלא שנאמר לו מפי
הגבורה..." 4

---

[2] Abraham Holtz, בעולם המחשבה של חז״ל, בעקבות משנתו של מ.קדושין (Israel: Sifriat Poalim, 1978).

[3] Abraham J. Heschel, *The Prophets* (Philadelphia: Jewish Publication Society of America, 1962), xiii.

[4] Heschel, *Torah min hashamayim*, 537–38.

The Study of Heschel and Kadushin in Israel

In the Torah is written: "As Moses approached the camp and saw the calf and dances, Moses was angered, threw down the tablets, and shattered them at the foot of the mountain" (Exodus 32:10). According to the *baraita* that we mentioned above, Moses shattered the tablets on his own initiative. But according to Rabbi Akiva, Moses shattered the tablets only after God told him to do so.

For some of the Orthodox participants in *Ma'agalim*, Heschel's emphasis on the extreme pluralism of *ḥazal* was challenging. But I was encouraged that a well-known *rav dati le'umi* who participated enjoyed Heschel's insights.

My second teaching session was on a follow-up question: מה איחד את חז"ל-לינו, למרות חילוקי הדעות? ("What united the Sages, in spite of their divergent opinions?") I based my response on Kadushin's analysis of rabbinic value concepts. Toward the beginning of *The Rabbinic Mind*, Kadushin explains what he means by "value concepts."[5] He contrasts value concepts with "defined concepts" and "scientific concepts." So far, so good. But he confused me when he contrasted value concepts with what he calls "cognitive concepts," which he defines as "terms we use in order to describe whatever we perceive through the senses." But if you Google "cognitive concept," you come up with something like: "processes that control mental functions, such as communication, learning, classification." What might be a better term?

Luckily, I came across Heschel's paragraph on "Descriptive and Indicative Words":

> The human mind is a repository of a variety of ideas, some of which are definite and expressive while others resist definition and remain ineffable. Correspondingly, there are two kinds of words: *descriptive* words, which stand in a fixed relation to conventional and definite meanings, such as the **concrete** nouns, chair, table, or the terms of science; and *indicative* words, which stand in a fluid relation to ineffable meanings and, instead of describing, merely intimate something which we intuit but cannot fully comprehend.[6]

---

[5] Max Kadushin, *The Rabbinic Mind*, 3rd ed. (New York: Bloch, 1972), 45–52.
[6] Abraham Joshua Heschel, *God in Search of Man, a Philosophy of Judaism* (New York: Harper and Row, 1955), 181, bold emphasis mine.

Through Heschel I understood Kadushin: defined, scientific, and "concrete" concepts are descriptive; value concepts are indicative. Holtz's *musagim qognitiviyim* became *musagim muḥashiyim*.

We then proceeded to examine *midrashim* from *Meḥilta, Parashat Beshalaḥ* on:

(שמות יג:יז) וַיְהִי בְּשַׁלַּח פַּרְעֹה אֶת הָעָם וְלֹא נָחָם אֱ–לֹהִים
דֶּרֶךְ אֶרֶץ פְּלִשְׁתִּים כִּי קָרוֹב הוּא כִּי אָמַר אֱ–לֹהִים פֶּן יִנָּחֵם
הָעָם בִּרְאֹתָם מִלְחָמָה וְשָׁבוּ מִצְרָיְמָה.

> Then it came to pass, when Pharaoh had let the people go, that God did not lead them by way of the land of the Philistines, although that was near; for God said, "Lest perhaps the people change their minds when they see war, and return to Egypt" (Exodus 13:17).

I based my teaching on Kadushin's *A Conceptual Approach to the Mekilta*,[7] emphasizing the following elements:

- Examples of rabbinic value concepts.

- Emphatic trends.

- *Ḥazal* were aware of the difference between *peshat* and *derash*.

- A midrash uses an (often minor) stimulus to emphasize one or more value concepts.

- Indeterminacy of belief (*emunah bilti mequba'at*) supports midrashim that diverge from the *peshat* and from one another.

- Even when *ḥazal* disagree on *halakhah* or *agadah*, they share a common universe of value concepts.

This time, it was the kibbutzniks in *Ma'agalim* who struggled with a paradigm change. They had grown up on the *Tanakh*, focused on understand-

---

[7] Max Kadushin, *A Conceptual Approach to the Mekilta* (New York: Jonathan David, 1969), 207–15.

ing the plain sense of narratives. Although they had learned *aggadah*, they judged the validity of a midrash by how close it was to the plain sense. Although some Haredim would probably be troubled by research that draws a dichotomy between *peshat* and *derash*, the Orthodox members of *Ma'agalim* had no problem with Kadushin on this issue.

The *Ma'agalim* theme for 5783 was *yaḥid vetsibur* ("individual and community"). Again, I taught Kadushin, this time drawing on one of my favorite Kadushin books, *Worship and Ethics*.[8] We started off with a review of value concepts, learning the first mishnah in Pe'ah (which has become part of *shaḥarit*):

אלו דברים שאדם אוכל פרותיהם בעולם הזה והקרן קימת
לעולם הבא...

One of the participants was critical of this mishnah combining into one list interpersonal, *bein adam leḥavero* value concepts (for example, *gemilut ḥasadim*, welcoming visitors, visiting the sick) with those *bein adam lamaqom* ("between humans and God"), such as prayer and learning Torah. But that was exactly Kadushin's point:

> The scope of the moral life, we repeat, cannot be described by a formula, not even by the formula "between a man and his fellow man." That phrase, or its equivalent, is used by the rabbis in one context and in one context only, and it is not a general designation for ethics or morality. However the statements in which the phrase occurs may differ in expression, the context in those statements is always the same, namely, the sins forgiven and the sins not forgiven by God.[9]

The "scope of the [Jewish] moral life" is mediated through the value concepts, not through generalizations.

Kadushin has a beautiful section on *berakhot* as *gemilut ḥasadim* ("blessings" as "acts of lovingkindness"),[10] which I used to teach the wedding *sheva berakhot* for my topic *"Zug, tsibur, vehaqadosh barukh hu"* ("The Couple,

[8] Max Kadushin, *Worship and Ethics: A Study in Rabbinic Judaism* (Chicago, IL: Northwestern University Press, 1964).
[9] Kadushin, *Worship and Ethics*, 55.
[10] Kadushin, *Worship and Ethics*, 151–59.

the Community, and God"). Kadushin points out that, in the fifth *berakhah*,

> [t]he *zibbur* as a whole engaged in an act of *gemilut ḥasa-dim* when, through the *ḥazzan* as deputy, it prayed for the bride and groom. "O make these loved companions greatly to rejoice, even as of old Thou didst gladden Thy creature in the Garden of Eden. Blessed art Thou, O Lord, Who makest bridegroom and bride to rejoice."[11]

Asking God to gladden the couple is a powerful example of *gemilut ḥasadim*.

So far, we have encountered several comparisons between the works of Heschel and Kadushin. Next, I would like to consider some more comparisons, with some surprising results.

Academic Rigor with Spiritual Relevance

It was important for both Heschel and Kadushin that their works be judged by academic standards. Because Judaism covers such a long time span, most academic scholars concentrate on (at most) one phase of Jewish history: biblical, rabbinic, medieval, or modern. But, as Samuel Dresner wrote of Heschel, "[h]e contributed major works in fields each of which required their own separate disciplines: Bible, rabbinics, philosophy, Hasidism, theology and ethics, among others."[12] Heschel and Kadushin both faced a number of religious challenges while remaining faithful to the academic context: drawing into their academic writings the reality of God that each experienced, searching for connections among the various stages of Judaism, and enabling moderns to find spiritual insight from our classic sources.

Heschel's doctorate, *Die Prophetie* limited its scope to the biblical prophets.[13] But the introduction he wrote when it was translated and adapted as *The Prophets* foreshadows the influence this work had on Heschel's social activism and on the civil rights movement: "The prophet was an individual who said No to his society, condemning its habits and assumptions, its complacency, waywardness, and syncretism."[14] In *Torah min hashamayim*, Heschel argued that rabbinic Judaism can be viewed as typified by diver-

---

[11] Kadushin, *Worship and Ethics*, 156.

[12] Samuel H. Dresner, "Heschel the Man," in *Abraham Joshua Heschel: Exploring His Life and Thought*, ed. John C. Merkle (New York: Macmillan, 1985), 16.

[13] Abraham Heschel, *Die Prophetie* (Krakow: Verlag der Polnischen Akademie, 1936).

[14] Heschel, *Prophets*, xix.

gence between the schools of R. Akiva and R. Ishmael. Although his starting point was the rabbinic period, Heschel found this schema useful for organizing later stages in Judaism into these two schools. For example, the rationalism of Maimonides is reminiscent of R. Ishmael and the Zohar and the Hasidism of R. Akiva. Fritz Rothschild wrote of Heschel: "In his writings on religion he combines the yearning for holiness and spirituality of his Hasidic ancestors with the yearning for free inquiry and objective truth of the modern Western scholar."[15]

Kadushin's background was Kaplanian rather than Hasidic.[16] But, as Jacob Neusner writes, "Kadushin left Kaplan's secularism for the sake of his own fidelity to rabbinic Judaism."[17] Kadushin's "fidelity to rabbinic Judaism" was the sometimes frustrating substructure of both of my classes with him during my years at JTS (1971–75). On several occasions, we students would ask how one might integrate the world of rabbinic value concepts into a modern Judaism. I do not recollect Kadushin's exact response, but it was probably something like "First make sure that you understand rabbinic Judaism."

Theodore Steinberg writes that Kadushin's personal Judaism was firmly rooted in rabbinic Judaism:

> On the closing page of *Organic Thinking*, Kadushin cautiously stated his emerging understanding of the nature of religious change and reinterpretation. Unlike Kaplan, he wrote not of a deliberate, experimental search for modern equivalents of old values—the heart of the Reconstructionist approach—but rather of an intricate, even mysterious process "...whereby the old organic complex is transposed in its entirety to a new level." In his subsequent books, Kadushin never mentioned the subjects of theological change and modernization, the two central themes of Reconstructionism.

---

[15] Fritz A. Rothschild, "Varieties of Heschelian Thought," in *Abraham Joshua Heschel: Exploring His Life and Thought*, ed. John C. Merkle (New York: Macmillan, 1985), 88.

[16] Theodore Steinberg, "Max Kadushin: An Intellectual Biography," in *Understanding the Rabbinic Mind: Essays on the Hermeneutic of Max Kadushin*, ed. Peter Ochs (Atlanta, GA: Scholars Press, 1990), 1–18.

[17] Jacob Neusner, foreword to in *Understanding the Rabbinic Mind: Essays on the Hermeneutic of Max Kadushin*, ed. Peter Ochs (Atlanta, GA: Scholars Press, 1990), ix n. 3.

Had Kadushin become a religious conservative? Years later, he reflected on this shift in his thinking, and stated that he had not become a "conservative," but rather an "unreconstructed partisan of tradition." His studies convinced him that the classical Judaism of the rabbinic era was neither outmoded nor anachronistic, but, on the contrary, quire durable and perennially relevant.[18]

All of Kadushin's works—but especially *Worship and Ethics*—are great aids to the spiritual life.

From the Tanakh to Modern Judaism

Not only do scholars of Judaism tend to concentrate on one phase of Jewish history, they often seem to feel that it is not valid to mention two different stages in the same breath. It is here that we encounter further common ground between Heschel and Kadushin. Kadushin's take on midrash, mentioned above, recognizes that connections between biblical *peshat* and rabbinic *derash* can be extremely tenuous. The rationale of *derash* is to emphasize rabbinic value concepts. However, Kadushin argues that "there is no rabbinic concept that does not have its roots in biblical thought."[19] He describes three types of rabbinic concepts, as far as their relationship to the Bible is concerned: First are concepts having conceptual terms that are not to be found in the Bible but are foreshadowed in the Bible. Second, concepts for which the conceptual term is the same as the biblical but with wider, more universal, connotations. And, finally, concepts for which the term appears in the Bible but for which there is no definite connection between the biblical term and the rabbinic term (*goy*, *nes*, and *tsedakah*, for example).

In general, "A living bond unites the Bible with rabbinic thought. Even though rabbinic thought possesses its own concepts, it remains in a state of continuous dependence on the Bible."[20] Many of Heschel's books span more than one period. The *Sabbath* draws on biblical, rabbinic, and mystical aspects of Judaism to suggest Shabbat as a spiritual cure for modern Jewry and Western civilization in general.[21] *God in Search of Man* builds

---

[18] Steinberg, "Max Kadushin," 7. The direct quote is from *Organic Thinking*, 261.

[19] Kadushin, *Rabbinic Mind*, 288.

[20] Kadushin, *Rabbinic Mind*, 298.

[21] Abraham Joshua Heschel, *The Earth is the Lord's* and *The Sabbath* (New York: Harper & Row, 1966 [1951]).

a philosophy of Judaism on the entire range of Jewish sources. And *Torah min hashamayim* focuses on the rabbinic period. But, as *ba'aspaqlariyah shel hadorot* ("as refracted through the generations"[22]) implies, Heschel argues that the approaches of Akiva and Ishmael offer an insightful way of categorizing post-rabbinic Judaism as well. Thus, both Heschel and Kadushin have managed to bridge the gaps between periods of Jewish history.

Kadushin and Heschel on Maimonides

There are both similarities and differences between Kadushin and Heschel on Maimonides. Above, I referred to Kadushin's criticism of Maimonides on the issue of *bein adam lamaqom/ bein adam leḥavero*. Although Kadushin points out that Maimonides himself qualifies the dichotomy in the *Guide*, there are many issues on which Kadushin emphasizes how greatly Maimonides and other philosophers diverge from rabbinic Judaism; see, for example, *The Rabbinic Mind* on the question of anthropomorphism.[23]

Heschel wrote a very sympathetic biography of Maimonides.[24] Yet he points out that "It was not the codifier and 'guide' Maimonides but the commentator Rashi who became the shaper, teacher, and educator of his people; it was not the metaphysics of Maimonides but the Cabala and Hasidism that molded the future."[25] In *The Prophets*, Heschel clearly diverges from Maimonides's denial of divine pathos, describing the prophetic response as one of sympathy with the divine pathos.[26] Rothschild points out that, on this issue, Heschel "has propounded a truly revolutionary doctrine, challenging the whole venerable tradition of Jewish and Christian metaphysical theology from Philo, Maimonides, and Thomas Aquinas to Herman Cohen, Etienne Gilson, and Paul Tillich."[27]

Torah min hashamayim is a work of research rather than a book of Heschel's philosophy. Yet, for one who grew up on *Man is not Alone* and *God in Search of Man*, reading *Torah min hashamayim* involves an ongoing search to discover on which issues Heschel's personal philosophy of Judaism was

---

[22] This is Gordon Tucker's felicitous translation; see Abraham Joshua Heschel, *Heavenly Torah: As Refracted through the Generations*, ed. and trans. Gordon Tucker (New York: Continuum, 2005).

[23] Kadushin, *Rabbinic Mind*, 325ff and 250 n. 95 for where Maimonides qualifies the dichotomy.

[24] Abraham Joshua Heschel, *Maimonides*, trans. Joachim Neugroschel (New York: Farrar, Straus and Giroux, 1982 [1935]).

[25] Heschel, *Maimonides*, 211.

[26] Heschel, *Prophets*, 307ff.

[27] Rothschild, "Varieties," 88.

closer to Akiva or to Ishmael.[28] Similarly—regarding Heschel's numerous citations of the works of Maimonides, often identifying him with the school of R. Ishmael—it is intriguing to speculate on Heschel's personal preference.[29] A systematic explication of this topic is beyond the scope of this article.

The God of Abraham, Isaac, Jacob, Ḥazal and Ḥasidut

When Blaise Pascal died in Paris in 1662, found sewn into the lining of his coat was a sheet of paper on which was written: "God of Abraham, God of Isaac, God of Jacob, not of the philosophers and the scholars. I will not forget thy word. Amen." Such a note in the lining of Heschel's coat might have read "The God of Abraham, Isaac, Jacob, Ḥazal and Ḥasidut, not of the philosophers and the scholars." Heschel wrote:

> Where an idea is the father of faith, faith must conform to the ideas of the given system. In the Bible the realness of God came first, and the task was how to live in a way compatible with His presence. Man's coexistence with God determines the course of history.[30]

> There are no proofs for the existence of the God of Abraham. There are only witnesses.[31]

Although Kadushin did not write a personal philosophy of Judaism, he gave the impression that rabbinic Judaism filled his spiritual needs. He described the nonphilosophical approach to the God of rabbinic Judaism as "normal mysticism."

> There is an experience of God in an act of rabbinic worship. To the individual who says a berakah, God seems so near that he addresses God with the pronoun "Thou," just as he would address a person facing him. "Thou" is the only word which can express the sense of God's nearness, yet the feeling of God's nearness is obviously different from

---

[28] Abraham Joshua Heschel, *Man is not Alone* (New York: Farrar, Straus and Young, 1951).
[29] Places where Heschel identifies Maimonides with the school of R. Ishmael, see, e.g., Heschel, *Torah min hashamayim*, 247.
[30] Heschel, *Prophets*, 16.
[31] Heschel, *Prophets*, 22.

anything the individual may feel when he addresses a fellow human being with the same pronoun.... We have, therefore, called the rabbinic experience of God normal mysticism.[32]

Heschel and Kadushin seem to be of one mind that experience of God— rather than philosophy—is the essence of Judaism.

Kadushin, Akiva, and Ishmael

Volumes 1 and 2 of *Torah min hashamayim* were published during Heschel's lifetime. Those volumes were a pleasure to read, but I felt the lack of a conclusion that put the differences between the schools of Akiva and Ishmael into a conceptual framework. David Feldman expressed this lack in his introduction to Heschel's posthumously published volume 3:

אלה שהגו בכרכים הראשונים העלו להם ידיעה רחבה בגלגול השיטות—אלא שלא מצאו בזה סיפוק כל צרכם. הם צמאו למשהו יותר קבוע ומכריע, למסקנות יותר מוחלטות של המחבר.[33]

> Those who studied the first volumes acquired a broad understanding of the two schools—but were left unsatisfied. They were thirsty for something more decisive, for more definitive conclusions of the author.[34]

But I still felt the lack of a conceptual conclusion after reading that 1990 version of volume 3. In 2021, Bondi published a revised version of volume 3 as part of the republication of the entire set.[35] He discovered that significant parts of volume 3 had been omitted, which he restored from Heschel's manuscripts. But, in spite of Bondi's restoration (and incisive foreward, chapter introductions, and summaries), I still felt the lack of a top-level conceptual context that would give coherence to each of the two schools.

I then began to reread *Torah min hashamayim* through the eyes of Kadushin, hoping that perhaps his categories might provide a conceptual context

---

[32] Kadushin, *Worship and Ethics*, 13–16.

[33] Abraham Joshua Heschel, תורה מן השמים באספקלריה של הדורות, ספר שלישי, ed. David Feldman (Jerusalem: Jewish Theological Seminary, 1990).

[34] Author's free translation.

[35] Heschel, *Torah min hashamayim*.

Jonathan Matt

for the differences between the schools of Akiva and Ishmael. So far, I have
found only partial success, which I share below. I am not alone in my quest
to see Heschel through Kadushin, as attested in a footnote in Shai Held's
Abraham Joshua Heschel, The Call of Transcendence.[36]

The Otherness of God

In *The Rabbinic Mind*, Kadushin examines whether Ḥazal were troubled
by anthropomorphisms in the Tanakh. "...the Rabbis apparently object to
biblical statements about God that appear to limit Him.... 'And the Lord
went before them by day (Exod. 13:21)'—is it possible to say so? Has it not
been said: "Do not I fill heaven and earth, saith the Lord" (Jer. 23:24)?"[37]
Kadushin's conclusion is:

> One of the prime characteristics of normal mysticism is...
> that God is like none other...."[38] But though these passages
> express the idea of the otherness of God, and hence do cul-
> tivate it, they do not stress it. The idea, in these instances,
> only serves as background, and against that background
> are stressed God's love and His justice.[39]

Throughout all of his works, Kadushin is careful to differentiate between
rabbinic conceptual terms (here *midat hadin*, or God's quality of justice, and
midat raḥamim, or God's quality of love) and his own terminology, such as
the "idea" of the otherness of God.

My sense is that the school of Ishmael could be described as emphasizing the otherness of God to a greater extent than the school of Akiva.[40] For
example:

'וֹאָהַבְתָּ אֵת ה' אֱ–לֹהֶיךָ' (דברים ו, ה). לְפִי פְּשׁוּטוֹ שֶׁל
מִקְרָא, אַהֲבַת אֱ–לֹהִים הִיא כְּלוֹת הַנֶּפֶשׁ אֶל הַבּוֹרֵא, דָּבָר
שֶׁבַּלֵּב. כְּנֶגֶד זֶה פֵּירְשׁוּהָ בְּבֵית מִדְרָשׁוֹ שֶׁל רַבִּי יִשְׁמָעֵאל

---

[36] Shai Held, *Abraham Joshua Heschel: The Call of Transcendence* (Bloomington: Indiana University Press, 2013), 29–30, 241 n. 18.

[37] Kadushin, *Rabbinic Mind*, 273.

[38] Kadushin, *Rabbinic Mind*, 303.

[39] Kadushin, *Rabbinic Mind*, 306.

[40] My brother, David Matt, points out that, by comparison, Akiva emphasizes the closeness of God, which jibes well with the account of Akiva as among ארבעה נכנסו לפרדס...רבי עקיבא יצא בשלום ("Four entered [the mystical] paradise.... [Only] Rabbi Akiva emerged unscathed," b. Hagigah 14b).

כדרך שפירשו את דבר הדביקות: אהבה היא מידת העושים
מעשים טובים...כנגד זה פירש רבי עקיבא את הכתוב
כפשוטו, ואמר על עצמו: "רחמתיה בכל לבי...".[41]

"Love the Lord your God" (Deuteronomy 6:5). According
to the plain sense of the text, love of God is the yearning
of one's soul for the Creator, a matter of the heart. But contrary to this, the school of Rabbi Ishmael explained it as
they did the matter of clinging to God: love [of God] is the
quality of those who perform good deeds. However, Rabbi
Akiva explained the verse according to its plain sense, and
said of himself: "I loved Him with all my heart."

And from Heschel's introduction to *Torah min hashamayim*:

זרה היתה למשנתו של רבי ישמעאל דעתו של רבי עקיבא,
שהקדוש ברוך הוא משתתף בצערן של הבריות, בצרתם של
יהודים ובצרה של האומה. דעה זו אינה הולמת את הכבוד,
ועלולה להביא לידי כפירה בגבורותיו של הקדוש ברוך
הוא. במשנתו של רבי ישמעאל, מידת הדין וגבורותיו של
המקום עיקר, ולא מידת הרחמים.[42]

Rabbi Akiva's position—that God shares in human pain, in
the suffering of Jews, and in the suffering of the nation—
was strange to the approach of Rabbi Ishmael. [According
to Ishmael,] such a position does not suit God's majesty and
may lead to denying the powers of the Holy One, blessed
be He. According to the approach of Rabbi Ishmael, *midat
hadin* and the powers of the Omnipresent are primary, not
midat haraḥamim.

It is tempting to generalize the preceding sentence into a claim that Akiva
consistently emphasized *midat raḥamim* and Ishmael *midat hadin*. Such
a generalization might have indicated that Kadushin's "value concept" terminology is helpful in differentiating between the two schools.[43] However,

---

[41] Heschel, *Torah min hashamayim*, 251.
[42] Heschel, *Torah min hashamayim,* 62.
[43] Kadushin, *Rabbinic Mind*, 15–26 identifies *midat raḥamim* and *midat hadin* as two of the
four rabbinic "tracer concepts."

in Heschel's chapter on *b'emah vepaḥad* ("with fear and tembling"), we learn that the dichotomy is not consistent: בפנים שמחות, בפנים מסבירות לרבי ישמעאל; בפנים זועפות, בפנים הדופות לרבי עקיבא ("A pleasant expression on the face of Rabbi Ishmael; an angry expression on the face of Rabbi Akiva").[44] And again of Ishmael: הוא נטה כלפי חסד ("He tended toward lovingkindness")[45]

Miracles

Another similarity between Heschel and Kadushin is the concept of miracles. Kadushin describes two phases of *nes*. One involves miracles that require a change in *sidre Bereshit*, and the other involves daily miracles. This second phase "also encompasses unusual happenings to the individual and striking events of importance to the nation, but these, too, are such as do not involve any change in *sidre Bereshit*."[46] In *Torah min hashamayim*, Heschel writes:

> דרשותיו של ר' עקיבא בדרך הפלגת הנסים לא היו תמיד
> לרצון בעיני חבריו. "וַתַּעַל הַצְּפַרְדֵּעַ וַתְּכַס אֶת אֶרֶץ מִצְרָיִם"
> (שמות ח, ב). רבי עקיבא אומר: צפרדע אחת היתה (והיא
> השריצה) ומלאה את כל ארץ מצרים. אמר לו רבי אלעזר
> בן עזריה עקיבא, מה לך אצל אגדות? כלה מדברותיך ולך
> אצל נגעים ואהלות! בעיקר התנגד רבי ישמעאל לדרשותיו
> אלה של רבי עקיבא.[47]

The *midrashim* of Rabbi Akiva expanding [biblical] miracles did not always find favor in the eyes of his colleagues. "'And the frogs [literally: frog] came up and covered the land of Egypt'" (Exodus 8:2). Rabbi Akiva said: It was a single frog that spawned and filled the land of Egypt. Elazar the son of Azaria said to him: Akiva, Why are you involved with *agadah*? Stop speaking; go deal with [impurities related to] skin diseases and tents." It was mainly Rabbi Ishmael who opposed such *midrashim* of Rabbi Akiva.

---

[44] Heschel, *Torah min hashamayim*, 226.
[45] Heschel, *Torah min hashamayim*, 233.
[46] Kadushin, *Rabbinic Mind,* 153–56.
[47] Heschel, *Torah min hashamayim*, 106–7.

In a footnote to this passage, Heschel cites the pages in *The Rabbinic Mind* that refer to Kadushin's description of the "rationalistic tendency" of some of the rabbis regarding the "change in *sidre Bereshit*" phase of *nes*, with Kadushin concluding: "The rationalistic tendency is not a dominant one."[48] In *God in Search of Man*, Heschel also writes of daily miracles:

> The profound and perpetual awareness of the wonder of being has become a part of the religious consciousness of the Jew. Three times a day we pray:
> We thank Thee...
> For Thy miracles which are daily with us,
> For Thy continual marvels....
> The sense for the "miracles which are daily with us," the sense for the "continual marvels," is the source of prayer.[49]

Communication between Heschel and Kadushin

In April 1939, Heschel received a lifesaving invitation to join the faculty of the Hebrew Union College (HUC) in Cincinnati, and he reached the shores of America and joined the institution in the spring of 1940. Heschel was at HUC for five years before his appointment as Professor of Jewish Ethics and Mysticism at JTS in 1945.[50]

Kadushin published his first work, *The Theology of Seder Eliahu* in 1932.[51] His following works—*Organic Thinking* (1938) and *The Rabbinic Mind* (1952)—were published by JTS.[52] However, Kadushin became part of the JTS faculty only in 1960, as Visiting Professor of Ethics and Rabbinic Thought. Kadushin served in this capacity at JTS until his death in 1980.

Kadushin and Heschel corresponded in November 1943 as Kadushin sought to submit his article "Aspects of the Rabbinic Concept of Israel" to the *Hebrew Union College Annual* (*HUCA*). Kadushin sent a draft of the article to Heschel, asking him to recommend it for publication in *HUCA*. In box 3 of the Max Kadushin Papers is Heschel's cordial response, with comments,

---

[48] Kadushin, *Rabbinic Mind*, 156 n. 20.

[49] Heschel, *God in Search of Man*, 48–49.

[50] John C. Merkle, *The Genesis of Faith: The Depth Theology of Abraham Joshua Heschel* (New York: Macmillan, 1985), 10–12.

[51] Max Kadushin, *The Theology of Seder Eliahu: A Study in Rabbinic Judaism* (New York: Bloch, 1932).

[52] Max Kadushin, *Organic Thinking: A Study in Rabbinic Thought* (New York: Jewish Theological Seminary of America, 1938).

and his conclusion: "I should be very glad to recommend your paper to the *HUCA*."[53] Kadushin's article appeared in *HUCA* two years later, even though Kadushin had not implemented Heschel's comment on *Torah* and *haTorah*.[54]

In *Torah min hashamayim*, Heschel cites Kadushin's article. With his exemplary *derekh erets*, Heschel handles Kadushin's decision not to implement his 1943 comment as follows:עַל פִּי דַעְתִּי, "הַתּוֹרָה" מַשְׁמַע כֹּל: הַתּוֹרָה, "תּוֹרָה" מַה שֶּׁנִּיתַּן בְּסִינַי ("In his opinion, *hatorah* implies the entire Torah, *torah* [only] what was given at Sinai").[55] Also intriguing in the 1943 letter is Heschel's "Some day I hope to have the opportunity of discussing with you the method which you apply in this paper." The opportunity was certainly there between1960 , when Kadushin joined the JTS faculty and Heschel's death in 1972. Although I have not yet discovered specific reports of close friendship between Heschel and Kadushin, Michael Graetz writes of the JTS faculty during those years: "There was friendship between all of them…. They lived close to each other, and usually we students would walk them home after Shabbat services (often with an invitation for schnaps or herring, etc.)."[56] There is at least one additional cross-reference to Kadushin in *Torah min hashamayim*.[57] In Kadushin's writings, I have come across two cross-references to works of Heschel.[58]

The Future of Heschel and Kadushin in Israel

Heschel is Heschel, and most of his major writings are now accessible in Hebrew, with Bondi now preparing a translation of *The Prophets*. Although it is unlikely that these volumes will become part of high school curricula under the current government, Bondi, Graetz, Green, and others are teaching Heschel to interested adult Israelis. In spite of all that Kadushin has to offer, Holtz's *be'olam hamaḥshavah shel ḥazal* is out of print, with no plans

[53] The Library of the Jewish Theological Seminary, New York, New York, ARC.1000.004. I have not yet come across either of Kadushin's letters to Heschel. Thanks to Dror Bondi for bringing the existence of this letter to my attention, and to Gordon Tucker for finding time to get a copy and send it to me.

[54] Max Kadushin, "Aspects of the Rabbinic Concept of Israel: A Study in the Mekilta," *Hebrew Union College Annual* 19 (1945–46), 57–96.

[55] Heschel, *Torah min hashamayim*, 491, n.40.

[56] Email from Michael Graetz to Jonathan Matt, June 13, 2023.

[57] Heschel, *Torah min hashamayim* ("*re'iyat penei hashkhinah*"), 372 n.12. That footnote cites Kadushin, *Rabbinic Mind*, 239ff.

[58] Kadushin, *Worship and Ethics*, 293 n. 177, citing *God in Search of Man* and Kadushin, *Rabbinic Mind*, 251–52 n. 126, citing Heschel's "עַל רוּחַ הַקּוֹדֶשׁ בִּימֵי הַבֵּינַיִים" in סֵפֶר הַיּוֹבֵל לִכְבוֹד אלכסנדר מַארְכְּס (נוֹיוֹרְק, תש"י).

to republish. I would like to translate *Worship and Ethics* into Hebrew and have begun exploring that option.

From teaching Heschel and Kadushin in Israel, I know that the insights of both can be helpful to Israelis searching for a Judaism that is both intellectually honest and spiritually inspiring. It is important that both become more influential in Israeli society. Are there signs of hope? Are there things we can do to encourage the process? Although Masorti has much in common with Israeli Reform, Israelis with a *dati le'umi* background seem to connect more easily with Masorti scholarship than with Reform. As Heschel and Kadushin were both on the JTS faculty, our continuing support of Schechter and Masorti congregations is certainly a part of the process. The upcoming Rabbinical Assembly convention in Israel will certainly contribute to the process.

The Israeli world has changed drastically since I wrote my first draft of this article in the summer of 2023. On October 8, my wife Noa and I drove out of our (Lebanese-border) Kibbutz Malkiya, warned that what happened on the Gaza border could also happen up north. We are now at Kibbutz Kramim in the eastern Negev, a relatively safe area. What brought us to Kramim was the combination of a government-funded stay at their country lodging with wanting to help Noa's daughter and her family, who live there. We are also developing friendships with refugees from the Gaza envelope to whom Kramim has opened its doors and its hearts. Although Kramim is not a *kibbuts dati*, it has an active *beit knesset*. It is a value-laden and pluralistic kibbutz, with members of all *'edot* and levels of observance. Israelis like those at Kramim give me further hope for the future of Israeli Judaism.

Jonathan Matt was ordained at JTS in 1975, and made Aliyah that summer. At times of peace, he and his wife Noa live at Kibbutz Malkiya, on the Lebanese border.

ממחסום לחומה

הפרדה מגדרית במקומות הקדושים היהודיים במדינת ישראל

דורון בר

בל"ג בעומר תשפ"א (אפריל 2021) התרחש אסון נוראי במירון, מקום קדוש יהודי ששוכן בצפון מדינת ישראל כשארבעים וחמישה אנשים, כולם גברים, קיפחו את חייהם. בסיום אירוע העלייה לרגל השנתי, המושך אליו מאות אלפים של משתתפים, נהרו המתפללים בדרכם אל מחוץ למתחם המקודש. בדוחק הרב שנוצר בשעת לילה מאוחרת נפצעו רבים ואחרים נדרסו למוות. בדיעבד התברר כי המעבר הצר שבו התרחש האסון, "שביל המהדרין," הוכשר בצורה לא חוקית לפני כ–20 שנים במטרה לאפשר לגברים להימנע ממגע עם הנשים הפוקדות גם הן את המקום הקדוש.[1] מסדרון זה הוא חלק ממערך נרחב של גדרות, מעברים וגשרים שנבנו במהלך השנים באתר הקבר המיוחס לרבי שמעון בר יוחאי במטרה להפריד בין גברים לבין נשים.[2] ההפרדה המגדרית הקיימת במירון מייצגת את המציאות ששוררת כיום ברבים מן המקומות הקדושים היהודיים במדינת ישראל, שם מתפללות נשים בנפרד מן הגברים.

אמנם אין בנמצא רשימה מסודרת ומלאה של כל המקומות הקדושים היהודיים במדינת ישראל, אך נראה כי מדובר במאות אתרי עלייה לרגל שמושכים אליהם קהל של מיליונים. רוב רובם של מקומות קדושים אלו הם קברים של מלכים, נביאים וחכמים הנזכרים בדפי המיתולוגיה היהודית ההיסטורית—תנ"ך, המשנה והתלמוד. רבים ממקומות אלו, כמאה ושלושים, מוכרים ומטופלים על ידי המרכז הארצי לפיתוח המקומות הקדושים (להלן המרכז). גוף ממשלתי זה, הוקם בשנת 1989 על ידי מדינת ישראל, על מנת לנהל ולטפל באתרים הקדושים ליהודים. מטרותיו העיקריות של המרכז – גיוס תרומות עבור פיתוח, תחזוקה ושמירת הסדר באתרים הקדושים. לאלו יש לצרף מאות קברים של צדיקים ורבנים בני זמננו שקודשו בדורות האחרונים על ידי אנשים פרטיים או על ידי ארגונים ואגודות דתיות–חרדיות. קברים אלו עלו גם הם על מפת הקדושה היהודית והפכו לאתרי עלייה לרגל בולטים.[3]

ברבים ממקומות קדושים אלה—רשמיים ומפוקחים על ידי מדינת ישראל, ועממיים ולא–רשמיים—מתפללים נשים וגברים בהפרדה מלאה. הפרדה זו מתעצמת ומתבלטת עוד יותר כאשר מתקיימים במקומות הקדושים הילולות שנתיות ואירועים רבי משתתפים כגון חגים, ימי צום, שמחות או תפילות הודיה. בזמנים אלו מתעצמת עוד יותר ההקפדה על ההפרדה וגוברת הדרישה להקפיד על "צניעות" הנשים. שלטים מורים למאמינות ולמאמינים את דרכם הנפרדת. שערים, מדרכות ומדרגות נפרדים מלווים את קהל המתפללות והמתפללים עד להגעה אל מוקד הקדושה,

1   חיים לוינסון, "השביל במירון שבו נמחצו למוות 45 בני אדם – נבנה בניגוד לחוק כדי להפריד גברים ונשים," הארץ, 6.5.2021.
2   לתיאור המצב במירון לפני האסון ראה: דניאל בכר, "הגדרות שאמורות למנוע מהנשים להידחק אל ציון הרשב"י," כיכר השבת, 28.4.2021; עידו חן, "הושלמה המלאכה: סיום החלפת גדר ההפרדה ההיסטורית במירון," המחדש, 28.4.2021.
3   Doron Bar, "Kivrei Tsadikim as holy places? The Tsadikification process of Jewish Cemeteries in the State of Israel," Journal of Modern Jewish Studies 2023, 22:4 (2023), 543–566

שחצוי תמיד לשניים באמצעות מחיצה.

השוואה לדתות אחרות בעולם מראה כי זו תופעה יוצאת דופן. בחלק מן הדתות מושתתות הגבלות על לבושן ועל התנהגותן של נשים במקומות קדושים, כמו גם על נוכחותן בהם. ישנם אף מקומות קדושים שכניסת נשים אליהם אסורה.[4] יחד עם זאת, באף לא אחת מדתות העולם לא בולטת ההפרדה המגדרית כמו במדינת ישראל. גם מבט היסטורי על המקומות הקדושים היהודיים בארץ ישראל מראה כי זו תופעה חדשה, מהדור או שניים האחרונים. כפי שאראה להלן, עד לפני כמה עשרות שנים כלל לא הייתה קיימת הפרדה בין המינים, וגברים ונשים התפללו במקומות הקדושים יחדיו ושטחו את תחינותיהם שכם אל שכם.

מטרת המאמר היא לעמוד על ההפרדה המגדרית המאפיינת כיום את המקומות הקדושים היהודיים במדינת ישראל, תופעה הקשורה בתהליכי הקצנה שעוברת החברה הישראלית. החר-דיזציה של המקומות הקדושים מובלת בחלקה "מלמעלה", על ידי זרועות דתיות שונות של מדינת ישראל הממומנת, מארגנות ומפקחות על ההפרדה זו. חלקו האחר של תהליך ההפרדה מגדרית זה צומח "מלמטה",, והוא תוצאה של פעילות פרטים וקבוצות חרדיות, אשכנזיות ומזרחיות, המקדמות החמרה בדרישות צניעות המושתתות על נשים יהודיות–ישראליות.

ההפרדה המגדרית הפיסית, הדרך שבה חברות שונות מונעות מנשים לפקוד מקומות מסוימים, מושכת בשנים האחרונות תשומת לב מחקרית רבה.[5] על אף זאת, מקומן ומעמדן השולי של נשים יהודיות במקומות קדושים לא זכה עד כה למיקוד במחקר, על אחת כמה וכמה לא שאלת קיומה של ההפרדה מגדרית בהם.[6] התנגשות זו בין ערכים אוניברסאליים של שוויון בין המינים אשר אמורים לשרור במקומות הקדושים, לבין מציאות של ערכים פרטיקולריים דתיים פרטיים וקהילתיים שמובילים את ההפרדה ואת הדרת הנשים, יש בה בכדי לשמש מקרה–מבחן ומקור להתבוננות השוואתית בינו לבין המתרחש בתחום זה במקומות קדושים אחרים בעולם.

---

[4] Nurit Stadler, *Voices of the Ritual: Devotion to Female Saints and Shrines in the Holy Land*, Oxford: Oxford University Press, 2020.

[5] Roel Meijer, "The Gender Segregation (ikhtilāṭ) Debate in Saudi Arabia: Reform and the Clash between 'ulamā' and Liberals," *Journal for Islamic Studies* 30 (2010), 2–32; Ruth Roded, "Middle Eastern Women in Gendered space: Religious Legitimacy and Social," *Hawwa* 10:1–2 (2012), 1–17; Reza Arjmand, *Public Urban Space, Gender and Segregation: Women-only Urban Parks in Iran* (Milton: Taylor and Francis, 2016); Aharon Rock-Singer, "The Salafi Mystique: The Rise of Gender Segregation in 1970s Egypt," *Islamic Law and Society* 23:3 (2016) 279–305; Fatemeh Salarvandian et. al, "How Women's Presence in Tehran's Public Spaces Compares to Shari'a Prescriptions, Old Tehran and Contemporary Tehran," *Hawwa* 19: 2 (2020), 223–253; ראו לגבי המרחב הישראלי: Michal L. Allon, "Gender Segregation, Effacement, and Suppression: Trends in the Status of Women in Israel," *Digest of Middle East Studies* 22:2 (2013), 276–291; Yofi Tirosh, "Diminishing Constitutional Law: The First Three Decades of Women's Exclusion Adjudication in Israel," *International Journal of Constitutional Law*, 18:3 (2020), 821–846.

[6] דו"ח הצוות המשרדי לבחינת תופעת הדרת הנשים במרחב הציבורי, מוגש ליועץ המשפטי לממשלה, משרד המשפטים, ירושלים: 2013. על הצוות נמנו שרית דנה, אבי ליכט, רז נזרי, אלי אברבנאל (פרקליטות המדינה) ואיל זנדברג, ראש תחום משפט ציבורי במחלקת ייעוץ וחקיקה. אין בדו"ח כל התייחסות להפרדת נשים מגברים במקומות הקדושים.

דורון בר

הפרדה בין גברים לנשים במקומות קדושים – מבט עולמי

נשים אמנם תופסות חלק משמעותי בקהל עולי הרגל למקומות קדושים,[7] אך על אף זאת מקומות
אלה הם גבריים מאד באופים ובתפקודם. גבריות זו באה לידי ביטוי בכך שאלו הם לרוב גברים
המנהלים אותם ומשמשים בהם כהני דת, ובכך שהם המעצבים את מרביתם מבחינה פיסית
והם שקובעים את אורחות הפולחן בהם. הגברים הם אלה הקובעים את קוד ההתנהגות במרבית
המקומות הקדושים (הכולל פעמים רבות כללים המגבילים את הנשים, העולות לרגל). הנשים
נתפסות על ידי הגברים כציבורי פסיבי המתארח במקום הקדוש, שאין לו מקום בעיצוב הפולחן
ובמראהו.[8]

גבריות המקומות הקדושים משרתת, לכאורה, ערכים של צניעות המאפשרת לבני שני המינים
לבקר במקום הקדוש תוך הימנעות מחיכוך זה עם זו ומפגיעה הדדית ברגשותיהם ובאמונתם
הדתית. אך ההפקעה הגברית של ניהול המקומות הקדושים והדרה, לפחות חלקית, של נשים
מהם נעשית "מעל ראשן", ללא הסכמתן וללא התחשבות ברצונן וברגשותיהן.[9] דחיקת נשים מן
המקומות הקדושים מביאה אותן פעמים לפקוד מקומות קדושים "שוליים" ולא ממוסדים, שם
לעתים שליטת הגברים מינורית יחסית והכללים הנהוגים בהם נוקשים פחות. שם הן יכולות לפתח
ריטואלים עצמאיים המותאמים להן.[10]

בקרב חלק מדתות העולם קיימת נטייה להפרדה מגדרית במבני תפילה. חלק מן הקהילות
היהודיות בעולם מפרידות את חלל בית הכנסת בין גברים לנשים, היושבות ב"עזרת נשים"; נשים
יושבות בדרך כלל נפרדות ומרוחקות מן הגברים במהלך התפילה במסגד (כלל זה נכון גם לגבי
מסגדים היסטוריים–מקודשים שמשמשים כיעד לעלייה לרגל);[11] בקרב חלק מן העדות הנוצריות
הייתה נהוגה בעבר ונהוגה כיום ישיבה נפרדת של גברים ונשים.[12] אך התמונה שונה בנוגע לביקור
במקומות קדושים. בקרב חלק מן הדתות קיימים אמנם לעתים אזורים מקודשים ומקומות קדושים

---

[7] על הקשר בין נשים לדת, ראו: Arvind Sharma (ed.) Religion and women (Albany, NY: State University of New
York Press, 1994); Yvonne Yazbeck Haddad and Ellison Banks Findly (eds.) *Women, Religion and Social
Change* (Albany, N.Y: State University of New York Press, 1985).

[8] Leigh Ann Craig, *Wandering Women and Holy Matrons: Women as Pilgrims in the Later Middle Ages*
(Leiden: Brill, 2009); Carlos Andres Gonzalez–Paz (ed.) *Women and Pilgrimage in Medieval Galicia* (Routledge: Oxon, 2016).

[9] אסתי רידר אינדורסקי, "מתחת להסכמה שבשתיקה להפרדה מסתתר כעס גדול של הנשים החרדיות," הארץ, 31.1.2020. מנגד
נשמעת טענה כי ההפרדה המגדרית במקומות הקדושים נוחה ורצויה למתפללות. על כך ראו: נויה רימלט, "הפרדה בין גברים לנשים
כהפליה בין המינים," על משפט, ג:1 (תשס"ג), עמ' 119–112.

[10] Aziza Ouguir, *Moroccan Female Religious Agents* (Leiden: Brill, 2020) 90–112; Nurit Stadler, "Land,
Fertility Rites and the Veneration of Female Saints: Exploring Body Rituals at the Tomb of Mary in Jerusalem," *Anthropological Theory* 15:3 (2015) 293–316.

[11] Shampa Mazumdar and Sanjoy Mazumdar, "In Mosques and Shrines: Women's Agency in Public Sacred
Space," *Journal of Ritual Studies* 16:2 (2002), 165–179; Marion Katz, *Women in the Mosque: A History of Legal
Thought and Social Practice* (New York, NY: Columbia University Press, 2014); Nevin Reda, "Women in the
Mosque: Historical Perspectives on Segregation," *The American Journal of Islamic Social Sciences* 21:2 (2004)
77–97 ; Line Nyhagen, "Mosques as Gendered Spaces: The Complexity of Women's Compliance with, And
Resistance to, Dominant Gender Norms, And the Importance of Male Allies," *Religions* 10:5 (2019) 1–15.

[12] Margaret Aston, "Segregation in Church," *Studies in Church History* 27 (1990), 237–294.

שאסורה כניסת נשים אליהם,[13] למשל מנזרי גברים.[14] אך לרוב, העלייה לרגל אל המקום הקדוש,
ההתקרבות אליו והתפילה בסמוך לו נעשים במשותף—גברים ונשים. חלק מן הדתות אף הפכו
את העלייה לרגל המשותפת לאידיאל—למשל הדת הבאהית, הדוגלת בשוויון מלא בין המינים גם
בנוגע לביקורו באתריה החשובים.[15] בדומה לכך מרבית הכתות בנצרות מעודדות ביקור משותף
של גברים ונשים במקומות קדושים דוגמת אתרי ניסים והתגלות, כנסיות ואתרי טבילה, ואין
בהם כל הפרדה בין המאמינים. ראשי הדת רואים ערך בחיבור בין שני המינים ומעודדים ישיבה,
אכילה ותפילה משותפות.

הקוראן אמנם איננו מצווה במפורש על הפרדה מגדרית. עם זאת, המסורת בחברות מוסלמיות
רבות שוללת אינטראקציה חברתית–פיסית בין גברים לנשים. לכן אם כן מתקיימת הפרדה מגדרית
ברבות מן המדינות המוסלמיות המגובה בפסקי הלכה. על אף זאת, קיום מצוות החאג' והעומרה,
העלייה לרגל למכה ומדינה וסדרת הטקסים הדתיים שמתקיימים שם, ובמיוחד טקס הקפת אבן
הכעבה נעשה במשותף, גברים ונשים יחדיו. אין במקום זה, כמו גם במקומות קדושים מוסלמיים
נוספים, מחסומים פיסיים שמפרידים בין המינים.[16] העדר ההפרדה המגדרית בולט במיוחד בדתות
המזרח, גם שם לא קיימת הפרדה מגדרית פיסית במקדשים המקודשים. נשים פוקדות בדרך כלל
מקדשים הינדים ובודהיסטים בהודו בצורה חופשית וללא כל הגבלות, וגם אצל הסיקים, הביקור
במקומות הקדושים מתקיימים במשותף.[17]

ההיסטוריה של המקומות הקדושים היהודיים בארץ ישראל

המידע על ההיסטוריה הקדומה של המקומות הקדושים היהודיים במדינת ישראל הוא חלקי ביותר.
איננו יודעים די על קיומם ועל מעמדם של מקומות קדושים במאות השנים שלאחר חורבן בית
המקדש השני, שבהן נשלטה הארץ על ידי האימפריה הרומית והביזנטית ומאוחר יותר על ידי
המוסלמים וגם איננו יודעים כלל על מקומן של נשים בפולחן.[18]
התקופה הצלבנית (מאות 12–13 לסה"נ) מרובה יחסית במסע בתיאורי עולי רגל יהודים
שפקדו את ארץ ישראל ומעידים על קיומו של מרחב מקודש יהודי.[19] בהמשך, עם דחיקת

[13] Kobayashi Naoko, "Sacred Mountains and Women in Japan: Fighting a Romanticized Image of Female Ascetic Practitioners," *Japanese Journal of Religious Studies* 44:1 (2017), 103–122.

[14] על איסור כניסת נשים למנזרי הר אתוס שביוון, ראו:Alice Mary Talbot, "Women and Mt Athos," A. Bryer and M. Cunningham (eds.) *Mount Athos and Byzantine Monasticism. Papers from the Twenty–eighth Spring Symposium of Byzantine Studies*, Birmingham, March 1994 (Aldershot: Variorum, 1996), 67–79.

[15] Susan Maneck, "Women in the Bahá'í Faith," Sharma, Arvind (ed.) Religion and Women (Albany, NY: State University of New York Press, 1994), 211–228.

[16] Marjo Buitelar, "Stepping in the footsteps of Hajar to bring home the hajj," Marjo Buitelaar, Manja Stephan–Emmrich and Viola Thimm (eds.) Muslim Women's Pilgrimage to Mecca and Beyond: Reconfiguring Gender, Religion, and Mobility (London: Routledge, 2021), 180–200.

[17] Rajinder S. Jutla, "The Evolution of the Golden Temple of Amritsar into a Major Sikh Pilgrimage Center," AIMS Geosciences, 2:3 (2016), 259–272.

[18] Elchanan Reiner, "From Joshua Trough Jesus to Simeon Bar Yohai- towards a Typology of Galilean Heroes," Neta Stahl (ed.) Jesus Among Jews: Representation and Thought (London: Routledge, 2012), 94–105.

[19] Elchanan Reiner, "A Jewish Response to the Crusades: The Dispute over Sacred Places in the Holy Land," A. Haverkamp (ed.) Juden und Christen zur Zeit der Kreuzzüge, Sigmaringen (Sigmaringen: Thorbecke, 1999), 209–231.

הצלבנים מן הארץ וביסוס השליטה המוסלמית בה, התגבש מערך נרחב של מקומות קדושים יהודיים בחלקים שונים של הארץ.[20] מקומות קדושים אלו, שהיו פעמים רבות בבעלות מוסלמית, ומאמינים מוסלמיים ויהודיים חלקו בהם, שירתו הן את הקהילה היהודית הארץ–ישראלית והן את עולי הרגל היהודיים שהגיעו מארצות האסלאם וממקומות ספרד ואשכנז.[21] ירושלים היוותה מוקד לעולי הרגל והתייחדה בכך שחלק גדול מטקסי העלייה לרגל התמקד בבכי על חורבן בית המקדש וביחולים לבנייתו מחדש. בולט במיוחד אזור הגליל המזרחי, שם זוהו וקודשו במאה השש–עשרה קבריהם של תנאים ואמוראים רבים.[22]

לא רק שיהודים ומוסלמים חלקו פעמים רבות מקומות קדושים אלו והתפללו בהם זה לצד זה אלא שנראה כי השפיעו והושפעו מן המוסלמים שנהגו לפקוד יחדיו, גברים ונשים, קברי קדושים.[23] החל מן המאה ה–16 יש בידינו תיאורים הולכים ומתרבים של נוכחות נשית במקומות הקדושים ושל תפילות נשים שם, אך אין בהם כל עדות להפרדה מגדרית. נוסע אלמוני שפקד את ארץ ישראל בשנת 1522–1523 דיווח כיצד "הלכנו כל הקהל כאחד אנשים ונשים להתפקד על כל ציוני הצדיקים אשר שם [באזור טבריה] והם רחוקים זה מזה מיל ויותר."[24] שמחה ב"ר יהושע מדווח בשנת 1774 כיצד "כל ספרדי ירא ה' והיכולת בידו הולך לא"י פעם אחת בימי חייו ומסבב והולך על קברי אבותינו הצדיקים והחסידים. וגם הנשים הולכות ומסבבות, ומוסרים עצמם בכל נפשם ובכל מאדם."[25] שמעון ברמן, המבקר בירושלים בשנת 1870–1871 מתאר כיצד בעלייה לרגל השנתית בל"ג בעומר לקבר שמעון הצדיק בירושלים "במערה כבר היו נאספים לערך 60 או 70 ספרדים, אנשים נשים וטף שבאו ממרחקים עוד אתמול ואתם חבילות ושקים, כלי מיטה וכלי בישול... הנשים הספרדיות מפטפטות, כי אינן יודעות לקרוא. הנשים המעטות מבין יהודי פולין קוראות תחינות לאור המנורות התלויות במערה"[26] בתיאורים אלו ואחרים אין כל עדות להפרדה מגדרית ונראה כי זו התקיימה רק לעתים רחוקות, למשל בימי עליה לרגל המוניים. בהילולת ל"ג בעומר במירון התפללו הגברים מול קבר רשב"י והנשים נאלצו להסתפק בתפילה בחדר סמוך. הן הודרו מן הזירה המרכזית של הטקס ולא השתתפו בתפילה, בשירה ובריקודים.[27]

במחצית השנייה של המאה התשע–עשרה, בעקבות השינויים הגיאופוליטיים הרבים שחלו בחלק המזרחי של אגן הים התיכון ועם שיפור תנאי התעבורה באזור, התרחבה בצורה משמעותית תנועת עולי הרגל היהודיים לארץ ישראל, מגמה שהתרחבה עם סיום מלחמת העולם הראשונה והתבססות השלטון הבריטי. הייתה זו תקופה של שגשוג ושל פיתוח המקומות הקדושים

---

20 אלחנן ריינר, "'מפי בני מערבא': על דרכי רישומה של מסורת המקומות הקדושים בארץ–ישראל בימי הביניים," רחל צרפתי (עורכת) מנחה שלוחה: תיאורי מקומות קדושים בידי אמנים יהודים, ירושלים: מחיאון ישראל, 2002, 17–9.

21 Josef W. Meri, The Cult of Saints Among Muslim and Jews in Medieval Syria (Oxford: Oxford University Press, 2002).

22 Daphna Levin, "Can Two Walk Together, Except That They Agree? R. Isaac Luria's Kabbalistic Initiation of R. Hayyim Vital," Daat: A Journal of Jewish Philosophy & Kabbalah 82 (2016), 211–250.

23 Mahmoud Yazbak, "The Muslim Festival of Nabi Rubin in Palestine: From Religious Festival to Summer Resort," Holy Land Studies 10:2 (2011), 169–198.

24 יהודה דוד אייזנשטיין, אוצר מסעות: קובץ תיורים של נוסעים יהודים בארץ–ישראל, סוריא, מצרים וארצות אחרות, רשימות עולי רגל לקברי אבות וקדושים, עם מפות, הערות ומפתח, ניוארק: י.ה. אייזנשטיין, תרפ"ז, עמ' 138.

25 שם, 240.

26 אברהם יערי, מסעות ארץ ישראל: של עולים יהודיים מימי הביניים ועד ראשית ימי שיבת ציון, רמת גן: מסדה, 1976, 609.

27 ראו למשל את תיאורו של יוסף מאנספעלד המובא על ידי ישראל דוד בית הלוי, תולדות יהודי קאליש, תל אביב: הוצאת המחברת תשכ"א, 324.

היהודיים,[28] עת שבה התרבו תיאורי המקומות הקדושים והעדויות על נוכחות נשים שם ועל מנהיגתן. אחד האתרים הבולטים מבחינה זו הוא קבר רחל ששמעו יצא למרחקים ומשך אליו נשים רבות. סיפור חייה התנ"כי הטרגי של רחל שימש עבור נשים רבות כמקור להזדהות שמשכה אותן לשם.[29] מצילומי קבר רחל, כמו גם מצילומי מקומות קדושים נוספים בני התקופה ניתן לראות בבירור כי לא קיימת הפרדה פיסית כלשהי בין גברים לנשים שמתפללים אלו בצד אלו.

הדבר נכון גם לגבי הכותל המערבי, המקום הקדוש היהודי הבולט ביותר בתקופה זו. מקורות היסטוריים, בהם גם צילומים, מצביעים על כך שבשלהי התקופה העות'מאנית (1917-1799) משך אליו הכותל המערבי נשים רבות שהתפללו בסמוך לגברים וללא מחיצה.[30] תופעה זו אפיינה גם את תקופת המנדט הבריטי (1948-1917), בתקופה שבה הפך הכותל המערבי לסלע מחלוקת לאומי בין יהודים למוסלמים. בשנים אלו אמנם ניסו גורמים יהודיים שונים להעמיד בלב הרחבה מחיצה, מציאות ששיקפה את רצונם להפריד בין המינים במהלך חגים והתכנסויות רבות משתתפים, אך דבר זה נאסר על-ידי שלטונות המנדט.[31]

העדר ההפרדה במקומות הקדושים נותר על כנו גם לאחר קום מדינת ישראל ועם ייסוד משרד הדתות, שאחד מעיסוקיו היה פיתוח מקומות קדושים. בתקופה זו נחלקה ארץ ישראל ונחסמה הגישה אל רבים מן המקומות הקדושים היהודיים שניצבו בחלקה המזרחי והירדני של המרחב. חוסר יכולתם של היהודים להגיע אל הכותל המערבי, קבר רחל ומערת המכפלה, הביאה לפיתוח מערך חלופי נרחב של מקומות קדושים, שבאף אחד מהם לא לא הפרידה מחיצה בין גברים לנשים.[32] תופעה זו הייתה עדיין נדירה למדי בכלל המרחב הציבורי הישראלי, ופה ושם נשמעו דעות של מי שצידדו בהפרדה זו בחופי הים ובבריכות שחייה.[33]

מלחמת ששת הימים, הכותל המערבי וחלוקת רחבת התפילה במחיצה

המקום הקדוש היהודי החשוב ביותר במדינת ישראל הוא הכותל המערבי, שריד מיתולוגי של בית המקדש היהודי שנחרב על ידי הרומאים בשנת 70 לסה"נ. המחיצה המפרידה בין שני המינים, הניצבת כיום בלב רחבת הכותל המערבי הוצבה שם ביולי 1967, מספר שבועות לאחר תום מלחמת ששת הימים. הכותל המערבי ובו המחיצה, הוא המקום הקדוש הראשון במדינת ישראל שבו הופרדו גברים ונשים, תקדים ונקודת מפנה משמעותית בתהליך ההפרדה המגדרית במקומות הקדושים הישראליים.

[28] דותן גורן, ובא לציון גואל: המאמצים היהודיים לקניית אחוזה במקומות הקדושים בירושלים וסביבותיה בשלהי התקופה העות'מאנית (1918-1840), ירושלים: הוצאת ספריית בית-אל, תשע"ז.

[29] Margalit Shilo, *Princess or Prisoner?: Jewish women in Jerusalem, 1840-1914* (Waltham, Mass: Brandeis University Press, 2005), 12-33.

[30] לביא שי, גיאוגרפיה היסטורית-תרבותית וצילום: התפתחות ירושלים כמקרה מבחן, 1948-1839, עבודת דוקטורט, האוניברסיטה העברית, 2011.

[31] *The Kotel Trail: A Report on the International Western Wall Committee* (Tel Aviv: Tel Aviv, 1931), 57

[32] דורון בה, לקדש ארץ: המקומות הקדושים היהודיים במדינת ישראל 1968-1948, ירושלים: יד יצחק בן צבי, תשס"ז, 149-129;
Doron Bar, "Reconstructing the Past: The Creation of Jewish Sacred Space in the State of Israel, 1948-1967," Israel Studies 13.3 (2008), 1-21

[33] ראו למשל: "יציעו מחיצה בין גברים לנשים," הארץ, 23.2.1958; "שיף דן בהתקנת מחיצה בבריכה," הארץ, 1.4.1958. חרדים הפגינו מדי פעם נגד פתיחתן של בריכות שחייה מעורבות כמו גלי גיל ברמת גן ועמק רפאים בירושלים ונגד חופי רחצה מעורבים ומעת לעת היה זה לכך הד בשיח הציבורי.

בשלהי התקופה העות'מאנית, כמו גם בתקופת המנדט לא הייתה קיימת הפרדה מגדרית פיסית בכותל המערבי. במהלך 19 שנות חלוקת העיר, בין השנים 1967–1948, ממילא נמנע ביקור חופשי של יהודים בכותל המערבי, מציאות ששונתה בחדות לאחר מלחמת ששת הימים ועם איחוד שני חלקי ירושלים. יצירת רחבת התפילה גדולת הממדים והשליטה הישראלית התקדימית עליה, חייבו את מדינת ישראל לקבוע את הגורם האחראי על הכותל המערבי ועל סדריו הדתיים.[34] בעקבות החלטת ראש הממשלה לוי אשכול כי "הסדרים על–יד הכותל המערבי ייקבעו בידי הרבנים הראשיים",[35] הועברה האחריות על המקום לידי משרד הדתות. שר הדתות, בעידוד הרבנות הראשית, שינה את 'מנהג המקום' שרווח שם לפני 1948 והחיל ברחבת הכותל המערבי כללי צניעות שהיו נהוגים בבתי–כנסת אורתודוקסיים. הדבר התאפשר בזכות השימוש ב'חוק השמירה על המקומות הקדושים 1967' שחוקק בסוף יוני 1967, שקבע כי שר הדתות ממונה על ביצוע החוק ורשאי להתקין תקנות להבטחת ביצועו.[36]

תקנות אלו נתנו תוקף חוקי לסדרים שנקבעו בכותל המערבי בשבועות שלאחר המלחמה ואפשרו לממסד הדתי להציב באמצע יולי 1967 מחיצה בלב הרחבה.[37] המחיצה הארעית הפכה תוך זמן קצר לקבועה והנציחה את חלוקת רחבת התפילה בין חלק גדול יותר שהוקצה לגברים ולבין חלק מצומצם שהועמד לרשות הנשים. בכניסות לרחבת התפילה הוצבו פקחי משרד הדתות שאכפו את ההפרדה בין נשים לגברים וכן לבוש 'צנוע' לנשים וכיסוי ראש לגברים.[38]

המציאות החדשה שנוצרה ברחבת הכותל המערבי עוררה ויכוח פנים–ישראלי עז בנוגע לשאלה למי שמורה הזכות לקבוע שם את כללי ההתנהגות הדתית. נשמעו מחאות כנגד חלוקתו המגדרית והועלו דרישות להסיר את המחיצה. יעקב ינאי, מנהל הרשות לגנים לאומיים, היה אחד מאלו שספק שאלו ספק התריס: "ממתי הכותל הפך למקום בו מבקרים רק דתיים? מדוע סבורים כי לכותל באים יהודים להתפלל? והחילונים בארץ – מדוע יאלצו אותם לעמוד ליד הכותל בלא נשותיהם? ומה יעשה אדם הרוצה לעמוד מול הכותל ולהתייחד עם עצמו – בשקט, ללא תפילה?"[39] "ומי קבע שלכותל המערבי אופי דתי בלבד? האין הוא שריד היסטורי לאומי? [...] לחוגים רחבים בעם כיום מחיצה בין גברים לנשים איננה מקובלת ובלתי נסבלת," נכתב בעיתון הארץ.[40]

שר הדתות, כמייצג הממסד הדתי, השיב לינאי ולשאר המבקרים כי החוק הוא שנותן בידו את הסמכות לקבוע מהו מקום קדוש ומהו מקום היסטורי (שבו לא הוחלה חלוקה מגדרית),[41] וכי הכותל המערבי היה מקום קדוש ליהודים לפני שהפך מקום היסטורי.[42] הוא קבע כי ההסדרים במקומות הקדושים היהודיים, ובכללם ההפרדה בין גברים לנשים הם עניין הלכתי שבסמכותם של

---

[34] Kobi Cohen-Hattab and Doron Bar, The Western Wall: The Dispute over Israel's Holiest Site 1967–2000 (Leiden: Brill, 2020).

[35] ארכיון מדינת ישראל [להלן אמ"י], גל–2603–2, דברי לוי אשכול בפגישה עם הרבנים הראשיים והמנהיגים הרוחניים של כל העדות במדינה, 7.6.1967.

[36] חוק השמירה על המקומות הקדושים, התשכ"ז–1967, ס"ח 499 מיום ה–28.6.1967.

[37] ע' בנזימן, "מכלאות ליד הכותל המערבי; משרד הדתות הופך רחבת הכותל לבית כנסת אורתודוכסי," הארץ, 19.7.1967.

[38] Meron Benvenisti, Jerusalem, the Torn City (Minneapolis: University of Minnesota Press, 1976), 136–139.

[39] צ' רימון, "חטפו את הכותל," ידיעות אחרונות, 23.7.1967.

[40] י' אליצור, "המחיצה ליד הכותל," הארץ, 12.7.1967; "ל"ע דורשת הסרת המחיצה," הארץ, 13.8.1967.

[41] Doron Bar, "Holy places or Historical sites? Defining Sacred על המתח בין מקומות קדושים למקומות היסטוריים: and Archaeological Sites in the State of Israel, 1948–1967," History of Religions 58:1 (2018), 1–23.

[42] "ורהפטיג מסביר את טיפול משרדו בבעיות הכותל," הארץ, 25.7.1967.

הרבנים הראשיים, והם שקבעו את העקרונות לשמירת כלל המקומות הקדושים והכותל המערבי בראשם.[43] שר הדתות אף טען כי מאחר שבזמן קיום בית המקדש הקפידו על הפרדה בין מינים, הרי יש לשמור על הפרדה כזו גם בכותל המערבי, שהוא שריד לאותו בית מקדש.[44] הרב הראשי האשכנזי איסר יהודה אונטרמן אישר כי "בוודאי צריכים מחיצה בין גברים לנשים כי זהו הצביון של בתי התפילה שלנו שאינם מחקים מחקים דרכי העמים, וזה לא ניתן לשינויים."[45] כאן התייחס הרב הראשי להעתקת המנהג מבית הכנסת, שם הייתה מקובלת בקרב חלק מקהילות ישראל ההפרדה בין גברים לבין נשים, אל הכותל המערבי.[46]

בשלהי 1967, ועל אף שהכותל המערבי לא שימש בעבר בית כנסת, נקבעה במקום הפרדה בין מינים נותרה בעינה עד ימינו. המחאות שהושמעו בשנים הראשונות שלאחר המלחמה כנגד הפרדה המגדרית הלכו ודעכו. האחיזה הדתית–חרדית במקום התבססה וההפרדה הפכה לאחד מסימני ההיכר הבולטים של המקום. בהמשך, במהלך שנות השבעים הלכו והתרחבו דרישות הצניעות אל עבר חלקים נוספים של הרחבה. נקבעו שערי כניסה נפרדים אל המתחם והמחיצה הלכה וגבהה והפכה למחסום פיסי בולט ומשמעותי.[47] בשלהי שנות השמונים של המאה העשרים הפך הכותל המערבי לזירת מאבק ייחודית שבה אותגרה לראשונה בתולדות מדינת ישראל ההפרדה המגדרית. פעילותן של "נשות הכותל" במקום מאז 1988 ומאבקן לאפשר חופש תפילה ברחבת התפילה, כמו גם שאיפתם של חברי התנועות הקונסרבטיבית והרפורמית לקיים שם תפילה משותפת הם חלק מן הניסיונות הנמשכים לאתגר את הסטטוס קוו שנוצר במקום לאחר 1967 והמנציח את חלוקת רחבת התפילה בין גברים לנשים.[48]

הפרדה מגדרית במקומות הקדושים היהודיים –
מ"למעלה" "למטה" ומ"למטה" "למעלה"

הפרדה מגדרית מאפיינת כיום רבים מן המקומות הקדושים היהודיים במדינת ישראל; הן מקומות מרכזיים וממוסדים כמו קבר שמעון בר יוחאי במירון, קבר רחל וקבר יהונתן בן עוזיאל בעמוקה,[49] והן אתרי קודש בעלי חשיבות מקומית או מגזרית כמו קבר רבי אבדימי בחיפה; קבר אליעזר שלמה שיק, הצדיק מיבנאל, וקברי אדמו"רי גור, אברהם מרדכי אלתר ובנו פינחס מנחם אלתר בירושלים.[50] בכל אחד ממקומות אלו מפרידות מחיצות בין שני המינים או שמוקצה להן עזרת נשים.

---

43 "המפד"ל מוחה בחריפות נגד המגמות להפקיע מקדושתו את הכותל המערבי," הצופה, 4.8.1967.

44 "בין הפטיש והדוכן– הכנסה דחתה ניסיונות לפגוע בסמכויותיה של הרבנות הראשית," הצפה, 20.6.1968.

45 אמ"י, חצ–4293–2, איסר יהודא אונטרמן, "חוות דעת," 12.3.1968.

46 שמואל ספראי, "האם הייתה קיימת עזרת נשים בבית הכנסת בתקופה העתיקה," תרביץ, לב: ד (תשכ"ג), 338–329; דוד גולינקין, מעמד האישה בהלכה – שאלות ותשובות, ירושלים: מכון שכטר למדעי היהדות, תשס"א, 204–179.

47 ריקי שפירא־רוזנברג, מודרות למהדרין: הפרדה בין נשים לגברים במרחב הציבורי בישראל, ירושלים: המרכז לפלורליזם יהודי, 2010, עמ' 12–11.

48 Yitzhak Reiter, "Feminists in the Temple of Orthodoxy: The Struggle of the Women of the Wall to Change the Status Quo," *Shofar* 34:2 (2016), 79–107; Yuval Jobani and Nahshon Perez, *Women of the Wall: Navigating Religion in Sacred Sites*, (New York, NY: Oxford University Press, 2017); Lihi Ben Shitrit, *Women and the Holy City: the Struggle over Jerusalem's Sacred Space* (Cambridge, Cambridge University Press, 2021).

49 נגה משל, "'ברכות בשקל': איך קרה שקברי צדיקים עברו מהפך ממקום קדוש לשוק פרוע?" דה מרקר, 24.10.2008; יוסי מזרחי, "הר הרווחות: אלפי מתפללים ובעיקר מתפללות פקדו את קברו של הצדיק יונתן בן עוזיאל ליד צפת," מעריב, 16.6.2004.

50 אלי אלון, "קברי אדמו"רי גור בחצר הישיבה בירושלים," מחלקה ראשונה, 10.5.2016.

קשה לקבוע מתי החל וכיצד התפשט תהליך זה ומי יזם את חלוקת המקומות בין גברים לנשים.
בניגוד לתהליך המתועד היטב בכותל המערבי, הרי ההתפשטות של ההפרדה המגדרית המאפיינת
את שאר המקומות הקדושים היהודיים איננה מתועדת במסמכים או במקורות אחרים. המקור
הבולט ביותר שמאפשר לנו לעמוד על התקבעות והתרחבות ההפרדה במקומות הקדושים הם
צילומיהם, מהם ניתן ללמוד על הזמן ועל הדרך שבה עוצבה בשנים האחרונות סביבתם והתבססה
ההפרדה בין גברים לנשים.

מצילומים של מקומות קדושים רבים, ובהם קבר שמואל הנביא שבקרבת ירושלים, קבר
הרמב"ם (רבי משה בן מימון) בטבריה, קבר רבן גמליאל ביבנה, קבר דוד בהר ציון וקבר הבבא
סאלי בנתיבות, עולה כי עד לשנות השמונים והתשעים של המאה העשרים לא הייתה קיימת
במקומות הקדושים כל הפרדה וגברים ונשים התפללו אלו בצד אלו. בהמשך הוצבו מחיצות
ברבים ממקומות אלו.[51]

אחד המרכיבים יוצאי הדופן והייחודיים של המקומות הקדושים במדינת ישראל היא העובדה
שחלקם מוכרים ומנוהלים על ידי משרד הדתות הישראלי. בניגוד למקומות אחרים בעולם, שם
שייכים המקומות הקדושים למסדרים דתיים, אגודות, הקדשים וארגונים שונים, הרי במדינת
ישראל מפקח המרכז על המקומות הקדושים היהודיים הבולטים. גוף ממלכתי זה, זרוע של משרד
הדתות, "שומר, מתחזק ומתפעל קרוב ל־130 אתרים המוכרים כקדושים לעם היהודי מדורי
דורות," ואחראי לא רק על פיתוח מקומות אלה אלא גם על "אכיפת הסדר במקום הקדוש."[52]

הגדרה זו מאפשרת לאנשי משרד הדתות, גוף שמנוהל מאז הקמת המדינה וכמעט ברציפות
מלאה על ידי מפלגות דתיות אורתודוכסיות שבהן ישנה דומיננטיות גברית, להגדיר את סדר היום
במקומות הקדושים היהודיים ולקבוע מסמרות בנוגע לנהליהם ולמנהיגהם. העובדה שגברים הם
אלו המובילים את המדיניות ואת הנורמות בגופים אלה שאין בהם כל ייצוג לנשים, היא המובילה
להפרדה בין המינים במקומות הקדושים. הדוגמאות לתופעה זו הן רבות ובאות לידי ביטוי ברבים
מן המקומות הקדושים המנוהלים על ידי גוף זה.

כך למשל קרה בקבר הרמב"ם שנמצא תחת אחריות המרכז. בצילומים מוקדמים של הקבר
השוכן בטבריה ניתן לראות כי האתר הקדוש פתוח לביקורי גברים ונשים כאחד ואין במקום כל
מחיצה אך בתחילת שנות האלפיים הוא חולק לראשונה באמצעות מחיצה שהפכה לקבועה בשנת
2017, אז עבר מתחם הקבר שיפוץ ביוזמה ובמימון של משרדי ממשלה שונים ושל המרכז. לגברים
הוקצה שטח רחב יותר ואף נבנה גרם מדרגות שיעד למתפללות בלבד[53] תהליך דומה עבר קבר
שמואל הנביא, מקום קדוש שהוא גם גן לאומי מוכר. רשות הטבע והגנים, גוף ממשלתי האמון
על שמירת ערכי הטבע והמורשת במדינת ישראל, אשר אחראי על המקום, לקח חלק פעיל בקביעת
ההפרדה המגדרית שם. כחלק מן הפיתוח של המקום הקדוש הוצבה במקום מחיצה המפרידה
בין גברים לנשים. לאלו ולאלו הוקצו כניסות נפרדות לקריפטה שבה שוכן חלל הקבר המחולק.[54]

מקום קדוש מרכזי נוסף שבו נכפתה הפרדה מגדרית הוא קבר דוד בירושלים. גם במקום זה

---

[51] "היערכות שיא להילולא של הרב מרדכי אליהו זצוק"ל," כיכר השבת, 15.6.2017.

[52] https://holy.org.il/about/

[53] זאב בלוי, "טיהר את עיר טבריה: תיעוד: קברי הצדיקים לאחר השיפוץ," חדשות JDN, 4.1.2018; יצחק גולדמן, "מתחם חדש
ומרהיב: קבר הרמב"ם בטבריה נחנך בטקס רשמי," חדשות הארץ, 26.12.2018.

[54] מעין סלומון גימון, "יחסי יהודים־מוסלמים בנבי סמואל: דו קיום או שקט יחסי המשרת אינטרסים," ישראלים 5 (תשע"ד),
131–114

ממחסום לחומה

לא התקיימה הפרדה מגדרית ונשים וגברים התפללו אלו בצד אלו אל מול ציון הקבר. אך בשנת
2005, ביוזמת המרכז, הופרדו הנשים והגברים (ישראלים ותיירים כאחד) אלו מאלו. האולם
המוביל אל הקבר וחלל הקבר עצמו חולקו לשניים באמצעות מחיצה ולגברים אף הוקצה חדר
תפילה מיוחד.[55] מקרים אלו ואחרים מצביעים על כך שרשויות שונות של מדינת ישראל—משרדי
ממשלה, זרועות ממשלתיות שונות, עיריות ומועצות מקומיות שונות—מעורבות בפיתוח הפיסי
של המקומות הקדושים ובביסוס ההפרדה המגדרית בהם.

בשנים האחרונות התרבו מאד המקרים שבהם יוזמים גברים, בדרך כלל באמצעות אגודות
ועמותות חרדיות, אשכנזיות ומזרחיות כאחד, את ה"גילוי," היצירה והפיתוח של המקומות
הקדושים ותוך כדי כך מפרידים פיסית בין גברים לנשים. גברים הם אלו המציבים גדרות ושלטים
במקומות הקדושים שמבססים את ההפרדה המגדרית, וזאת לעתים כבר בשלבים המוקדמים של
"גילוי" המקום הקדוש ופיתוחו לקראת פתיחתו לביקור המתפללים.

חרדיזציה זו של המקומות הקדושים מובלת הן על ידי קבוצות חרדיות-חסידיות שבדור
האחרון גברה מאד מעורבותם בפיתוח המרחב המקודש היהודי והן על ידי עמותות וקבוצות
מקרב בני עדות המזרח.[56] מתיניותם הדתית של אלו הוחלפה בשנים האחרונות בהקצנה דתית
שבאה לידי ביטוי, בין היתר, בטיפוח ההפרדה המגדרית במקומות הקדושים.[57]

דוגמה לתהליך הפרדה מגדרית אשר נוצר "מלמטה" היא בקבר הבבא סאלי שבנתיבות, בנגב
המערבי, מתחם שמנוהל על ידי "הקרן להנצחת הבבא סאלי."[58] הרב ישראל אבוחצירא נפטר
בשנת 1984 ונקבר בבית הקברות בנתיבות. בשל מעמדו הרם והילת הקדושה שאפפינה אותו
עוד בימי חייו, בנו בני משפחתו מעל קברו מבנה בולט ובתוך זמן קצר הפך מתחם הקבר לאחד
מאתרי פולחן הקדושים הפופולריים במדינת ישראל והוא מושך אליו מאז קהל אלפים. הקרן
להנצחת הבבא סאלי שיפצה את מתחם הקבר בשנת 2005 ואז גם הופרדו הנשים מן הגברים
באמצעות שערים נפרדים ומחיצה שהוקמה בחלל הקבר.[59]

גם בקבר רחל אשת רבי עקיבא אשר בטבריה ניתן לראות כיצד הביאה יוזמה מלמטה, פרטית
וקהילתית, לחלוקת הקבר בין גברים לנשים.[60] בשנת 1994 החל הרב רפאל כהן, חבר מועצת
טבריה ויושב ראש עמותת בני מרדכי לפתוח את מתחם הקבר ההרוס למחצה והעמיד במרכזו
מצבה שהפרידה בין גברים לנשים. קבר רחל הפך לאטרקציה דתית שמשכה אליה מאמינים
מכל רחבי מדינת ישראל, רבות מהן נשים שהגיעו למקום בשל סגולות הזיווג ששויכו לרחל.[61]

גם מתחם קברו של הרב גדליה משה גולדמן, הרבי מזוויעל, שנפטר בשנת 1949 ונקבר בבית
הקברות שיח' באדר שנמצא מאחורי בניין בית המשפט העליון בירושלים, עבר בשנים האחרונות
תהליך דומה של מגדור. משך שנים רבות לא משך קבר הרב תשומת לב רבה והוא שימש כיעד

---

55 "שינויים באתר קבר דוד לתועלת המבקרים," ערוץ 7, 22.10.2005.
56 ראו לדוגמה את הקמת מחיצת העץ בקבר הרב משה אהרון פינטו באשדוד: לכבוד ההילולה ה-34 להרה"צ רבי משה אהרון
פינטו זצ"ל: שיפוץ כללי בציון הקדוש בבית העלמין בעיר, אתר המועצה הדתית אשדוד.
57 נסים ליאון, חרדיות רכה: התחדשות דתית ביהדות המזרחית, ירושלים: יד יצחק בן צבי, תש"ע, 131–128; בנימין בראון, מדריך
לחברה החרדית, אמנות וזרמים, תל אביב: עם עובד, תשע"ז, 157–108.
58 https://www.babasali.org.il/
59 Hadas Shadar, "The Poetics and the Politics of the Contemporary Sacred Place: Baba Sali's Grave Estate in
Netivot, Israel," Buildings and Landscapes: Journal of the Vernacular Architecture Forum 16:2 (2009), 73–85.
60 יערי, מסעות ארץ ישראל, 157.
61 Nimrod Luz, "Materiality as an agency of Knowledge: Competing Forms of Knowledge in Rachel's Tomb
in Tiberias," Journeys 21:1 (2019), 63–84.

73

תפילה עבור חברי הקהילה החסידית הקטנה. אך בשנת 2008 התחולל בבית קברות זה מפנה משמעותי והמקום עלה על מפת העלייה לרגל החרדית.[62] כמו במקרים אחרים בארץ שבהם "נגאלו" מקומות קדושים יהודים "מלמטה" וכתוצאה מדיווח על חלומות והתגלויות וביוזמה פרטית,[63] כך קרה גם כאן. מיתוס הקדושה שטופח בהצלחה במקום גרס כי אלו שיפקדו את קבר הצדיק ברציפות בימי שני, חמישי ושני (ימי חול שבהם קוראים מהתורה) יזכו לסגולות רבות. העלייה לרגל לקבר האדמו"ר הפכה להמונית וחתצת מגזרים דתיים ואל בית הקברות מגיעים בימי העלייה לרגל המרכזיים, שני וחמישי, מאות מבקרים, רבות מהם עולות רגל. הביקור במקום נעשה בנפרד לאחר שנבנתה במקום תשתית של מעברים וגדרות.[64]

השפעת תהליך ההפרדה המגדרית על המקומות הקדושים היהודיים בתפוצות

בדור האחרון גברה מאד נטיית מאמינים יהודים (תושבי מדינת ישראל והתפוצות כאחד) לפקוד קברים קדושים במרוקו, פולין, תוניסיה, אוקראינה וארצות הברית.[65] אם בעבר הרחוק הייתה למקומות הקדושים ההיסטוריים בארץ ישראל ובסביבתה בלעדיות,[66] הרי שבמאות ה-19 וה-20 התפתחו מוקדי קדושה נוספים במקומות נוספים.[67] כך קרה בין השאר בכמה מארצות צפון אפריקה, דוגמת מרוקו ותוניס, ובכמה מדינות במזרח אירופה ובהן אוקראינה, בלארוס, צ'כיה, הונגריה ופולין. במקומות אלו קידשו קהילות חסידיות קברים שהפכו לאתרי עלייה לרגל. רוב גברי אפיין התכנסויות דתיות אלו, אך ניכר כי נשים התפללו בצד הגברים ללא הפרדה פיסית.[68]

גלי ההגירה הגדולים של המאה התשע–עשרה והתוצאות הנוראיות של השואה הביאו לריקון אזורים אלו מאוכלוסייה יהודית, אז נותרו רבים מן הקברים הקדושים ללא קהל מאמינים. כך קרה גם בצפון אפריקה, שם הביאה הגירת היהודים במחצית השנייה של המאה העשרים לנטישת בתי הקברות ובהם הציונים הקדושים.

אך בדור–שניים האחרונים ניכרת תופעה של "חזרה לשורשים" והתגברה מגמת הביזור של

---

[62] עידן יוסף, "אטרקציה חדשה בכנסת: קבר האדמו"ר מזוויל," בחדרי חרדים, 23.11.2008.

[63] Yoram Bilu, "The Role of Charismatic Dreams in the Creation of Sacred Sites in Present–day Israel," Benjamin Z. Kedar and R.J. Zwi Werblowsky (eds.) Sacred Space: Shrine, City, Land, (London: Macmillan, 1998), 295–315.

[64] נעם דביר, "הפרדה בקבר: גברים ימינה – נשים שמאלה," ידיעות אחרונות, 1.12.2013.

[65] Shlomo Deshen, "Near the Jerba Beach: Tunisian Jews, an Anthropologist, and Other Visitors," Jewish Social Studies 3.2 (1997), 90–118; David M. Gitlitz and Linda Kay Davidson, Pilgrimage and the Jews (Westport, Ct.: Praeger Publishers, 2006); Hanane Sakkat, "Jewish Tourism in Morocco: "Hilloulot" as case study," European Judaism 52.2 (2019), 156–164.

[66] אברהם בן יעקב, קברים קדושים בבבל: תיאורים של קברי אישים מתקופת התנ"ך, התלמוד והגאונים, ירושלים: מוסד הרב קוק, תשל"ה.

[67] Elliott S. Horowitz, "Speaking to the Dead: Cemetery Prayer in Medieval and Early Modern Jewry," Journal of Jewish Thought & Philosophy 8.2 (1999), 303–317; Lucia Raspe, "Sacred Space, Local History, and Diasporic Identity: The Graves of the Righteous in Medieval and Early Modern Ashkenaz," Ra'anan S. Boustan, Oren Kosansky and Marina Rustow (eds.) Jewish Studies at the Crossroads of Anthropology and History (Philadelphia: University of Pennsylvania Press, 2011), 148–163; Arthur Green et. al. "A Little Townlet on its Own": The Hasidic Court and its Inhabitants," in Hasidism: A New History (Oxford: Oxford: Oxford University Press, 2018), 426–429.

[68] ראו לדוגמה צילומים משנת 1931 של בית הקברות היהודי בקרקוב שם מתפללים גברים ונשים יחדיו מול קברו של רבי משה איסרליס: National Digital Archives in Warsaw, collection 1–R–1040–25.

המרחב המקודש היהודי. יהודים צפון–אמריקאים פוקדים עתה לא רק קברי צדיקים המצויים שם,[69] אלא גם נוסעים לבקר בקברי רבנים ואדמו"רים במזרח אירופה.[70] יהודים צרפתיים עו־רכים מסעות שורשים למרוקו ולתוניסיה ופוקדים קברים שם,[71] וחסידי חב"ד ישראלים טסים לארצות–הברית בכדי לפקוד את קברו של הרב מנחם מנדל שניאורסון. נשים לוקחות גם הן חלק בתנועה נרחבת זו.[72]

תופעה זו היא תוצאה של הנוחות היחסית לנוע ממקום למקום, של הירידה היחסית במחיריהן של טיסות המאפשרת ליותר מבקרים פוטנציאליים לממן סיורים כאלו, ובעיקר של השינויים הדמו־גרפיים הרבים המאפיינים את העולם היהודי מאז המחצית השנייה של המאה העשרים. התחזקותן של קהילות יהודיות שונות ברחבי העולם, עליית מעמדן של קהילות חסידיות במדינת ישראל ובמקומות נוספים בתפוצות, מעודדות תופעה זו. "תנועה חזרה לשורשים" זו בולטת במיוחד בשני אזורים, מרוקו ומזרח אירופה. שם, ובמיוחד לאחר נפילת מסך הברזל בשנת 1989, הפכו מספר קברי צדיקים בולטים ל'אקוניים' והם מושכים את מאמיני כל המגזרים (כולל בני עדות המזרח).

חוץ מקבר רבי נחמן מברסלב באומן,[73] גם קברי מייסד תנועת החסידות הבעש"ט במז'יבוז' והרב לוי יצחק מברדיצ'ב (שלושתם באוקראינה), וקבר הרב אלימלך וייסבלום בליז'נסק (בפולין) מושכים קהל רב. בנוסף לאלו פרוסים במזרח אירופה עשרות רבות של קברים קדושים המהווים אבן שואבת עבור בני שושלות חסידיות ספציפיות כמו סדיגורה, צנז, ויז'ניץ, חב"ד, סלונים ובלז.[74] התחזקות תנועה זו באה לידי ביטוי בביקורי פרטים וקבוצות מאורגנות, רובן של גברים, בבתי קברות אלו, בשיקום נרחב של מבני הציונים החרבים ובבנייה חדשה מעל ציונים אחרים שאותרו בשנים האחרונות במאמץ רב.[75]

לבניית הציונים, במיוחד אלו הפופולריים המושכים קהל נרחב ומעורב, נלווית פעמים הפרדה מגדרית כאשר חלל הקבר מחולק בין נשים לגברים ולחילופין מוקמת עזרת נשים לידו. כמו במדינת ישראל, גם במקומות אלו מהווה ההפרדה המגדרית חידוש גמור. כך למשל הוקמה בשנת 2012 עזרת נשים בקבר רבי נחמן מאומן, שם מתפללות הנשים המגיעות לעיירה. אך ארבע פעמים בשנה, לקראת ה"התקבצויות" והעליות לרגל השנתיות, אז מתאסף במקום קהל של עשרות אלפי גברים, נשללת מידי הנשים הזכות להתפלל שם.[76] עזרת נשים הוקמה גם בקבר רבי שניאור זלמן

---

[69] למשל חסידי סאטמר הפוקדים את קברו של הרב יואל טייטלבוים, האדמו"ר מסאטמאר, הקבור בבית הקברות קרית יואל במונרו, ניו יורק, וחסידי חב"ד העולים לקברו של אדמו"רם מנחם מנדל שניאורסון, אף הוא בניו יורק. ראו: יונה לאנדא, קונטרס קברי צדיקים בארה"ב וקאנאדא, ברוקלין: ועד הנסיעה לקברי צדיקים בארה"ב וקאנאדא, תש"ג.

[70] יוסף חיים גרינוואלד, ספר פרדס הצדיקים: קברי צדיקים, ברוקלין: הוצאת פרדס הצדיקים, תש"ע; ספר בדרכי אבות: תולדות, הנהגות ועובדות, סיפורי קודש ואמרות טהורות מקדושים אשר בארץ המה במדינות אוקריינא ופולין, ווילאמסבורג: מערכת בדרכי אבות שע"י קהל תורת חיים וויזניץ, תש"ע.

[71] André Levy, "To Morocco and Back: Tourism and Pilgrimage among Moroccan–Born Israelis," Eyal Ben-Ari and Yoram Bilu (eds.) *Grasping Land: Space and Place in Contemporary Israeli Discourse and Experience* (Albany, N.Y: State University of New York Press, 1997), 25–46.

[72] ואני תפילתי: קובץ תפילות ומידע לנוסע» לקברי צדיקים, ירושלים: חברת דרך צדיקים, תשנ"ה.

[73] Shlomo Resenfeld, "Prayer at Saint's Tombs and especially on the tomb of Rabbi Nachman of Breslov," *Asif* 1 (2004), 249–268.

[74] Adam S. Ferziger, "Holocaust, Hurban, and Haredization: Pilgrimages to Eastern Europe and the Re-alignment of American Orthodoxy," *Contemporary Jewry* 31:1 (2011), 25–54.

[75] Alla Maksimovna Marchenko, "Hasidic Pilgrimage as a Cultural Performance: the Case of Contemporary Ukraine," *Judaica Ukrainica; Annual Journal of Jewish Studies* 3 (2014), 60–79.

[76] שמעון איפרגן, "אומן: נשים הורשו להתפלל רק מחוץ לגדר", מאקו, 3.10.2019.

מליאדי, מייסדה של שושלת אדמו"רי חב"ד. סביבת הקבר, שממוקם בעיירה האוקראינית האדיטש, נרכשה על ידי ארגון 'חסדי יוסף' ואלו הובילו בשנת 2003 את בניית "קריית האדמו"ר הזקן בעל התניא", הכשרתו לביקורי המונים, ואת הקמת עזרת הנשים בקומה שמעל למבנה הקבר.[77] אגודת "אוהלי צדיקים" המנהלת את מתחם קבר הבעל שם טוב במז'יבוז' שבאוקראינה, מתכננת לעצב מחדש את סביבת הקבר. כחלק משינויים אלו תוקם במקום עזרת נשים עם כניסה נפרדת.[78]

במרוקו, לעומת זאת, לא קיימת הפרדה מגדרית בקברי הצדיקים, אותם פוקדות בשנים האחרונות קבוצות רבות של עולי רגל שהן לעתים עם רוב נשי מובהק.[79] בניגוד לעלייה לרגל לקברי אדמו"רים, הזיארה, כפי שמכונה הביקור בקברי הצדיקים שבמרוקו, הייתה מאז ומתמיד תופעה בעלת אופי משפחתי וקהילתי, ולנשים היה בה תפקיד חשוב ומרכזי.[80] הביקור בקברים קדושים אלה איפשר לנשים לבטא את אמונתן ודבקותן הדתית בצורה שוויונית יחסית ולקחת חלק בפולחן הצדיקים.[81] לכך גם הוסיפה הקרבה הדתית היחסית בין היהודים למוסלמים והעתקת מנהג העלייה לרגל המשותפת לקברי הקדושים.[82] מרכיבים היסטוריים אלו, כמו גם אופייה הדתי של קהילת יהודי מרוקו בימינו, משפיעים מאד על העלייה לרגל לקברי הצדיקים במרוקו. הביקור בהם הוא סקטוריאלי ורבים מעולי הרגל הם בני הדור השני והשלישי של העולים שהיגרו למדינת ישראל ולצרפת בשנות החמישים והשישים. אלו לא מרגישים כל צורך להפריד בין המינים והעלייה לרגל נעשית לרוב בצורה מעורבת וללא כל הפרדה בין גברים לנשים.

דיון וסיכום

אחת התופעות הדתיות הבולטות ביותר במדינת ישראל היא נהירתם של מאות אלפים לבקר במקומות קדושים יהודים. מתופעה חברתית–דתית שולית יחסית הפכה בשנים האחרונות העלייה לרגל לקברי צדיקים לאחד הריטואלים הדתיים הבולטים ביותר.

הגידול הניכר בפולחן הקברים קשור קשר הדוק בתהליך מקביל של גידול האוכלוסייה הדתית והחרדית במדינת ישראל והוא גם השפיע בצורה ניכרת על אופי העלייה לרגל המסורתית. המעורבות ההולכת וגוברת של רבנים ספרדים, של אגודות ועמותות של בני עדות המזרח כמו גם של קבוצות חסידיות בפיתוח המרחב המקודש היהודי הביאה לשינוי באופי העליות לרגל ובמראה האתרים הקדושים. אם בעבר נחגגו העליות לרגל אל הקברים הקדושים בצורה עממית וההתכנסות שם לוותה פעמים רבות באכילת ארוחות משפחתיות משותפות ליד המקום הקדוש, בריקודים ובשירה, הרי שמסורתיות זו חוסלה במהלך השנים. מירידים צבעוניים ומשפחתיים הפכו רבות מן העליות לרגל לאירועים דתיים מאופקים ושמרנים שנשמרים בהם כללים הלכתיים

---

[77] http://arh-uk.com/%D7%94%D7%A6%D7%99%D7%95%D7%9F–%D7%94%D7%A7%D7%93%D7%95%D7%A9/

[78] שלום אומן, "עזרת נשים וגישה לכהנים, הדמית האוהל החדש בקבר הבעש"ט בעיירת מעז'בוז'", חדשות ברסלב, כ"ח סיוון תשע"ט.

[79] Hanane Sekat, "Jewish Tourism in Morocco: Hilloullot as a Case Study," *European Judaism*, 52:2 (2019), 156–164.

[80] יששכר בן עמי, הערצת הקדושים בקרב יהודי מרוקו, ירושלים: הוצאת הספרים ע"ש י"ל מאגנס, תשמ"ה. בן עמי דן בביקורי נשים בקברי הקדושים במרוקו ומביא עדויות רבות של עולות רגל אך איננו מזכיר הפרדה מגדרית.

[81] Yoram Bilu, *The Saints' Impresarios: Dreamers, Healers, and Holy Men in Israel's Urban Periphery* (Boston: Academic Studies Press, 2010), 25–26.

[82] Fatima Mernissi, "Women, Saints, and Sanctuaries," *Signs* 3:1 (1977), 101–112.

ממחסום לחומה

קפדניים והנוכחות הנשית בהם הלכה ופחתה. אחד הביטויים הבולטים של חרדיזציית המקומות הקדושים היהודיים היא ההפרדה המגדרית המאפיינת אותם בשנים האחרונות.

אין זו תופעה היסטורית המושרשת במסורת היהודית אלא תופעה חדשה בתולדות המקומות הקדושים היהודיים, בת דור אחד או שניים, שהולכת ומתעצמת לנגד עינינו. מתופעה אקראית ויוצאת דופן עד לפני כמה עשרות שנים, הפכה ההפרדה בין המינים במקומות הקדושים לנורמטיבית. שלטי "גברים" ו"נשים", גדרות, מעברים וגרמי מדרגות כפולים המפרידים בין המתפללים והמתפללות והמוליכים אותם אל עבר הקבר הקדוש שגם סביבתו מחולקת באמצעות מחיצה רמה הפכו לנורמה. המרחב שמוקדש לנשים הוא תמיד קטן יותר מזה המוקצה לגברים.

אלו הן רשויות רשמיות של מדינת ישראל—משרדי ממשלה, עיריות ומועצות מקומיות— הממממנות ומקדמות את הקמת הגדרות, המדרגות, והשערים כמו גם ארגונים ועמותות דתיות שמקדמות את ההפרדה במקומות רבים נוספים. כאשר העמדת המחיצות נעשית "מלמטה," הן נבנות פעמים רבות מגיבוב של מחסומים, פחים, גדרות ומעקות. כאשר המדינה, על זרועותיה השונות, מעורבת בהפרדה המגדרית, הרי פעמים רבות המחיצה מתוכננת ומעוצבת היטב. תוצאת תהליך זה, בין אם הוא מגיע מ"למעלה" או מ"למטה," הוא הפיכת מרבית המקומות הקדושים היהודיים למרחבים מופרדים מגדרית. ההפרדה מוצגת כמחויבת מן הדת ורשויות המדינה מקבלות עמדה קיצונית זו כמייצגת את העמדה הדתית המונוליתית והבלתי משתנה.

גברים הם ללא יוצא מן הכלל אלו המנהלים את מכלול העמותות, המרכזים והמשרדים המפתחים ומטפלים במקומות הקדושים. גברים הם אלו השולטים בפעילות הדתית במקום הקדוש, קובעים שם את כללי ההתנהגות ואת הנורמות הדתיות שבאות לידי ביטוי בדחיקת רגלי הנשים. פעילות זו נעשית בכדי להגן על "אותנטיות" המקומות הקדושים ועל המנהגים ה"עתיקים" שמתקיימים שם. הפרדה זו, שנסמכת על תפישות הלכתיות שמרניות, נועדה בראש ובראשונה להגן על הגבר מפני האישה, שמיניותה נתפסת על ידי הפוקדים את המקומות הקדושים כמכשלה. הפסוק מספר תהילים "כל כבודה בת מלך פנימה" (מה, יד) משמש כצידוק לצניעות הנדרשת מן הנשים המושגת על ידי הצבת מחסומים פיסיים במקומות הקדושים.[83]

הדרת נשים מן המרחב הישראלי הולכת ומתרחבת. היא אמנם מאפיינת בעיקר את הישובים והשכונות שבהן חיה ופועלת החברה החרדית. ישובים אלו מתוכננים כיום מראש מתוך שיקולי צניעות תוך שכלל מבני הציבור (בתי כנסת, מוסדות חינוך, מוסדות בריאות ועוד)[84] מופרדים. אך בשנים האחרונות מגמה זו מפעפעת אל המרחב הציבורי הכלל–ישראלי ובאה לידי ביטוי במגוון דרכים.[85] קווי מהדרין, שבהם יושבות הנשים בחלק האחורי של אוטובוסים;[86] מוסדות חינוך שונים, כולל גם באקדמיה הישראלית, שמתקיימים למידה נפרדת;[87] אירועי תרבות שמתקיימים

[83] Franses Radai, "Modesty Disrobed: Gendered Modesty Rules under the Monotheistic Religions," Marie A. Failinger, Elizabeth R. Schiltz, and Susan J. Stabile (eds.) *Feminism, Law and Religion* (Farnham, Surrey: Ashgate, 2013), 284–306.

[84] שלומית שהינו-קסלר, מלכה שנאאו ויהודית מילצקי, תדריך לתכנון עירוני של שכונות לאוכלוסייה החרדית, ירושלים: משרד הבינוי והשיכון, המכון החרדי למחקרי מדיניות, 2020.

[85] "עזרת נשים: בקווי אוטובוסים, בשלטי פרסומת ואפילו בבתי קברות – נשים בישראל שוות הרבה פחות," ידיעות אחרונות, 2.12.2011.

[86] נויה רימלט, "המשפט כסוכן של רב–תרבותיות: על אוטופיה ומציאות בפרשת ההפרדה באוטובוסים," משפטים 42:3 (2012), Zvi Triger, "The Self-Defeating Nature of 'Modesty'-Based Gender Segregation," *Israel Studies* 834–773; 18:3 (2013), 19–28

[87] אור קשתי, "בג"ץ הכשיר לימודים בהפרדה מגדרית באקדמיה, אך קבע: לא ניתן להדיר מרצות, הארץ," 12.7.2021; Jan

בהפרדה.[88] שעות רחצה נפרדות מוקצות בבריכות ציבוריות;[89] כללי צניעות המושתים על חיילות שמירותים ביחידות שונות בצבא הישראלי; ולכך מתווספת השחתה קבועה ורחבה של דמויות נשים בשלטי פרסומת.[90] תופעות אלו, על אף שנעשות רווחות בשנים האחרונות, אינן מתקבלות כמובן מאליו ומתקיים דיון ציבורי ישראלי ולעתים משפטי.

בניגוד לכך ההפרדה המגדרית במקומות הקדושים, המרחב הציבורי הישראלי הבולט ביותר שבו קיימת הפרדה מגדרית, התקבלה כמעט ללא כל איתגור, לא מצד הציבור החילוני במדינת ישראל וגם לא מצדם של המסורתיים. המחיצה, שהוצצה לפני כמה עשרות שנים באחדים מן המקומות הקדושים ומטרתה העיקרית אז הייתה למנוע מעבר מצד לצד של המקום הקדוש, הפכה היום למרכיב קבוע ומהווה מחסום שמונע גם החלפת מבט וראיה.

מדובר בתהליך "היסטורי" קצר יחסית, בן כמה עשרות שנים, שבמהלכו התבססה נורמת החלוקה בין הגברים לנשים. הפיכת המחיצה ברחבת הכותל המערבי לנורמטיבית; הקמת המרכז לפיתוח המקומות הקדושים; מינוי רב חרדי הממונה על המקומות הקדושים; כוחן הפוליטי הגובר של המפלגות החרדיות האשכנזיות והספרדיות שאין בהן ייצוג נשי; ושליטתם הממושכת של גורמים חרדים על משרד הדתות השפיעו בצורה דרמטית על התרחבות והתבססות ההפרדה המגדרית במקומות הקדושים. גם העובדה שהתפיסה הציבורית הישראלית הרווחת רואה את המקומות הקדושים כ"שייכים" לציבור הדתי–חרדי והעובדה שטקסים דתיים יהודיים הם טאבו שבתי משפט לא עוסקים בהם,[91] היא המאפשרת והמבססת את ההפרדה המגדרית הרווחת בהם.

Professor Doron Bar (President of the Schechter Institute of Jewish Studies 2015-2022) is engaged in the research of Jewish holy places and the development of national holy sites in the State of Israel. His recent books include: Landscape and Ideology: the Reinterment of Renowned Jews in the Land of Israel 1904-1967; The Western Wall: The Dispute over Israel's Holiest Site 1967-2000 *(with Kobi Cohen-Hattab) and* Yad Vashem: the Challenge of Commemorating the Holocaust in Jerusalem's Mount of Remembrance, 1942-1976.

Feldman, "Public Purposes at Cross–Purposes: Can Segregation Lead to Integration? What We Can Learn from Israel," *Israel Studies* 26:2 (2021), 29–56.

[88] גלי מרקוביץ-סלוצקה, "בית המשפט קבע: חומת ההפרדה תישאר: מוסד המריבות בבית שמש," *מעריב*, 5.9.2015; קורין אלבז-אלוש, "המשיח ניצח את העירייה: האירוע של חב"ד יתקיים הערב כמתוכנן," *ידיעות אחרונות*, 25.6.2018; אור קשתי, "מחיצה כבר לא מספיקה: אירוע במימון ציבורי מפנה נשים לאולם נפרד," *הארץ*, 18.10.2018.

[89] "בג"ץ קיבל עתירה נגד הפרדה מגדרית ב"בריכת המריבה" בקרית ארבע," *גלובס*, 7.10.2020.

[90] יורי ילון, "ירושלים: שלטים עם דמויות נשים הושחתו," *ישראל היום*, 8.12.2020.

[91] Pnina Lahav, "Israel' Rosit the Riveter: Between Secular Law and Jewish Law," *Boston University Law Review* 93 (2013), 1063–1083.

Museos Judíos Latinoamericanos[1]

Tamara Kohn

Introducción

La presencia de museos judíos en las ciudades más importantes del mundo y donde existen grandes (o pequeñas) comunidades judías, es un fenómeno que a muchos hoy nos puede parecer natural - ya sea un museo de arte judío, de la historia de la inmigración o uno dedicado a la historia del Holocausto. Sin embargo, no fue hasta comienzos del siglo XX que estos museos surgieron en Europa, ante la necesidad de los judíos de compartir con las sociedades que los rodeaban, la historia de su pueblo. Solamente medio siglo después, aparecen los primeros museos judíos en América Latina.

Para la tradición judía, la colección de objetos rituales era una tarea de la sinagoga y la accesibilidad a los mismos era limitada. Los objetos rituales eran generalmente vistos por la comunidad, solamente durante su uso en la sinagoga en las ocasiones para las que se habían creado. El punto de inflexión en la colección y exposición de este tipo de artefactos ocurre cuando la mayor parte de la judería de Europa Occidental y Europa Central logra finalmente la Emancipación legal en los diferentes estados europeos. Adquieren derechos civiles y no dependen de la comunidad para ser representados ante el Estado. Es decir, que esto sucede durante el proceso de su aculturación e integración a la sociedad moderna.

Una exhibición o un museo sirve como un espacio público de encuentro para gentiles y judíos de igual manera, saliendo del contexto litúrgico religioso, en el espíritu de la cultura y como apreciación hacia la cultura judía. La primera exposición de Arte judío en Europa fue realizada por Isaac Strauss (1806-1888), un judío francés de la corte de Napoleón III, que expuso 82 objetos rituales judíos en el Palacio Trocadero, siendo un pionero en la presentación pública de una colección privada de este tipo. A esta primera exposición en Francia le siguieron la Exposición Histórica Anglo-judía en el Albert Hall en Londres en 1887, la Exhibición de Arte Judío y Antigüedades en la Whitechapel Art Gallery en 1906, y otras tantas muestras que se van desarrollando en la Europa de Fin de siècle[2].

---

[1] Este trabajo es una adaptación y revisión de la ponencia presentada en *III Jornada internacional de museología y gestión de museos, Asociación internacional para la protección del patrimonio cultural*, Buenos Aires, 16 de septiembre 2022.

[2] Richard I. Cohen, *Jewish Icons: Art and Society in Modern Europe*, (Berkeley: University of

Richard Cohen sostiene que más allá de las razones personales que podrían haber llevado a Strauss a montar esta colección, este evento ha demostrado ser un punto de referencia y un testimonio del desarrollo de la vida judía en Europa Occidental y Central, desde la Revolución Francesa.[3] Por primera vez artefactos rituales judíos eran presentados como un fenómeno histórico y estético, más allá de su contexto de la práctica religiosa. Cohen afirma que, con esta exposición, un nuevo aspecto de la vida judía se ha objetivado.[4]

Sin embargo, las instituciones comunitarias judías estaban poco interesadas en la colección y la preservación de arte y artefactos judíos en los años previos a la Primera Guerra Mundial. La mayoría de los museos judíos de Europa se fundaron en el período de entreguerras, muchos fueron destruidos por el nazismo, y luego reaparecieron como continuación o nuevos museos, desde la inmediata posguerra en adelante.

Exposición e institucionalización del arte judío en América Latina

En nuestra región el proceso por el cual los objetos pasan de la esfera privada y comunitaria a la pública, es posterior a la Segunda Guerra Mundial y cuenta con el antecedente de la existencia de museos judíos en Europa, así como de espacios de exposición comunitarios.

Este trabajo propone la presentación de una cronología y categorización de los espacios de exposición y "museos judíos" en Latinoamérica, con el objetivo de visibilizar la multiplicidad de museos judíos con enfoques completamente diferentes, sobre la historia y la cultura judía en relación a su presencia en la región.

Cabe destacar que, a diferencia de Norteamérica y Europa, donde existen asociaciones que nuclean a los museos judíos (CAJM y AEJM), estas no existe en nuestra región, por lo que el relevamiento se hizo a partir de la información disponible y es una investigación que continúa desarrollándose día a día.[5]

California Press, 1998), pp. 155.

[3] Strauss había pasado la mayor parte de su vida adulta alejado de la comunidad judía y emprende un viaje por Europa Central donde comienza su colección de arte, a la que luego añade la colección de *judaica*. Cohen relaciona este hecho con el concepto de nostalgia y el intento de preservar un pasado que está desapareciendo con la modernidad. Cohen, 155.

[4] Cohen, 155.

[5] CAJM es la sigla para Council of American Jewish Museums y AEJM es la Association of European Jewish Museums. Si bien al día de hoy no existe una organización regional ni nacional que nuclee a todos los museos judíos, en 2020 se creó la red LAES (Red Latinoamericana para la

Museos Judíos Latinoamericanos

Historia de los museos judíos en América Latina
A diferencia de lo que ocurre en Europa, el proceso de integración de los judíos a la sociedad general en la modernidad es diferente. No existe la salida de los guetos (en el sentido de los barrios judíos) sino que una inmigración masiva que ocurre hacia fines del siglo XIX y comienzo del XX y se completa con la llegada de refugiados y sobrevivientes del nazismo hacia mediados de siglo XX.

El primer museo judío del que se tiene registro es el Museo Maurycy Minkowski, conocido como museo del IWO (Instituto judío de investigación). Fue fundado en 1940 y es una excepción frente al resto de los museos relevados, ya que se crea durante el período de la Segunda Guerra Mundial. Su patrimonio consiste en pinturas, esculturas, objetos de *judaica* y cotidianos, relacionados con la vida judía en Europa del Este y la cultura Idish en Argentina. Dentro de su colección se destacan las obras del pintor judío polaco Maurycy Minkowski y los objetos de *judaica* rescatados del Holocausto y enviados a la Argentina en la posguerra, por la JCR (Jewish Cultural Reconstruction). En 1945 el IWO mudó su sede a la AMIA, ocupando el tercer piso del edificio. Al momento del atentado, la colección fue dañada y parte de ella rescatada, pero no volvió a contar con un espacio propio de exposición, fuera de los salones del Archivo y Biblioteca de IWO, por lo que se encuentra actualmente cerrado. A pesar de ello, el museo Maurycy Minkowski continuó exponiendo en espacios externos, como es el caso de la muestra de Minkowski en el Museo Sivori en la Ciudad de Buenos Aires, que se llevó a cabo en 2012.

Es recién en los años 60 cuando se funda el primer Museo Judío, el Museo Judío de Buenos Aires, siguiendo el modelo europeo. Creado en 1967 por Salvador Kibrick, se encuentra en el edificio adyacente a la sinagoga de la Congregación Israelita Argentina (CIRA). Al mismo tiempo, en Montevideo se funda en 1960, el Museo de la Shoá Uruguay, el primero en toda Sudamérica. Y es recién hacia finales de la década de 1980 que aparecen los primeros museos de las colonias, dedicados a la inmigración judía.

Estos primeros museos van a sentar el antecedente para los tipos de museos judíos que van a surgir en la región a lo largo de las décadas. El primer

---

Enseñanza de la Shoá) que nuclea a nueve instituciones de diferentes países de América latina: el Museo del Holocausto de Buenos Aires (Argentina), el Museo del Holocausto de Curitiba (Brasil), el Museo Interactivo Judío de Chile, el Museo de la Comunidad Judía de Costa Rica, el espacio Ana Frank de Guatemala, la fundación Emet de Panamá, el Centro Educacional Holocausto y Humanidades como parte del Museo Judío del Perú, el Museo Memoria y Tolerancia de México y el Museo de la Shoá de Uruguay. Además, algunos museos latinoamericanos son miembros de las asociaciones norteamericana y europea.

modelo es el del Museo judío tradicional, adyacente a una sinagoga, centro de vida comunitaria. El segundo modelo es el del Museo del holocausto. Y el último el del museo de la inmigración. Podemos identificar un cuarto tipo de espacio de exposición en los salones de arte.

El modelo tradicional del museo adyacente a la sinagoga es el más popular en la región, y tal vez, en todo el mundo. Naturalmente, estos museos surgen como un espacio de preservar la memoria y la historia comunitaria que se puede adecuar a grandes urbes y pequeños pueblos, ya que la sinagoga funciona como marco institucional para la creación de los mismos. Esto permite, a lo largo de la segunda mitad del siglo XX, el continuo desarrollo y fundación de este tipo de museos, desde los ejemplos más tempranos como el de Buenos Aires, pero también con los casos más recientes como el Museo de los Judíos Alemanes, en Santiago de Chile (2022), el Museo Sefaradí de Tucumán, San Miguel de Tucumán (2022) y el Museo judío Virtual de Córdoba (2021). Si nos extendemos a otras áreas de la región, también aparecen casos similares en Panamá, Perú, Paraguay y Costa Rica.

Los museos de la inmigración judía, en el caso de Argentina, responden a una característica muy interesante, que es el hecho de que sean museos comunales, es decir, de carácter público. Dentro de esta categoría nos encontramos con dos subtipos de museos: los museos que cuentan la historia del pueblo donde se encuentran, incluyendo una sección sobre la historia judía con la agrupación de algunos objetos rituales judíos o museos completamente dedicados a ello, como lo son el Museo Rabino Aaron Goldman, ubicado en Moisesville, prov. de Santa Fe, y el Museo de las Colonias Judías del Centro de Entre Ríos. Para el primer subtipo nos encontramos con el caso del Museo de Carlos Casares, por ejemplo.[6]

En cuanto a la historia de la shoá, resulta esta temática más o menos relevante según la locación y el relato del museo. En el caso de la Ciudad de Buenos Aires, existe un Museo del Holocausto creado con ese fin y una filial de La Casa de Anne Frank, en la misma ciudad, por lo que los museos judíos existentes en la ciudad se dedican a otros temas. Pero en el caso de Santiago de Chile, existe el Museo Judío de Chile, que se encuentra junto a una sinagoga y que abarca tanto el tema migratorio, como la historia y tradición judía, como la historia del Holocausto. Esa misma función cumple el Museo Judío del Paraguay "Dr. Walter Kochmann", en Asunción y el Museo judío de Perú y Centro de Estudios del Holocausto, en Lima.

---

[6] Michele Migliori (Bar-Ilan University), "Museos y muestras permanentes de interés judío en el interior argentino" en *20 International Research Conference, Latin American Jewish Studies Association* (online), July 6th, 2023, https://www.youtube.com/watch?v=OWkgzEej9zQ

Un último espacio de exposición, consiste en salones y espacios de arte dedicados al arte en general, no necesariamente judío, pero promovidos por instituciones de la comunidad. Tal vez el caso más famoso sea el espacio de arte de la Sociedad Hebraica Argentina (SHA), que en la década de 1960 estaba absolutamente integrado a los circuitos de arte contemporáneo locales. Por ejemplo, en 1967 se llevó a cabo la muestra "Estructuras Primarias II" donde se expusieron obras de artistas contemporáneos argentinos, pioneros del minimalismo. Esta muestra histórica, formó parte del programa del circuito del Arte Avanzado organizado por el Instituto Torcuato Di Tella y fue en respuesta a la muestra "Primary Structures" expuesta en el Museo Judío de Nueva York el año anterior.[7]

Cabe destacar que la presencia de los tempranos ejemplos del Museo Minkowski y el espacio de arte de SHA en Buenos Aires, son una excepción al desarrollo de los museos judíos en el resto del mundo, donde generalmente surgen a partir del primer modelo mencionado.

En cuanto al enfoque y el contenido de los museos, a medida que pasa el tiempo se identifican dos tendencias: la especialización o la inclusión de los tres modelos en uno. Es decir, la creación de museos especializados en temas específicos, como la shoá o la inmigración, o la inclusión de tres secciones dentro de un mismo museo. Estas secciones suelen incluir la historia del pueblo judío previo a su llegada a América, por medio de los artefactos religiosos, un sector dedicado a la historia del holocausto, y por último una sección relacionada con la inmigración judía y su desarrollo en comunidades locales e integración a la sociedad general.

Conclusiones

Luego del relevamiento de datos sobre más de 30 museos judíos en América Latina podemos concluir que existe una cantidad significativa de museos dedicados a la historia del pueblo judío. A veces nos encontraremos con centros educativos destinados a la historia de la shoá que comparten el edificio con el museo de la historia judía y de la comunidad pero que funcionan como identidades separadas. En otros casos el foco estará en la historia de la inmigración, como símbolo del inicio de un nuevo capítulo en la historia del pueblo judío en el que se fusiona e integra a una sociedad

---

[7] Tamara Kohn, " `Primary Structures II:' A bridge between North and South, the Jewish community and the art world" in Building Bridges in the Americas, *2022 Biennial Scholars Conference on American Jewish History, The Academic Council of the American Jewish Historical Society,* Tulane University, May 15-17, 2022.

Tamara Kohn

Relevamiento de Museos Judíos y espacios de exposición en America Latina

Año de creación	Nombre	Ciudad	País
1940	Museo Maurycy Minkowski (IWO)	CABA	Argentina
1947	Sociedad Hebraica Argentina	CABA	Argentina
1965	Museo de la Shoá Uruguay	Montevideo	Uruguay
1967	Museo Judío de Buenos Aires	CABA	Argentina
1970	Museo Judío de México	Ciudad de México	México
1977	Museo Judaico Río de Janeiro	Rio de Janeiro	Brasil
1989	Museo de las colonias judías de Entre Ríos, Villa Dominguez	Villa Dominguez, Entre Rios	Argentina
1989	Museo Histórico Comunal y de la Colonización Judía, Rabino A. H. Goldman	Santa Fe	Argentina
1994	Museo Sefardí	Santiago de Chile	Chile
1996	Villa Clara	Entre Rios	Argentina
1999	Museo del Holocausto	CABA	Argentina
1999	Museo Sefaradi de Caracas Morris E. Curiel	Caracas	Venezuela
2000	Salon de Arte Tarbut	CABA	Argentina
2003	Museo judío de Santa Fe	Santa Fe	Argentina
2004	Espacio Arte AMIA	CABA	Argentina
2005	El Museo de la Comunidad Judía de Costa Rica	San Jose	Costa Rica
2007	Museo Judío de Entre Rios	Concordia, Entre Rios	Argentina
2009	Casa Ana Frank	CABA	Argentina
2010	Museo judío de Perú y Centro de Estudios del Holocausto	Lima	Peru
2010	Museo de la memoria y la tolerancia	Ciudad de México	Mexico
2011	Museo del Holocausto Curitiba	Curitiba	Brasil
2012	Arte Lamroth	CABA	Argentina
2013	Museo Judío del Paraguay "Dr. Walter Kochmann"	Asunción	Paraguay
2014	Museo Judío de Chile	Santiago de Chile	
2017	LABA Buenos Aires	CABA	Argentina
2019	Museo judío de Villa María	Codoba	Argentina
2020	Museo judío virtual de Córdoba	Córdoba	Argentina
2021	Museu Judaico de Sao Paulo	San Pablo	Brasil
2021	"Museo Judío Alemán de Santiago	Santiago de Chile	Chile
2022	Museo sefaradí de Tucumán	San Miguel de Tucumán	Argentina
	Museo judío de Sosúa	Sosúa	República Dominicana
	Museo judio de Panamá	Ciudad de Panamá	Panamá

Museos Judíos Latinoamericanos

Renovación	Categoría	Afiliación	Tema
	Museo institucional		Arte y Arte judío
	Espacio de arte		Arte
2014	Museo institucional	CIRA- Judaica	Judaica e inmigración
	Museo comunal		Inmigración
	Museo comunal		Inmigración
	Museo comunal		Inmigración
	Museo independiente		Holocausto
	Museo institucional		Historia judía
	Salon de arte		Arte contemporáneo
	Museo institucional	Kehila de Santa Fe	Historia judía
	Espacio de arte		Arte
	Museo independiente		Holocausto
	Museo institucional		Historia judía y holocausto
	Museo institucional		Holocausto
	Salon de arte		Arte contemporáneo
	Museo institucional		"Historia judía
	Museo privado		Historia judía y holocausto
	Studio		Arte contemporáneo
	Museo institucional		Historia judía
	Museo institucional	Kehilá Sefaradita de Tucumán	Judaísmo sefardi
En proceso de renovación	Museo institucional	Kaal shearit israel	Historia de los judios de Panama

donde son minoría. Luego de 1990 y en el siglo XXI los museos donde se expone la historia de la shoá tomaron especial protagonismo.

Todos tienen en común que miran hacia el pasado cumpliendo un rol de memoria, pero también hacia el futuro, al actualizarse y buscar atraer a las nuevas generaciones. En un mundo donde la discriminación y xenofobia no cesan, estas instituciones buscan narrar la historia de un pueblo que siendo minoría y víctima de persecuciones en el pasado, supo reconstruirse en diferentes momentos de su historia en las diferentes sociedades latinoamericanas a las que se integraron y formaron parte de ellas rápidamente. Al fin y al cabo, el guion curatorial de cada uno de estos museos busca conectar el pasado con el tiempo presente y su ubicación geográfica. Esto último adquiere principal importancia en un contexto en el que la virtualidad toma protagonismo.

Tamara Kohn is a researcher, curator, and Jewish art lecturer at the Seminario Rabinico Latinoamericano Marshall T. Meyer. She graduated from the Hebrew University of Jerusalem and obtained an MA in Jewish Art and Visual Culture at JTS in 2011. She was part of the research and curation teams for the renewal of the permanent exhibition at the Jewish Museum of Buenos Aires (2012-2014) and the Holocaust Museum of Buenos Aires (2018-2020). Currently, she is writing her dissertation on the ritual art and material culture of Jewish refugees from Nazism in Argentina as objects of memory. She also coordinates the LAJM project (Latin American Jewish Museums), aimed at creating a regional association of Jewish museums and professionals in Jewish art.

Redemptive Mourning

The Sages' Seder at Benei Braq and the Productive Act of Memory

Daniel Stein

In his famous meditation on Jewish history, *Zakhor*, Yosef Haim Yerushalmi laments what he considers to be a lacuna of "historiography" in rabbinic literature. "Classical rabbinic literature," he writes, "was never intended as historiography, even in the biblical, let alone the modern, sense, and it cannot be understood through canons of criticism appropriate to history alone."[1] Yerushalmi follows Hannah Arendt in drawing a distinction between Jewish history and memory. History, he argues, is focused on constructing linear narratives with defined teleologies. Memory, on the other hand, is less concerned with chronology and is "by its nature, selective."[2] Memory, Yerushalmi asserts, and not history was the sustaining force behind the Jewish people prior to the advent of modernity. Yerushalmi expresses anxiety that in the modern period the pendulum has swung in the opposite direction: while there is no shortage of historical writing, Judaism has failed to create a metahistorical narrative that functions as memory once did. This failure of synthesis, he asserts, pushes the community toward a crisis.[3]

What if, though, the rabbis of the Talmud had a different approach to history and historical memory—one that is perhaps obscured by its very synthesis? We might argue that asynchronous tales of rabbinic literature are models of what Walter Benjamin famously called "the tradition of the oppressed."[4] In reading such traditions, one of Benjamin's translators, the philosopher Susan Buck-Morss has argued for privileging the fragmentary over the linear. "The detail that counts," she writes, "is the one that arrests the reader because it does not fit that narrative."[5] Such fragments, she asserts, can function as the Paris arcades did for Benjamin, as "a passageway that

---

[1] Yosef Haim Yerushalmi, *Zakhor: Jewish History and Jewish Memory* (Seattle: University of Washington Press, 1982), 18.

[2] Yerushalmi, *Zakhor*, 8–15.

[3] Yerushalmi, *Zakhor*, esp. 137.

[4] Walter Benjamin, "Theses On the Philosophy of History," trans. Harry Zohn in Walter Benjamin, *Illuminations*, ed. Hannah Arendt (New York: Schocken, 1969), 257.

[5] Susan Buck-Morss, "Translations in Time," *October* 172 (Spring 2020): 149.

pierces through the street facade of the present, providing an entry point into the past."[6] Perhaps we could be even bolder in contemplating the role of rabbinic literature in the Jewish tradition: Could it be the passageway from the past that provides an entry point into the present moment?

This approach to memory challenges the nostalgia typologies recently explored by literary theorist Svetlana Boym.[7] Boym sees acts of memory as either restorative, embracing a dangerous desire to restore a simulacrum of a past that never was, or reflective, forever trapped in a narcissistic sense of loss. Indeed, recent interest in the fragmentary nature of rabbinic literature—a literature born out of the cataclysmic destruction of the Second Temple that Benay Lappe has called "The Crash"—may herald a contemporary renewal of the praxis of Jewish memory.[8]

In this essay, I will reread a famous tale from the Passover Haggadah, the account of the sages' *seder* at Benei Braq, seeking to understand the implications of reading this tale as such an entry point into the past. I hope that reflecting on this famous rabbinic narrative evidences a different and less pathologized form of memory than those Boym contemplates. The rabbis knew of a kind of memory that engages neither in narcissistic melancholy nor in restorative fantasy. Instead, we witness a trend in rabbinic literature that seeks to memorialize the past in order to redeem the present. As we will discuss below, and following Benjamin's understanding of melancholia, critical theorists Judith Butler and Enzo Traverso have named this kind of memory either "productive" or "fruitful" melancholia."[9]

Toward the beginning of the Haggadah, we read:

> A story is told of Rabbi Eliezer, Rabbi Yehoshua, Rabbi Eleazar ben Azariah, and Rabbi Akiva, who were reclining in B'nai B'rak, and were telling of the Exodus from Egypt all of that evening, until their students came and said to them: Our Rabbis, the time has arrived to recite the morning *shema*.[10]

---

[6] Buck-Morss, "Translations," 148.

[7] See, inter alia, Svetlana Boym, *The Future of Nostalgia* (New York: Basic, 2002).

[8] Benay Lappe, "An Unrecognizable Jewish Future: A Queer Talmudic Take," Eli Talks (May 2014), https://www.myjewishlearning.com/eli-talks/an-unrecognizable-jewish-future-a-queer-talmudic-take/.

[9] Enzo Traverso, *Left-Wing Melancholia: Marxism, History, and Memory* (New York: Columbia University Press, 2016), 21.

[10] All Haggadah citations are from Mordechai Leib Katzenelbogen, ed., *Passover Haggadah: Torat Hayim* (Jerusalem, Israel: Mosad Harav Kook, 1998) (Hebrew).

Redemptive Mourning

This tale appears in the Haggadah as a response to the preceding passage: "All who expand on the telling of the Exodus from Egypt are considered praiseworthy." In our story, we see many of the great sages of their generation doing exactly that—expanding on the story at such length and with such fervor that their students must interrupt their study for the only ritual obligation that could take precedence: the recitation of the morning prayers. The story of the sages is also linked to Eleazar ben Azaria's legal statement, which immediately follows it, and which may be understood, at least in this context, as a continuation of the story itself. This is markedly different than the way the story of Eleazar ben Azaria appears in the Mishnah.[11] There, Eleazar ben Azaria is responding to the legal statement that the exodus be recalled in the evening. Here, the Haggadah presents the legal statement alongside the narrative material as a single literary unit, generating further interpretive implications.

The reception tradition around the Haggadah has long been fascinated with this gathering, which brings together many—but not all—of the greatest rabbinic sages of the first century at a time of great upheaval. Is there a deeper meaning to this grouping of sages? Can we say with precision when exactly they met? Why did they apparently travel from their homes to the town of Benei Braq? Did their gathering signify anything at all beyond what is stated explicitly in the text?

One of the most well-known answers to these questions is of recent origin. In *Ḥagim umo'adim* (*Holidays and Festivals*, 1943), Yehuda Leib Maimon wonders why the sages' students are absent from the seder and appear only at the very end of the meal. He offers this hypothesis:

> I speculate, therefore…that this party, which gathered the sages of Israel from a variety of locations, had a double purpose: while its expressed goal was to engage with the memories of the past in the form of the Exodus from Egypt, the sages also hoped to discuss the issues of the day from their national-religious (*datit-leumit*) perspective. They were especially concerned with the rebellion against the Roman Empire, which had recently started to develop in secret among the Jews of Israel and which would culminate in the Bar Kokhba Revolt and the Hadrianic War.[12]

---

[11] m. Berakhot 1:5

[12] Yehuda Leib Maimon, *Holidays and Festivals* (Jerusalem: Mossad Harav Kook, 1943), 206 (Hebrew).

Maimon was an important Zionist religious and political leader. He was a founder of the Mizrahi movement, one of the most significant religious Zionist political organizations. He also founded Mosad haRav Kook, a religious research organization named after Israel's first chief rabbi, and served as Israel's first minister of religion. In Maimon's reading of the gathering of sages at Benei Braq, we see clear reverberations of a Zionist mythology that emerged at the end of the nineteenth century. He introduces an element not found in the text—that the seder is no longer simply a religious gathering but a clandestine conclave planning revolt against Rome. Rabbi Akiva assumes a central role in this reading for his endorsement of Simon Bar Kokhba, the military leader whose doomed campaign against Rome marked the final chapter of Jewish life in Palestine and the true beginning of exile. This interpretive choice is reflective of broader trends; as Yael Zerubavel has observed, the Zionist movement rehabilitated the personage of Bar Kokhba, perhaps in countervalance to the rabbinic tradition:

> The transformation of Bar Kokhba from a dubious leader of a failed revolt to a prominent heroic figure from Antiquity is an important feature of the Zionist reshaping of the past.... National pride was a central Zionism theme, and the revolt was important because it symbolized the ancient Hebrews' proud and courageous stand.... The Zionist commemorative narrative thus shifts its focus from the *outcome* of the revolt to the act of rebelling.[13]

Maimon's reading, then, may be a kind of historical artifact; it is revelatory in helping to understand the early Zionist worldview but does little to help us understand the literary context that generated the Haggadah. A more compelling interpretation can be found in the commentary of Maimon's teacher, Yechiel Michael Epstein, widely known as the *Arukh hashulkhan* after his composition of the same name. In Epstein's commentary on the Passover Haggadah, he observes:

> We must look into this—for rabbi Eliezer lived in Lod, Rabbi Yehoshua lived in Peki'in, and Rabbi Akiva lived in B'nei B'rak. For what purpose did they gather at Rab-

---

[13] Yael Zerubavel, *Recovered Roots: Collective Memory and the Making of Israeli National Tradition* (Chicago, IL: University of Chicago Press, 1995), 96.

bi Akiva's home in B'nei B'rak?...It appears, in my humble opinion, that this story should be read in accordance with this account in the Talmud.[14]

Here, Epstein points the reader to this famous narrative in b. Makkot:

Once, Rabban Gamliel, Rabbi Elezar ben Azariah, Rabbi Yehoshua, and Rabbi Akiva...were coming up to Jerusalem together, and just as they came to Mount Scopus, they saw a fox emerging from the Holy of Holies. They fell a-weeping and R. Akiba seemed merry. "Wherefore," said they to him, "are you merry?" Said he: "Wherefore are you weeping?"- Said they to him: "A place of which it was once said, 'And the common man that draws nigh shall be put to death,' is now become the haunt of foxes, and should we not weep?" Said he to them: "Therefore am I merry; for it is written, 'And I will take to Me faithful witnesses to record, Uriah the priest and Zechariah the Son of Jeberechiah' [Isaiah 8:2]." "Now what connection has this Uriah the priest with Zechariah? Uriah lived during the times of the first Temple, while [the other,] Zechariah lived [and prophesied] during the second Temple; but Holy-Writ linked the [later] prophecy of Zechariah with the [earlier] prophecy of Uriah. In the [earlier] prophecy [in the days] of Uriah it is written, 'Therefore shall Zion for your sake be ploughed as a field etc.' [Micah 3:12]. In Zechariah it is written, 'Thus saith the Lord of Hosts, There shall yet old men and old women sit in the broad places of Jerusalem' [Zechariah 8:4]." "So long as Uriah's prophecy had not had its fulfilment, I had misgivings lest Zechariah's prophecy might not be fulfilled; now that Uriah's prophecy has been fulfilled, it is quite certain that Zechariah's prophecy also is to find its literal fulfilment."Said they to him: "Akiba, you have comforted us! Akiba, you have comforted us!"[15]

---

[14] Yechiel Michael Epstein, *Passover Haggadah: A Night of Vigil* (Warsaw 1889), 17 (Hebrew).
[15] Translation of the talmudic passage cited here, b. Makkot 24b, is taken from I. Epstein, ed., *The Babylonian Talmud: Tractate Makkoth* (London: Soncino, 1935).

Epstein, then, offers this gloss on the tale:

> Therefore, I say that it was for this reason that the sages
> gathered at Rabbi Akiva's home: he strengthened the hopes
> of the House of Israel *immediately* after the destruction
> of the temple. Therefore, they all came to the city and the
> house of Rabbi Akiva—except for Rabban Gamliel, who
> did not come because he was the *Nasi*.[16]

By setting the Haggadah's seder within the larger narrative context of the
Talmud, Epstein's reading invites us to explore foundational questions. What
was the relationship between these sages? Was there something significant
about Rabbi Akiva's personality that caused his colleagues to travel to his
home instead of their own? And can we read anything at all into the absence
of their colleague Rabban Gamliel—who is absent from Rabbi Akiva's seder,
but whose voice is essential to the Haggadah? Following Epstein, I would
like to a suggest a reading that asks us to situate the story of the seder at
Benei Braq alongside the Babylonian Talmud specifically and rabbinic literature more generally. I will also suggest a hermeneutic for understanding
this rabbinic gathering and argue that, in recalling narratives of liberation,
the rabbis may have been engaged in a task even more revolutionary than
planning a revolt against their Hadrianic oppressors.

To understand the seder at Benei Braq, then, I suggest that we read the
tale as part of a series of narratives that Daniel Boyarin has called "The
Yavneh Cycle." Boyarin argues that the Babylonian Talmud's stories of the
rabbinic academy at Yavneh are meant to be read collectively, and that
Yavneh serves as an "icon of the Stammaitic yeshiva" of the fifth century.[17]
Following Boyarin, Moshe Simon-Shoshan has argued that Yavneh func-
tioned as a "narrative world" for the redactors of the Talmud, who "established the norms on which the society of the *beit midrash* is founded and
the ground rules by which rabbinic study, dispute, and decision-making
are to be conducted."[18]

The Talmud famously tells the tale of how the academy at Yavneh was

---

[16] Epstein, *Passover* Haggadah, 18.

[17] Daniel Boyarin, "The Yavneh-Cycle of the Stammaim and the Invention of the Rabbis," in
Creation and Composition: The Contribution of the Bavli Redactors (Stammaim) to the Aggada,
ed. Jeffrey L. Rubenstein (Tübingen: Mohr Siebeck, 2005), 237–89.

[18] Moshe Simon-Shoshan, "Creator of Worlds: The Deposition of Rabban Gamliel and the
Creation of Yavneh," *AJS Review* 41, no. 2 (2017): 287–313.

founded. During the Roman siege of Jerusalem, Rabbi Eliezer and Rabbi Yehoshua, the first two protagonists mentioned in our story, hid the great sage Rabbi Yoḥanan ben Zakkai in a coffin and smuggled him out of the city. The story goes to relate how, while leaving the city, the trio encountered the Roman emperor Vespasian, and the quick-witted rabbi Eliezer was able not only to sweet talk his way out of trouble, but also to extract additional promises from the emperor. He secured the protection of Yavneh and guaranteed the safety of Rabban Gamliel, a descendent of both King David and Hillel the Elder, who would serve as *nasi*, leader of the rabbinic court, after Rabbi Yoḥanan. [19]

The other sages at our seder represent a younger, so-called second generation of sages. Rabbi Eleazar ben Azaria and Rabbi Akiva are the students in our story and are listed second to illustrate their subordinate position in the chain of transmission. Yet, according to the Talmud, three of the four sages mentioned do share at least one thing in common: they were participants in the controversy that led to the removal of Rabban Gamliel as *nasi*.

Several stories in the Talmud relate how Rabban Gamliel could be particularly cruel, especially to his contemporary, Rabbi Yehoshua. In one well-known incident, Rabban Gamliel disagrees on the calculation of Yom Kippur. Using his authority as the *nasi*, Rabban Gamliel orders Rabbi Yehoshua to appear before him with his staff and purse on the date Rabbi Yehoshua considered to be Yom Kippur. Rabbi Yehoshua is humiliated and distraught at having to violate the most sacred day of the year, as he understood it, to appease the *nasi*. It took the intervention of Rabbi Akiva to resolve the dispute, appease Rabbi Yehoshua, and honor Rabban Gamliel.

In another famous incident, Rabban Gamliel was deposed from leadership of the rabbinic academy. Here, again, in a dispute with Rabbi Yehoshua over whether the evening prayer was obligatory or optional, Rabban Gamliel humiliates his contemporary. He forces the aging Rabbi Yehoshua to stand for hours in the study hall and ultimately compels him to publicly recant his previous teaching. This shaming is more than his fellow can bear. The assembled sages—including Rabbi Yehoshua, Rabbi Akiva, and Rabbi Eleazar ben Azaria—lock Rabban Gamliel out of the study house and appoint Rabbi Eleazar ben Azaria as *nasi* in his place.[20]

---

[19] b. Gittin 56a–56b and Avot deRabbi Natan 4:5.

[20] b. Berakhot, 27a–28b. For a rich exploration of the comforting role of Rabbi Akiva, see Miriam Gedwiser, "Rabbi Akiva the Comforter," Drisha Institute, https://drisha.org/audiolibrary/rabbi-akiva-the-comforter/. On the deposition of Rabban Gamliel, see Avi Poupko, "Lighting Up the Night: The Revolutionary Mandate of a Rabbinic Coup," *Ateret Tzvi Prize 5778* (2018),

Perhaps this rift explains Rabban Gamliel's absence from at Benei Braq. While Rabbi Akiva again intercedes to restore harmony, suggesting a rotating leadership of the academy, the damage has been done. Rabban Gamliel's absence from the seder suggests that he is unable or unwilling to celebrate Passover with the other sages. The association of the seder at Benei Braq and Rabban Gamliel's deposition is suggested by the Haggadah itself. The text that immediately follows is a quote from the Mishnah that begins "Rabbi Eleazar ben Azariah said, 'Behold, I am *like* a man of seventy, and yet I did not know that the Exodus from Egypt was to be remembered in the evening." The Talmud is captivated by the word "like." It views it as superfluous and uses the irregular language as hook for another legend. I share the story below, in Emmanuel Levinas's telling:

> Rabban Gamliel, head of the rabbinic academy, was too strict a master. He was dismissed for that very excess of severity. A replacement is sought, and Eleazar ben Azaria is designated. He possesses wisdom, material independence and nobility—being descended from Esdras [Ezra] in the tenth generation; responsible for an exceedingly glorious spiritual heritage. Everything seems to portend an eminent role for him. But he is only eighteen years old—without one white hair. Can one teach without innovating? But can one innovate without reference to a tradition, without remaining the contemporary—real or apparent—of the discourse of the past? A miracle was needed! Eighteen rows of white hair appeared on Eleazar ben Azaria's head—who, at the age of eighteen, henceforth looked seventy, in order that all innovation should derive from earlier forms.[21]

While at first glance, it may appear that Rabbi Eleazar ben Azaria's statement—and therefore the legend of his overnight maturation—appears independent, disconnected from the story of the sages' seder that precedes it in the Haggadah, the manuscript tradition suggests reading the two texts together. While the majority of Haggadot today follow the text of Rabbi Eleazar ben Azaria's statement as preserved in the Babylonian Talmud, most

https://www.hadar.org/torah-tefillah/resources/lighting-night.
[21] Emmanuel Levinas, "Beyond Memory: From Tractate Berakhot 12a–13b," in *In the Time of Nations*, trans. Michael B. Smith (London: Continuum, 2007), 64–79.

extant geniza fragments of the Haggadah offer a reading with a critical addition, which is also preserved by Maimonides in his Haggadah text. They all add the word לֹהֶם, "to them," so that the line reads "Rabbi Elazar ben Azariah said **to them**, 'Behold I am like a man of seventy...'" This addition demands that the reader understand this paragraph as continuation of the story that precedes it.

A second text also asks us to imagine the sages at Benei Braq as being in dialogue in some ways with the legal and political attitudes that led to the deposition of Rabban Gamliel. While Rabban Gamliel is absent from the seder in the Haggadah, the Tosefta shares a story of his own all-night seder:

> A story is told of Rabban Gamliel and the Sages: Once they were reclining at the house of Boethus ben Zonim in Lydda and were occupied with *the laws* of Passover all evening until the early morning [*kerot ha'gever*]. They removed [the table] from before them, gathered themselves and went to the study hall.[22]

While this narrative differs in several ways from the seder in the Haggadah, perhaps the most critical distinction is in the contents of the Passover service. At the seder in Benei Braq, the sages spend the evening telling the story of the exodus, while Rabban Gamliel and the unnamed sages with him spend the evening "engaged with the laws of Passover." How are we to understand the difference in practice between these two groups?

Barry Wimpfheimer has argued for the importance of deconstructing the division between so-called halakhah (legal) and aggadah (narrative) in reading rabbinic literature. At a minimum, he maintains that narrative material should be read within a legal context and vice versa.[23] This methodology is useful here. Immediately prior to the story of the sages, the Haggadah enjoins the act of communal memory: "Even if we were all sages—even if we all knew the Torah, we would still be obligated to tell of the Exodus from Egypt. And all who expand in their telling of the story is deemed praiseworthy." Rabban Gamliel's seder, though, comes as an example of fidelity to a different legal tradition cited in the Tosefta: "One should not

---

[22] Tosefta (Liberman) Pesahim 10:12. On the expression *kerot hagever*, see Avraham Yoskovich, "Keroth Ha-Gever (A Cock Crow) in Rabbinic Literature" (paper presented at the World Union of Jewish Studies, 2013).
[23] Barry Wimpfheimer, *Narrating the Law: A Poetics of Talmudic Legal Stories* (Philadelphia: University of Pennsylvania Press, 2011).

Daniel Stein

consume dessert, such as nuts, dates, or roasted grains, after the [eating]
the Passover offering. A person is obligated to occupy themselves with the
laws of Passover all evening, whether with his son, his students, or even with
himself alone."[24] We have, then, two traditions about what the content of the
Passover seder should be, one that privileges the study of the law and one
that centers the seder around the telling of a story. It is perhaps surprising
that the Passover Haggadah ultimately embraced the second approach. If
legal dispute is at the heart of the rabbinic tradition, why did the rabbis
choose narrative and memory as the most appropriate modes of discourse
for Passover?

S. Daniel Breslauer has argued that the two narratives reflect divergent
ethical traditions within rabbinic literature. Rabban Gamliel's seder "focuses
on actions rather than on thought, on deed rather than on motivation." The
Seder at Benei Braq, conversely, is an example of Rabbi Akiva's messianic
optimism, even if it predates his revolutionary activities: "The purpose of
telling stories is to motivate political action," Breslauer argues. "Political
action does not precede but depends upon theology. In such a case, theology can succeed even when the political action fails." He understands the
Haggadah's call to remember the exodus as an example of Abraham Joshua
Heschel's "depth theology," which he understands to mean "the sense of
divine challenge and the desire of human beings to answer that challenge."[25]
Or, as Heschel writes, "[t]heology declares. Depth theology evokes...the-
ology deals with permanent facts. Depth theology deals with moments."[26]

Similarly, Levinas asserts that the memory of a singular event—the exodus—becomes the very *breath* of Jewish existence. Reflecting on Eleazar
ben Azaria's enjoinment to recall the exodus in the evening that follows the
seder in the Haggadah, he writes:

> The going forth from Egypt—the Exodus—and the evo-
> cation of that exodus in which freedom was given to a
> people, the coming to the foot of Mount Sinai where that
> freedom culminated in Law, constituted a privileged past,
> the very form of the past, as it were. But by the same token
> it is a thought virtually obsessed by the theme of freeing

---

[24] Tosefta Pesahim 10:7.
[25] S. Daniel Breslauer, "When Halakha is Haggadah: The Ethics of the Passover Seder," *Shofar* 3, no. 4 (1985): 5–18.
[26] Abraham Joshua Heschel, *The Insecurity of Freedom: Essays on Human Existence* (New York: Noonday, 1967), 118.

slaves…. Here we have a dimension of the memorable and as it were the spirituality—or the respiration—of consciousness, which already, in its content of presence, is memory of affranchisement, and lived concretely as the soul of freedmen. The Jew is free qua affranchised: his memory is immediately compassion for all the enslaved or all the wretched of the earth, and a special flair for that wretchedness that the wretched themselves are prone to forget.[27]

Perhaps, by including the seder at Benei Braq and excluding Rabban Gamliel's seder at Lod, the editors of the Haggadah were simply preserving the tradition best known to them by its transmission in the Babylonian Talmud. It is plausible, though, that the text is also making a claim about the function of memory as a redemptive act.

In the rabbis' telling, the two Passover meals come at a time of crisis for the Jewish community: the Jerusalem temple lays in ruins, and Jewish ritual practice must find a way to move forward. In recalling the specific laws of Passover as they would have been carried out in the temple, Rabban Gamliel is recalling a recent past to which he was a direct witness. A psychoanalytic reading might suggest that Rabban Gamliel is trapped in a pathologized melancholy; he longs to maintain and restore those customs and rituals that were central to his identity when the temple stood. This perhaps contributes to the lack of empathy he displays toward his contemporaries. In Rabban Gamliel's world, there is no room for the kind of innovative teaching that Levinas sees manifest in Rabbi Eleazar ben Azaria. How can one innovate? "The footrest of our God is burnt in fire. Should we not weep!"

In the seder at Benei Braq, though, another mode of memory prevails. Where Rabban Gamliel weeps, Akiva laughs. These sages are no less traumatized—they are products of the same calamity as Rabban Gamliel. They deploy, though, a messianic vision of history that sees the world not through the lachrymose lens of recent destruction but with an eye—or, better, soul—toward past and future redemption. Telling the tale of redemption is an act of defiance against destruction. Seen this way, the purpose of historical narrative is not to create linear arcs, but to disrupt them.

---

[27] Levinas, "Beyond Memory."

Daniel Stein

Fruitful Melancholia and Jewish Memory

In *Mourning Becomes the Law*, philosopher Gillian Rose reflects on the perseverance of narrative in Jewish thought, even in the midst of catastrophic loss. She cites a famous Hasidic tale that she learned from Elie Wiesel:

> When the great Rabbi Israel Baal Shem-Tov
> Saw misfortune threatening the Jews
> It was his custom
> To go into a certain part of the forest to meditate.
> There he would light a fire,
> Say a special prayer,
> And the miracle would be accomplished
> And the misfortune averted.
> Later when his disciple,
> The celebrated Magid of Mezritch,
> Has occasion, for the same reason,
> To intercede with heaven,
> He would go to the same place in the forest
> And say: "Master of the Universe, listen!
> I do not know how to light the fire,
> But I am still able to say the prayer."
> And again the miracle would be accomplished.
> Still later,
> Rabbi Moshe-Leib of Sasov,
> In order to save his people once more,
> Would go into the forest and say:
> "I do not know how to light the fire,
> I do not know the prayer,
> But I know the place
> And this must be sufficient."
> It was sufficient and the miracle was accomplished.
> Then it fell to Rabbi Israel of Rizhyn
> To overcome misfortune.
> Sitting in his armchair, his head in his hands,
> He spoke to God: "I am unable to light the fire
> And I do not know the prayer;
> I cannot even find the place in the forest.

All I can do is to tell the story,
And this must be sufficient."
And it was sufficient.[28]

Rose comments:

> The tale plus the comment which questions the continuing
> ability to tell the tale is the tale renewed by the questioning
> of its transmission in spite of the loss of its truth. Not to
> tell the tale of perhaps not being able to tell the tale would
> make the loss of the tale and the occurrence of the catastro-
> phe absolute: it would fix the catastrophe as the meaning,
> or, rather, as the devastation, of meaning.[29]

Rose would have perhaps been delighted to learn that the tale she cites here, one that she hopes "countless others" would also relate, has a rich history of its own—one that, ultimately, helps us finally understand Rabbi Akiva's seder.

The letters between Benjamin and Gershom Scholem, both philoso-phers, bear witness to the growth of and ultimately the tragic demise of a friendship that developed during the most catastrophic moments in world history. Despite this—or perhaps because of it—they also display a consis-tent theme: the urgent desire the two men shared to write and hopefully publish books of lasting impact.[30] While Benjamin's influence has ascended in recent years, he died tragically, before seeing his mature works through to fruition. Scholem, on the other hand, published arguably his most important book, *Major Trends in Jewish Mysticism* (1946), just after the conclusion of World War II. It carries this dedication:

TO THE MEMORY OF
WALTER BENJAMIN
(1892–1940) The friend of a lifetime whose genius united
the insight of the Metaphysician, the interpretative power

---

[28] Elie Wiesel, *Souls on Fire*, trans. Marion Wiesel (Harmondsworth: Penguin, 1987), quoted in Gillian Rose, *Mourning Becomes the Law* (Cambridge: Cambridge University Press, 1996), 99.
[29] Rose, *Mourning*, 100.
[30] Gershom Scholem, ed., *The Correspondance of Walter Benjamin and Gershom Scholem*, trans. Anson Rabinach (Cambridge, MA: Harvard University Press, 1992).

of the Critic and the erudition of the Scholar.
DIED AT PORT BOU (SPAIN)
ON HIS WAY INTO FREEDOM[31]

In the afterward to the collection of lectures that formed *Major Trends*, Scholem concludes with the same Hasidic tale cited by Rose. It is, to my knowledge, the first time the story appears in English. Scholem, though, does not attribute the tale to Martin Buber's famous collections of such tales. Instead, he notes that he heard the story from Shmuel Yosef Agnon, the Hebrew author who, in the 1920s, had served as a kind of spiritual mentor to Scholem and Benjamin in their early studies of Judaism in Berlin.[32] This is how Scholem understood the story:

> You can say if you will that this profound little anecdote symbolizes the decay of a great movement. You can also say that it reflects the transformation of all its values, a transformation so profound that in the end all that remained of the mystery was the tale. That is the position in which we find ourselves today, or in which Jewish mysticism finds itself. The story is not ended, *it has not yet become history*, and the secret life it holds can break out tomorrow in you or in me.[33]

How are we to understand such an approach to memory?

Traverso has contemplated the fate of Marxism after the collapse of the Soviet Union and has suggested an approach to mourning that might also be applied to Rabbi Akiva: "This melancholia does not mean lamenting a lost utopia, but rather rethinking a revolutionary project in a nonrevolutionary age. This is a fruitful melancholia that, one could say with Judith Butler, implies the transformative effect of loss."[34] Traverso also offers a moving example of this kind of "fruitful melancholia":

---

[31] Gershom Scholem, *Major Trends in Jewish Mysticism* (New York: Schocken, 1946, 1995), dedication page.

[32] Cynthia Ozick, "The Heretic," *New Yorker* (August 25, 2002), https://www.newyorker.com/magazine/2002/09/02/the-heretic.

[33] Scholem, *Major Trends*, 264–65.

[34] For Butler's construction of such melancholia, see Judith Butler, "After Loss, What Then," in *Loss: The Politics of Mourning*, ed. David Eng and David Kazanjian (Berkeley: University of California Press, 2003), 467–73.

One of the most significant examples of a fruitful work of
mourning that, instead of paralyzing action, stimulates it in
a self-reflexive and conscious way deals with the reactions
of gay activists to the disruptive consequences of AIDS, a
pandemic whose outbreak coincided with the fall of com-
munism.... Rather than escaping melancholia, [activists]
channeled it toward a fruitful work of reconstruction, creating medical centers, assuring psychological care, defending recently achieved rights, and rebuilding a network of
associations. Act Up [The AIDS Coalition to Unleash Power—an early HIV-AIDS advocacy group] was the product
of a fruitful, political melancholia.[35]

Rabbi Akiva's approach to memory is similarly productive. As Rose notes,
the act of telling stories is an act of resistance against catastrophe. For Rabbi
Akiva and his fellows, telling the tale of redemption and plunging its interpretive depths while experiencing their own personal loss inspires them
to work for a better future. Instead of striving to rebuild an irreplaceable
past, their memories remind them of what was and allow them to envision
the world as it might be. As Levinas asserts, the exodus is evidence that it
is possible, against all odds, to move from suffering to freedom. In renewing this memory, then, Rabbi Akiva and his fellows were simultaneously
bearing witness to a redeemed past and calling on each other to be agents
in creating a holier future. It is in this way that Akiva brings comfort to his
colleagues. And it is perhaps for this reason that new approaches to Jewish
memory are ascendant today. We live in a turbulent time, when the impacts
of catastrophes beyond name are regularly experienced by so many. While
petty tyrants may call on their followers to seek refuge in imagined pasts that
never were, Rabbi Akiva's seder teaches us that embedded within crisis is
the promise of redemption, if we only seek it out and heed its call to action.
As Scholem writes, "The story is not ended, it has not yet become history,
and the secret life it holds can break out tomorrow in you or in me."

---

*Rabbi Daniel Z. Stein is the spiritual leader of Congregation B'nai Shalom in Walnut Creek,
California and a doctoral student at the Graduate Theological Union, Berkeley. He is the
2023–2024 Daniel Jeremy Silver Fellow at the Harvard University Center for Jewish Studies.*

[35] Traverso, *Left-Wing Melancholia*, 21.

From Despair to Hope: A Torah Model

Rachael Turkienicz

One of the most challenging instances in life is when we begin to move from sadness to despair. This transition often involves feelings of isolation and hopelessness. Once despair sets in, a person's perspectives can narrow, and the ability to move beyond the despairing moment minimizes. The Torah narrative of Hagar's exile into the wilderness with her son, Ishmael, portrays her journey toward despair, as well as her journey toward its resolution: hope. By carefully reading the verses that detail Hagar's exile, consulting with parts of Psalms, rabbinic literature, and modern psychological approaches, a model for transitioning from despair to hope can be seen.

From Sadness to Despair

Unlike moments of sadness or grief, despair has a far more all-encompassing aspect to it. According to the American Psychological Association's dictionary, despair is: "the emotion or feeling of hopelessness, that is, that things are profoundly wrong and will not change for the better. Despair is one of the most negative and destructive of human affects." There is a narrative within Torah, the exile of Hagar and Ishmael (Genesis 21:14–21), that portrays the human journey from despair to healing.[1] The beginning of the text outlines the dilemma and the beginning stages of despair (Genesis 21:14–16):

וישכם אברהם בבקר ויקח לחם וחמת מים ויתן אל הגר
שם על שכמה ואת הילד וישלחה ותלך ותתע במדבר באר
שבע ויכלו המים מן החמת ותשלך את הילד תחת אחד
השיחם ותלך ותשב לה מנגד הרחק כמטחוי קשת כי אמרה
אל אראה במות הילד ותשב מנגד ותשא את קלה ותבך

And Abraham arose early in the morning, and he took bread and a goatskin of water, and he gave them to Hagar, placed it on her shoulder, with her son, and sent her. She

[1] The author wishes to thank Rabbi Elliot Dorff and Rabbi Brad Artson for their insights and encouragement in writing this article.

All translations are original to the author.

went and erred in the wilderness of Beersheba. And the water in the goatskin ceased, and she sent the boy under one of the bushes. And she went and sat by herself opposite, at the distance of an arrow from a bow, because she said, "I must not see the death of the boy." As she sat opposite, she raised her voice, and she wept.

The description of events, as well as the choice of images and words, paints the picture of someone who is beginning to despair. The Torah depicts increasing challenges, as well as a mindset of personal responsibility, both of which lead to the conclusion of personal failure. Repeated images, as well as words of battle and confrontation, are used to indicate the locked perspective of conflict that repeats in the worldview playing repeatedly in the mind.

Textual Images and Word Choices

On a careful reading of the Hagar narrative, we can see that the Torah presents key signs of a despairing person: an overwhelming load, feelings of being lost and rejected, a narrowing of perception, and an effort to position oneself in opposition to or in conflict with one's surroundings. We see in Hagar a person who has descended to the lowest spiritual and psychological levels. If such a person is left alone, there is a strong possibility of extreme outcomes.

The Load is Overwhelming

Hagar has been exiled into the wilderness with her son, and with limited supplies. The order of phrases in Genesis 21:14 indicates that Abraham has placed two warm things on Hagar's shoulders. The Hebrew word for "goatskin of water" contains the word "warm" in it (חמת מים), and her son, Ishmael, has the warmth of a living child. Hagar is now carrying the water they will need to survive, as well as the life for which she is responsible, on her shoulders. Both these responsibilities are emitting heat as she is cast into the desert, where heat is a primary threat. By playing with this image of warmth and wilderness, the Torah shows that the things normally viewed as reinforcing survival are now being viewed as growing threats.

Although it is Abraham who is exiling her, Hagar never blames him or expresses anger toward him. This may also be explained by the description of Abraham placing these things on her shoulders. Once placed, Hagar

Rachael Turkienicz

bears both the water of their future survival and the child she birthed from the waters of her womb on both her shoulders. This image also shows the shift from carrying Ishmael in her womb to now carrying Ishmael on her shoulders. While he was in her womb, Hagar could provide water for him constantly; now that he is on her shoulder, she cannot give him what he needs, and she now sees this as her failure, not Abraham's.

Losing the Way

The Torah tells us that, before running out of water, Hagar lost her way in the desert. Hagar is an Egyptian woman and may have been able to return to Egypt had she not become disoriented in the desert. The problem she faces begins not with a lack of resources (water) but with a lack of direction or control. The water running out is now the last measure of loss in that Hagar, the mother, can no longer provide the waters of life for her son. Hagar's entire focus is on her relationship with her son, which becomes apparent because the loss of water is equally a threat to her own life, but she does not see it.

Rejection

When Abraham rejects Hagar, the verb used is וישלחה, "and he sent her"; when Hagar leaves Ishmael under a bush, the verb used is ותשלך, "and she sent." This is a strange verb choice for Hagar, as it literally means "to send," but in her case she seems to be laying her child under the bush. The deliberate use of this verb, especially because it is a constrained use, hints at the place of rejection within despair. Abraham has rejected Hagar by sending her away. Hagar will subsequently reject all meaningful relationships in her life, mirroring the rejection that triggered her despair. A key component of despair is a sense of isolation and rejection, which leads to a narrowing of perspective and connections.[2]

A Narrowing of Perception

Once the water has stopped, Hagar places Ishmael "under one of the bushes" (Genesis 21:16). In other words, Hagar is sitting at an oasis that has living bushes, a clear sign of the presence of water. The solution to her dilemma

[2] V. Brown, T. Morgan, and A. Fralick, Isolation and Mental Health: Thinking outside the Box," General Psychiatry 34, no. 3 (2021): 1–4, 34:e100461, doi: 10.1136/gpsych-2020-100461.

104

is sitting all around her, but Hagar is unable to see it. Hagar's perceptions have narrowed, such that she is able to process the crisis but cannot see the opportunities for resolution.

Words of Opposition and Conflict

Once Hagar has placed Ishmael under the bush, the Torah says that she sat at a distance from him (Genesis 21:16). The exact description is ותשב לה מנגד, which literally means "and she sat in opposition." In fact, the phrase repeats later in the same verse, emphasizing that she has positioned herself in conflict with, or opposition to, the events. The language becomes stronger when the distance being described is כמטחוי קשת, "like the distance of an arrow from a bow." The text has used the image of a weapon to describe the measure of Hagar's distance. A bow and arrow would be used either to attack or to hunt. In either case, Hagar is feeling that she is being preyed upon, as if she has been targeted.

The Portrait of Despair

Abraham Maslow's Pyramid (1943) represents a hierarchy of human needs beginning with a broad base structure of physiological needs. This base covers the essential needs of food, warmth, water, and rest. The pyramid builds upward through needs of safety, belongingness and love, esteem, and culminates with self-actualization. According to Abraham Maslow's hierarchy of human needs, Hagar has been deprived of all stages listed on the hierarchy. The resulting psychology is one of despair, a struggle to survive.

There is a commonly accepted notion that a person needs to "hit rock bottom" before rebuilding. The idea is that, while sitting at the bottom, they would understand that there is only one direction of movement, and that is upward. However, there is a second option to someone in this position: rather than choosing to move upward, the person might choose to opt out entirely. It is important to recognize when the spiral has reached its lowest point, since connecting in that moment may make all the difference in which choice the person will make. Connecting means meeting the person where they are without offering platitudes of how things will get better.[3]

---

[3] This example of connection will be seen in the angel's opening words to Hagar when she is asked to share her perspective first: "What is [upon you]?" (Genesis 21:17).

Rachael Turkienicz

The Torah's Response to Hagar

The Torah's response to Hagar's despair is related in the verses that immediately follow the incident (Genesis 21:17–19):

וישמע א–להים את קול הנער ויקרא מלאך א–להים אל
הגר מן השמים ויאמר לה מה לך הגר אל תיראי כי שמע
א–להים אל קול הנער באשר הוא שם: קומי שאי את הנער
והחזיקי את ידך בו כי לגוי גדול אשימנו: ויפקח א–להים
את עיניה ותרא באר מים ותלך ותמלא את החמת מים
ותשק את הנער:

> And God heard the voice of the lad, and an angel of God
> called to Hagar from the sky and said to her: "What [is
> upon] you, Hagar? Do not be afraid, for God has heard
> the voice of the lad from where he is. Rise up, carry the lad,
> and strengthen your hand with his, for I will place him as
> a great nation." And God opened her eyes and she saw a
> well of water, and she went, filled the goatskin of water, and
> fed water to the lad.

As the narrative progresses, we are told that Ishmael has also been despairing and crying out: "And God heard the voice of the lad." In fact, the angel
tells Hagar: "God has heard the voice of the lad from where he is." Although
we are told of Hagar's dilemma, we must not forget that Ishmael is doing
worse and is at death's door. The focus now shifts from Hagar as the victim
to Hagar as the support person.

Moving toward Hope

The Torah now outlines the initial stages involved in approaching Hagar
and changing her perspective. The first words spoken are words of inquiry:
"What [is upon] you?" is an open-ended question of outreach that allows
the person to describe what they are seeing and feeling—or, conversely, what
they are not seeing or feeling.

The angel immediately proceeds to give instructions to Hagar and explain
what she must do to save Ishmael. The instructions are simple and easy to
follow: stand up, walk over to him, touch him, cradle him, hold his hand.
Each step on its own is small but addresses parts of the isolation Hagar

must overcome to help her son—to simply be present with him, no words exchanged except the offer of companionship, and to move from there to caring gestures such as touching hands, in order to strengthen each other with the power of presence and contact. Throughout it all, the angel does not tell Hagar to say anything, because sometimes words can themselves become the barriers.

Michelle Friedman, a psychiatrist who founded and directs the pastoral program at Yeshivat Chovevei Torah, notes: "What clergy do wrong is leaning forward and talking too much. In their own anxiety, they are not believing in the power of pastoral listening and hospitality. People feel like they have to make it better, to fill the space with words. They really need to quiet down."[4] This subtle sentiment is also present in Jewish traditions of visiting mourners at a shiva house. It is the presence of the visitor that is comforting, not necessarily the words of comfort, which can sometimes sound like platitudes. The person visiting—or, in the Hagar text, the person supporting—initially takes the role of listener. At times, subtle and small physical gestures of contact breach the isolation far more effectively than words.

Although we hear that Hagar raised her voice to sob, we are told that God heard the voice of Ishmael. Genesis Rabbah 53,19 comments on this change of subject and connects it to the phrase "from where he is": באשר הוא שם. בזכות עצמו. יפה תפילת החולה לעצמו יותר מכל, "'From where he is.' On his own merit. The prayer of the one who is ailing is preferred over all others." Genesis Rabbah states that God hears Ishmael's cries first because Ishmael is more desperate than Hagar in this moment. The midrash clearly states that a person must be strengthened to reach out on their own behalf. Empowerment can be found in self-advocacy, in finding one's own voice.

This concept is reinforced in the Talmud, Bava Metzi'a 33a: אבדתו ואבדת אביו אבדתו קודמת אבדת אביו ואבדת רבו שלו קודם, "We learn (Mishnah), his own lost article and the lost article of his father, his own lost article takes precedence. And [as regards] the lost article of his rabbi, his own takes precedence." The Talmud lists the comparisons between us and those people in our lives we have been commanded to respect and revere. Although one might assume that the commandment to respect a father or a rabbi would be prioritized first, it is self-care that gains importance when feeling dis-

4 Michelle Friedman and Rachel Yehuda, The Art of Jewish Pastoral Counseling: A Guide for All Faiths (London: Routledge, 2017). Cited in Sandee Brawarsky, "The Key to Pastoral Care: 'Quiet Down,'" New York Jewish Week (May 16, 2017), https://www.jta.org/2017/05/16/ny/the-key-to-pastoral-care-quiet-down.

advantaged.

The same midrash in Genesis Rabbah (53,19) also discusses the latitude of assessment in the moment of despair. It is not about what was or what will be; it is singularly about what is within this moment. Genesis Rabbah presents a discussion between God and the angels as God is preparing to save Ishmael:

אמרו לפניו רבון העולמים אדם שהוא עתיד להמית בניך
מצמא, את מעלה לו באר? א״ל עכשו מה הוא, צדיק או
רשע? אמרו לו, צדיק. א״ל איני דן את האדם אלא בשעתו.

> They said before Him: "Master of Eternities, a person who is destined in the future to kill your children by thirst, You raise a well for him?" He said to them, "Right now, what is he, righteous or wicked?" They said to Him, "Righteous." He said to them, "I do not judge a person except for in his [present] moment."[5]

Genesis Rabbah has narrowed the context to be this moment of time, while ruling out a discussion of the future. To begin the support for someone who is despairing is to enter the current moment of despair with them, not to begin with predicting a future. Only once the support person is standing alongside them can the discussion entertain unknown futures.

When the angel says "For I will place him as a great nation" (Genesis 21:18), the angel is now introducing a future that looks quite different than either the present moment or even what logical hope might have predicted. The statement explores the aspect of creating the possibility of the unknown. It broadens the narrow perspective on the moment and invites the person to imagine what could be.

The Torah then states that God opens Hagar's eyes so she can see the well of water. It does not say that God creates a well; rather, the well had been there all along, but Hagar's despair made her blind to its existence. Once the angel opens the door of possibility in her mind, Hagar can entertain the opportunities that are around and see them as possibilities.

The final verse has Hagar refilling the water from the well, an endless source of water, and seeing herself again as the protective mother to her son.

---

[5] The word עולם in "Master of Eternities" is used to mean both "world" and "eternity" and often gains its meaning from the context. In this instance, they are discussing elements of present and future, a temporal argument, so I have translated it as "Eternities."

From Despair to Hope: A Torah Model

This image is solidified when the text says את הנער ותשק, which means "she fed him water," but the verb also alludes to a kiss. She is now giving Ishmael water both from the well and from her lips—the physical and the emotional/spiritual are replenished.

While the Torah provides the basis for understanding this portrait of despair and hope, it is only the outline within which the remaining texts find their expressions.

The View from Within: Psalms Can Enter the Moment

Following the example of the Torah and the midrash, an important step in supporting someone is to enter the moment they are experiencing, rather than try and force them to enter yours. The book of Psalms is filled with texts that speak to the moment of sadness from within and allow the reader to unapologetically explore its realms. It is to enter the human heart and walk around.

The psalms that describe the despairing heart from the inside validate its pain. The psalmist does not retreat from the recognition that a person can legitimately feel abandoned, isolated, and betrayed. These verses can be used to sit together with a person and enter the heartache they feel. We see this, for example, in Psalm 22:

(ב) א-לי א-לי למה עזבתני רחוק מישועתי דברי שאגתי:
(ג) א-להי אקרא יומם ולא תענה ולילה ולא דומיה לי: (ד)
ואתה קדוש יושב תהלות ישראל:...(ח) כל ראי ילעגו לי
יפטירו בשפה יניעו ראש:...(י) כי אתה גחי מבטן מבטיחי
על שדי אמי: (יא) עליך השלכתי מרחם מבטן אמי א-לי
אתה: (יב) אל תרחק ממני כי צרה קרובה כי אין עוזר:

My God, my God, why have you abandoned me, far from helping me when I roared my words? My God, I call to You all day and You do not answer, and at night, and You make no appearance to me. But You are the Holy One who sits on the praises of Israel... All those who see me will mock me, they will open with their lips and they will shake their head... Because You drew me from the womb, You gave me promise at my mother's breast. I was cast upon You from the womb, from my mother's womb You are my God. Do not make Yourself far from me, because crisis is close, and

there is no one there to help me.

The psalm begins with the validation of feeling abandoned, alone, and betrayed. It incriminates God for remaining silent in the face of beseeching
words. The verbs of the first four verses speak of a present and ongoing un-
answered outreach. There is no reprieve, whether it is day or night. Sitting
with no answer, the psalmist reminds God that God sits on Israel's praises.
The unspoken disconnect is the complete divine disengagement from the
painful outreach of someone who belongs to those who praise.

The psalm continues to explore the details of the human rejection experienced by the writer. It is in their spoken words and in their body language;
it is both overt and subtle, but it is present and unending. The verbs now
change to future tense. It reflects the viewpoint of a person in despair who
believes that what is currently happening will continue to happen endlessly,
with no change or improvement. To this point, the words of the psalm, when
shared with a person in pain, creates a point at which the support person
can enter the pain through validation, with no comfort offered. Any words of
comfort would be understood as undermining the reality of the experience
in its personal and spiritual depth and trauma.

The psalmist then expresses the reality that life exists because God wills
it, and the writer therefore has no choice but to feel bonded with God. God
was present at birth and through infancy, as the writer was sheltered and
nourished by his mother's breast. The psalm explains that an acceptance of
God occurred in those most gentle moments when the world was reduced
to God and the mother, both anchoring the new life. The fact that no one
else is mentioned in the poem excludes all those who mock and will continue to mock. They have never been part of the essential picture. They are
insignificant.

The language of the psalm now switches to the imperative verb form. It
does not beseech but demands—אל תרחק, "Do not make Yourself far!"—
ultimately stating that God's presence is the constant, and God must stand
beside him.

Modern religious pastoral care teaches clergy to understand how and
when to bring God into the discussion. Theresa Clement Tisdale, Carrie E.
Doehring, and Veneta Lorraine-Poriere[6] present a case study outlining the
following steps for pastoral support and care:

---

[6] Theresa Clement Tisdale, Carrie E. Doehring, and Veneta Lorraine-Poriere, "Three Voices,
One Song: A Psychologist, Spiritual Director, and Pastoral Counselor Share Perspectives on
Providing Care," Journal of Psychology and Theology 31, no. 1 (2003): 52–68.

The importance of listening to the theological language used by the person. Entering the moment of despair to stand with the person affected includes listening first to establish common theological language and perspective.

Once the language is established, the discussion can explore the theological structure within which the person views the crisis: one of sin; personal or societal; is there promise in redemption; does the person believe in personal salvation etc.

Throughout the conversations, it is important to note if the person has maintained or changed their understanding of God in their lives, and whether the crisis has affected this or triggered it.

By using the Psalm 22 excerpts or similar verses, the discussion around God and the person's feelings of religious context can be explored and validated. It is important to allow the suffering person to articulate spiritual feelings, and this can be encouraged by asking questions such as: What were they and what are they now? When did the change occur? What would be the ideal picture? Where do they feel God's absence?

The journey of the psalmist toward empowerment, self-advocacy, and direct theological dialogue now includes the perspectives presented within modern pastoral literature.

Words of Comfort Can Become Words of Pain

Even as a support person might intend to bring comfort and relief, it is often easy to fall back on long held cultural beliefs that may no longer hold true. "Misery loves company" can lead someone to offer examples of suffering, believing that this will soothe the sufferer. This strategy often backfires, as it may end up adding more pain or fear to the situation or rendering the uniqueness of their moment less important.

Chapter 14 of Avot deRabbi Natan describes a situation of crisis and the responses it received:

כשמת בנו של רבן יוחנן בן זכאי נכנסו תלמידיו לנחמו
נכנס רבי אליעזר וישב לפניו ואמר ליה רבי רצונך אומר
דבר אחד לפניך. אמר לו אמור. אמר לו אדם הראשון היה
לו בן ומת וקבל עליו תנחומין, ומנין שקבל עליו תנחומין

שנאמר וידע אדם עוד את אשתו (בראשית ד׳ כ׳ה) אף
אתה קבל תנחומין. אמר לו לא די לי שאני מצטער בעצמי
אלא הזכרת לי צערו של אדם הראשון. נכנס רבי יהושע
ואמר לו רצונך אומר דבר לפניך. אמר לו אמור. אמר לו
איוב היו לו בנים ובנות ומתו כולם ביום אחד וקבל עליהם
תנחומין אף אתה קבל תנחומין. ומנין שקבל איוב תנחומין
שנאמר ה׳ נתן וה׳ לקח יהי שם ה׳ מבורך (איוב א׳ כ׳א).
אמר לו לא די לי שאני מצטער בעצמי אלא שהזכרת לי
צערו של איוב. נכנס רבי יוסי וישב לפניו אמר לו רבי
רצונך אומר דבר לפניך. אמר לו אמור. אמר לו אהרן היו
לו שני בנים גדולים ומתו שניהם ביום אחד וקבל עליהם
תנחומין שנאמר וידם אהרן (ויקרא י׳ ג׳) אין שתיקה אלא
תנחומין ואף אתה קבל תנחומין. אמר לו לא די לי שאני
מצטער בעצמי אלא שהזכרתני צערו של אהרן. נכנס רבי
שמעון ואמר לו רבי רצונך אומר דבר לפניך. אמר לו
אמור. אמר לו דוד המלך היה לו בן ומת וקבל תנחומין
ואף אתה קבל תנחומין ומנין שקבל דוד תנחומין שנאמר
וינחם דוד את בת שבע אשתו ויבא אליה וישכב עמה ותלד
בן ויקרא את שמו שלמה (שמואל ב׳ י׳כ כ׳ד) אף אתה
רבי קבל תחנומין. אמר לו לא די שאני מצטער בעצמי
אלא שהזכרתני צערו של דוד המלך. נכנס רבי אלעזר בן
עזריה...וישב לפניו ואמר לו אמשול לך משל למה הדבר
דומה לאדם שהפקיד אצלו המלך פקדון. בכל יום ויום
היה בוכה וצועק ואומר אוי לי אימתי אצא מן הפקדון הזה
בשלום. אף אתה רבי היה לך בן קרא תורה מקרא נביאים
וכתובים משנה הלכות ואגדות ונפטר מן העולם בלא חטא
ויש לקבל עליך תנחומין כשהחזרת פקדונך שלם. אמר לו
רבי יוחנן, אלעזר בני נחמתני כדרך שבני אדם מנחמין.

When Rabban Yoḥanan ben Zakkai's son died, his disciples came to comfort him. Rabbi Eliezer entered, sat before
him, and said, "Master, by your will, may I say one thing to
you?" He said to him, "Speak." Rabbi Eliezer said, "Adam
had a son who died, yet he accepted comfort over him.
And from where do we learn that he accepted comfort?
'And Adam knew his woman again' (Genesis 4:25), now
you too must accept comfort." He said to him, "Is it not
enough that I have my own sorrow, but now you remind
me of the sorrow of the first human being?" Rabbi Joshua

entered, and he said to him, "By your will, may I say one thing to you?," and he said to him, "Speak." He said to him, "Job had sons and daughters, and they all died on one day, and he accepted comfort over them. Now you must accept comfort. And from where do we know that Job accepted comfort? As is written, 'God gave and God took, may the Name of God be blessed' (Job 1:21–22)." He said to him, "Is it not enough that I have my own sorrow, but now you remind me of the sorrow of Job?" Rabbi Yosi entered and sat before him. He said to him, "My Master, by your will, may I say one thing to you?," he said to him, "Speak." He said to him, "Aaron had two grown sons, and the two of them died on the same day and Aaron accepted comfort, as is written 'And Aaron was silent' (Leviticus 10:3), there is no [other meaning] for silence other than comfort. Now you, too, must accept comfort." He said to him, "It is not enough that I have my own sorrow, but now you remind me of the sorrow of Aaron?" Rabbi Shimon entered, and he said to him, "My master, by your will, may I say one thing to you?," he said to him, "Speak." He said to him, "King David had a son who died, and he accepted comfort. From where do we know that David accepted comfort? As is written, 'And David comforted Batsheva, his wife, and he came to her and he lay with her, and she delivered a son, and he called his name Solomon' (2 Samuel 12:24). Now you too must accept comfort." He said to him, "It is not enough that I have my sorrow, but now you remind me of the sorrow of King David?" Rabbi Eleazar ben Azaria entered…and sat before him. He said to him, "I will draw an analogy for you. To what does this compare? To a man with whom the king entrusted something. Each and every day he would cry and shout 'Woe to me, when will I be safely relieved of this trust?' Even you, my master, You had a son who read Torah, he read Prophets and Scrolls, Mishnah, laws, and legends, and he is now departed from the world without sin. It is upon you to receive comfort that you returned your trust whole." He said to him, "Rabbi Eleazar, my son, you have comforted me in the way that a human being should be comforted."

The midrash presents Rabban Yoḥanan ben Zakkai as an inconsolable parent in the face of losing his son. As each rabbi enters to offer comfort, they engage in what they think he would find most comforting: rabbinic discourse. Each of the examples offered is an example from text, and the emotional arguments they present are all accompanied with prooftexts. It is the day-to-day exchange in which they all engage; it is the discourse of their lives. They are seeking to offer comfort through the security of routine.

But ben Zakkai rejects each one, not on the basis of the argument, but on the basis of the lack of humanity within the argument. He points out to them that empathy would result in increased sorrow, not comfort. The suffering of others is not a textual exchange. It is a human moment that must be recognized in the uniqueness of each one. To consider that "misery loves company" is to argue that all suffering and misery is the same and can therefore be grouped together to form some kind of community in which comfort can be found. Ben Zakkai refutes each attempt by telling his interlocutor that they are adding to his pain.

When ben Azaria gives his analogy, he is speaking in human terms, with no texts and no prooftexts. He offers the story of the human condition and the ongoing responsibility of parenting. In his final words to ben Zakkai, ben Azaria offers him comfort in the idea that, throughout his son's life, he met his parental responsibility of providing care, knowledge, depth of insight, and guidance for a life without sin. The loss is still there, but the self-blame and doubt has been comforted. Ben Zakkai addresses ben Azaria as "my son" and by doing so offers the response that ben Azaria spoke to him from within the relationship he shared with his lost son—ben Azaria had entered the realm of ben Zakkai's pain and spoke to him from there. In the end, the comfort is accepted because it is "the way a human being should be comforted"—it entered the human moment and spoke from within.

Conclusion

The Torah brings a powerful portrait of despair, presenting the details and steps through which Hagar's journey leads her there. Once despair sets in, Hagar can no longer see opportunities or hope; she feels hunted and lost and has given up. The nuances of the Torah text are reinforced through modern psychological lenses of depression and despair. Once the biblical narrative changes Hagar's role from victim to support person, we become aware of the voice of the suffering child, Ishmael. Rabbinic literature enters the text in discussing the power of self-advocacy and the importance of finding your own voice.

The ability to enter the heart, into the reality of the despairing person, is accessible through the excerpts from Psalms. Once we have validated the suffering and all the emotions that accompany it, a candid exploration of God's presence in life or perceived absence can be discussed. The perspectives of modern psychiatric and pastoral care providers include the questioning and discussion of God, as well as the changing spiritual relationships that are important in a life journey. The importance of listening rather than speaking is crucial to creating and maintaining a supporting connection.

Ultimately, rabbinic literature shows how words of comfort that are offered must recognize the uniqueness of each person and their experiences. A moment of despair breaks the mold of the mundane; mundane words will therefore only make it worse. It is the human bond, the recognition of the suffering in its uniqueness, that can begin a discussion that moves toward comfort and hope.

Hagar, in her despair, and an angel with but a few words open a deeper understanding in us all. In allowing these texts to connect with each other, each bringing a different crucial element to the human moment, the journey from despair to hope broadens. Through this model, the Torah and all supporting texts and examples brought here allow us to recognize when someone moves closer to despair, and how we might enter that moment with them to begin a journey toward hope.

Rachael Turkienicz is currently the rabbi at the Beit Rayim Synagogue in Vaughan, Ontario, Canada. She holds a Ph.D. in rabbinic literature and was on faculty at York University for many years. Turkienicz founded and leads a Canadian learning center focusing on Jewish texts and musar studies. She is one of the founders of the Toronto Heschel School, a Jewish day school with an integrated general studies and Judaic program.

When God's "Yes" is "No" and God's "No" is "Yes"

Righting God's Law, Revealing the Divine Moral Conscience

Daniel Z. Siegel

In a late seventeenth-century text, entitled *Meï'ah berakhot* (*One Hundred Blessings*), we read:

> Blessing when Purchasing Slaves
> When an Israelite purchases a slave, he must recite a blessing, saying: "Have mercy and remember, master of this slave, to rejoice in his deeds and to enslave him and his children after him" as it says, 'You shall make them an inheritance for your children after you, to inherit as a possession in perpetuity, them shall you enslave' (Leviticus 25:46). 'Praised are You Who is good and does good'" (m. Berakhot 9:2).[1]

The author, Rabbi Avuhav da Fonseca, was then serving as chief rabbi of the Sephardic community of Amsterdam, which included Jewish slaveholders (and traders), as did the Dutch colony, Recife, in which he previously served as rabbi of the Portuguese Jewish community.[2]

While, in light of present-day sensibilities, we might find it morally repugnant for one to acquire or own a slave, let alone recite such a blessing, from biblical times into the nineteenth century (and beyond) one can hear an echoing of the sentiment expressed by the second–third century Babylonian Amora, Samuel: "Whoever emancipates his non-Jewish slave transgresses

---

[1] P. 184 (Amsterdam 1687). The title of this work reflects the rabbinic rendering of the biblical verse "Israel, what (*mah*) does the Lord your God require of you?" (Deuteronomy 10:12) as "Israel, one hundred (*meï'ah*) [blessings, daily] does the Lord your God require of you" (b. Menaḥot 43b).

[2] Jonathan Schorsch, Jews and Blacks in the Early Modern World (Cambridge: Cambridge University Press, 2004), 93–101.

a positive commandment" (b. Gittin 38a–38b).[3] Indeed, the assertion *Deo Vindice*, "God Will Vindicate Us," adopted as the motto of the seceding slaveholding Confederate States of America, points to this same biblical commandment referenced by Samuel and cited in *Mei'ah Berakhot*.

Beyond slavery, there remain today not a few biblical prescriptions/proscriptions and rabbinic sanctioning of the same whose viability and validity, although questioned on moral grounds, still meets with a response akin to that of Samuel or with the cry of *Deo Vindice*, voiced by those who would "uphold" the divine word against the "mistaken" moral onslaught of those who could only succeed in "dishonoring" it. For Hasidic Grand Rebbe Tsvi Elimelekh Spira of Dinov (1783–1841), whose reflections on the conflict of Jewish law and morality are the subject of this article, not only should we not cite the Torah as grounds for divine vindication in defending a law that would otherwise be deemed repugnant, but we should also not vindicate God in upholding this commandment, for that, in truth, would be a violation of the Divine will.

Tsvi Elimelekh, who lived in the period following the appearance of

---

[3] Slavery, of course, persists globally in various forms; see Lev Meirowitz Nelson, "Fighting Modern-Day Slavery: A Handbook for Jewish Communities," Truah (2014), https://truah.org/resources/fighting-modern-day-slavery-a-handbook-for-jewish-communities and "What Is Modern Slavery?," Anti-Slavery, https://www.antislavery.org/slavery-today/. Interestingly, Rabbi Avuhav's contemporary, Rabbi Ya'akov Hagiz, provides the following response to the query if one should say the blessing "Who makes diverse creatures" (Tosefta 6:3 and b. Berakhot 58a) upon seeing a black person (kushi): "It seems that one should [say this blessing] when [seeing] one who was born black (kushi) but his mother and father are white. But, for the children of blacks (kushim) it seems that one should not bless ('Who makes diverse creatures'). For the former [case] we are sorry, but the latter [case] reflects the way of the world, that a black (kushi) bears a black (kushi). But, if they are black (kushim) and gave birth to a white...then one may say [the blessing] 'Blessed is He who is good [and does good]'"; see Halakhot Ketanot (Jerusalem 1895), 44a (Part I, Query no. 240). Feeling sorry (for the parents or the child) when White parents give birth to a Black child, one says the blessing "Who makes diverse creatures." If Black parents give birth to a White child, however, then one may say "Blessed is He who is good and does good." Perhaps the sensibility that construes Black as negative and White as positive and elicits the blessing "Blessed is He who is good and does good" regarding Black parents bearing a White child reflects the same sensibility that causes one to say "Blessed is He who is good and does good" upon acquiring a (Black) slave: It is good for the less fortunate (or "inferior") Black and the more fortunate (or "superior") White. On the interplay within the Jewish community and Jewish tradition of slavery and color (and the curse of Ham) with regard to Blacks, see Schorsch, Jews and Blacks, 116–65. Even as they are feared for the presumed power they possess, albino Blacks, who were and continue to be shunned, persecuted, and killed within the Black communities of Africa, would offer a different perspective on the blessings of white Blacks. See the documentary film In the Shadow of the Sun (2012), directed by Harry Freeland, and Standing Voice, https://StandingVoice.org.

Mei'ah berakhot and shortly before the abolitionist movement came to the fore, is not alone within our Jewish tradition in arguing that divine law and morality must coincide. Challenging God for what might be deemed questionable, unjust, and/or destructive is not foreign to our biblical or rabbinic tradition. Well known are the words of the biblical Abraham when seeking to save Sodom from God's (indiscriminate) destruction: "It would be a profanation (*ḥallilah*) for You; would the judge of all the earth not do justice"? (Genesis 18:25).[4] When Moses saves the Israelite people from destruction by an angry God, following the golden calf incident, the rabbis have God Himself contrast the consequences from the generation of the flood, when no intercessor rose up to challenge Him:

> The Holy One Blessed be He says: "When I win, I lose and when I lose, I win. I won at the generation of the flood, but I lost in destroying all those people. And so it was with the generation of the dispersion [of the races, in the tower of Babel] and the people of Sodom. But, at the [golden] calf, Moses prevailed over Me and I won" (*Pesiqta Rabbati*, pisqa 40).[5]

Prophets with "boundless audacity" such as Moses, our tradition tells us, exemplify true servants of God in being "His Majesty's loyal opposition."[6] Within the Hasidic sphere in particular, confronting God was both laudatory and to be expected. The famous Berditcher Rebbe, Rav Levi Yitschak, is known as the "Defender of Israel" in that he is the "Prosecutor of God." In "The Kaddish of Reb Levi Yitschak" or "A Din Toyre mit Gott," this leader of his community rebukes God for the great, unjust suffering of his people.[7] In our time, Elie Wiesel, of Hasidic lineage, explains that his play, *Trial of God*, set in the fictitious seventeenth-century Ukranian town of Shamgorad, found its inspiration in witnessing a court of three rabbis in Auschwitz placing God on trial and declaring Him guilty for allowing the massacre of His people.[8]

---

[4] On ḥallilah see Targum Jonathan (and Rashi).

[5] Pesiqta Rabbati, ed. Meir (Ish Shalom) Friedmann(Vienna: Yosef Kaiser,1880).

[6] Yochanan Muffs, "Who Will Stand in the Breach? A Study of Prophetic Intercession," Love and Joy (New York: Jewish Theological Seminary of America, 1992), 11.

[7] *Samuel Dresner, Levi Yitzhak* of Berditchev: Portrait of a Hasidic Master (New York: Hartmore House, 1974), 85–90.

[8] Elie Wiesel, Trial of God (New York: Schocken, 1979), xxv.

When God's "Yes" is "No" and God's "No" is "Yes"

In being an upstander—in challenging rather than vindicating God— Rabbi Elimelekh is thus not exceptional. He may prove to be more distinctive in his creative interweaving of, on the one hand, the biblical and rabbinic portrayal of God as desiring or responding positively to the human challenge, as refracted through the biblical narrative, or *aggadic* portions of our tradition's texts, and, on the other hand, the call for human beings to take up the cause, presented through prescriptive and exhortative statements found within our Torah and halakhah. It is to him that we will now turn.

We will explore Rabbi Elimelekh's contention that, moved by our moral conscience and as prescribed by His law, we are required to call God to account and effect the necessary changes. The central passage we will consider is found within his commentary on the Bible entitled *Agra dekallah*. Noteworthy are the concluding remarks of his introduction to this volume, wherein he states that "these words of mine" are to be "safeguarded" by the "ḥaverim makshivim" for whom they are intended and are not for those seeking to "attack" God and "to render defective [*lehatil mum*], God forbid, the Holy Divine."[9] The *ḥaverim maqshivim* are those "companions attending (to your voice)", appearing in Song of Songs, a biblical book that the rabbis presented as an allegory of Israel seeking God. For Elimelkeh, his teachings, in *Agra dekallah*, when properly understood and applied, will make for a union of God and His people rather than provide a cause to rupture the divine-human relationship.[10]

---

[9] Tsvi Elimelekh, Agra dekallah (Lemberg, 1868), introduction.

[10] In this introduction, Elimelekh explains that most of the book's contents derive from his Shabbat lectures, thus its title, Agra dekallah, "means aseiphat shabbat kallah," or the ingathering/ collection of the Shabbat kallah. The term kallah here hearkens back to the mass assemblies of Babylonian students in talmudic times who gathered to learn from renowned teachers during the months of Elul and Adar. Agra as a gathering or collection would reflect the verse from Proverbs (10:5) in which the root letters alef, gimel, and resh are employed: "A wise son gathers (oger) in the summer while a shameful son sleeps during the harvest." At the same time, the word agra, in consonance with the book's full title, is Aramaic and reflects the talmudic expression Agra dekallah (b. Berakhot 6b), the reward of (attending) the kallah. This title has a more esoteric allusion as well, as indicated when Elimelekh says that these words of the kallah "were said and taught in the assembly of the ḥaverim makshivim." As noted, the phrase ḥaverim makshivim derives from Song of Songs 8:13 ("The initiates/companions [ḥaverim] attend [makshivim] to your voice"). This book, according to rabbinic tradition, speaks of Israel seeking and finding union with God, her beloved. In this context, the kabbalistic tradition speaks of the coming together of God (associated with tiferet, the divine male principle) and His Shekhinah, or divine indwelling (associated with malkhut, the divine female principle), which is often identified with Knesset Yisrael, or the congregation of Israel, and called kallah, or the divine bride. Shabbat, perceived as a propitious time for this union, is called Shabbat ha-malkah or Shabbat kallah. Agra sometimes also means "to unite, or bind," as does the word ḥaver. Thus the ḥaver, or one who will properly understand this book, will receive the reward, or experience the union, of

Daniel Z. Siegel

The textual teaching that will be our focus appears in Elimelekh's commentary on the Torah portion *Re'eih*, which begins with the words "Behold, I have set before you today a blessing and a curse—the blessing if you heed the commandments of the Lord your God, and the curse if you do not heed the commandments of the Lord your God" (Deuteronomy 11:26–28). After subsequently noting that, upon entering the Land, Israel is to "utterly destroy all the places where the nations you are to dispossess served their gods... And you shall break down their altars...and you shall destroy their name out of that place" (Deuteronomy 12:2–3), the Bible warns: *lo ta'asun kein l'adonai elohekha*, "You shall not do thus to the Lord your God" (Deuteronomy 12:4).

This latter verse, based upon its context, is generally understood as part of the Deuteronomist's call for centralization of the cult, as further evidenced in the verses that immediately follow it (Deuteronomy 12:5–6) and/or as warning against erasing God's name or destroying (a stone of) the altar, in contrast with the actions prescribed in the verses preceding it. Our Hasidic rebbe, however, reads this negative commandment in a remarkably surprising way:

> *lo ta'asun kein...* [The word] *kein* is to be explicated as meaning just (*tsedeq*) and right (*nakhon*, firmly established). For God, may He be praised, desires that the righteous (*tsadiqim*) annul His decree for that is His delight (*sha'ashua'v*) rather than that the righteous one (*tsadiq*) would say "certainly His laws, may He be praised, are just and how can I bring charges (*meqatreig*) against my Master." He should not say thus (*kein*)! That is [the meaning of] *lo ta'asun kein* [*l'adonai elohekha*], "Do not make just and right (*kein*) His laws [when they are not so]" (Elimelekh, *Agra dekallah*, 320b).[11]

---

the kallah. These words, or teachings, then, are to be guarded by the ḥaverim for whom they are gathered, lest they fall into the hands of those who will use them against heaven. Elimelekh, *Agra dekallah*, end of introduction.

[11] The word sha'ashu'a is associated in the Bible with God's Torah (toratkha sha'ahu'ai, "Your Torah is my delight") and mitsvah (mitsvotekha sha'ahu'ai, "Your commandments are my delight"), as well as with Israel (yeled sha'ashu'im, "delightful child"); see Psalm 119 and Isaiah 31:19; cf. Jeremiah 5:7. The kabbalistic tradition tells us: "The Holy One Blessed be He enters the Garden of Eden to take delight (le'ishta'ashe'a) with the righteous (tsaddiqim). At this time [midnight] one is to rise to take delight (le'ishta'ashe'a) in the Torah. For the Holy One Blessed be He and all the righteous in the garden of Eden all listen for his voice, as it is written (Song of Songs 8:13): "O, you who linger in the garden, the companions are listening (ḥaverim makshivin)

When God's "Yes" is "No" and God's "No" is "Yes"

Applying his explication *lo ta'asun kein* directly to the words of the verse, we thus read: "Do not make just/right the Lord your God." In an otherwise radical exegesis of this verse, Elimelekh replaces "the Lord your God" with "His laws" thus stopping short of (directly) impugning God. This would not escape his readers, who, on the basis of Elimelekh's rendering of this verse, are told to challenge and "bring charges" against the "Master." For purposes of presenting the whole of the verse in terms of his exegesis, we shall read it "Do not make just (the laws of) the Lord your God."

Significantly, Elimelekh's exegesis of *kein*—whereby one is not to be God's "yes man" by finding just what is unjust—is based upon the biblical episode of the daughters of Zelophehad. Immediately before his above-cited exposition of this verse, he writes: "*Lo ta'asun kein... kein* as in the expression *kein beinot Tselofḥad*, meaning right and just [are the daughters of Zelophehad]" (Elimelekh, *Agra dekallah*, 320b). The daughters of Zelophehad are recorded as bringing the following grievance:

> Then the daughters of Zelophehad drew near...and stood before Moses and before Eleazar the priest, and before the princes and the entire congregation at the entrance of the tent of meeting, saying: "Our father died in the wilderness, but he was not among the assembly, Korah's assembly, that banded together against God...and he had no sons. Why should our father's name be lessened among his family because he has no son? Give us a holding among our father's brothers" (Numbers 27:1–4).

Not unexpectedly, as this was apparently their intent in presenting themselves before the tent of meeting, their claim as daughters to inherit as do the sons of other Israelite fathers is brought before God:

---

for your voice, cause me to hear it" (Zohar 1:92a and 2:46a). Using here the word sha'ashu'a, Elimelekh suggests that in letting God hear our voice—through faithful engagement in Torah, which at times requires us to challenge Him—we help bring about and experience the union of the "Community of Israel" (Kenesset Yisra'el/Shekhinah) with God. Indeed, the text further relates that, when the "Community of Israel comes and takes delight in (mishta'ashe'a) the Holy One, Blessed be He, He extends to her the scepter of mercy," intimating, as the kabbalist Abraham Galante notes, "that the secret of union and copulation (sod hayiḥud vehazivvug) is called sha'ashu'a." For an extended discussion of the term sha'ashu'a in kabbalistic sources, including the citation from Galante, see Elliot Wolfson, Language, Eros and Being: Kabbalistic Hermeneutics and Poetic Imagination (New York: Fordham University Press, 2004), 132ff. Cf. Elimelekh, Agra dekallah, 126a and 45a.

> Moses then brought their cause before the Lord. And the Lord said to Moses: "Justly/Rightly (*kein*) do the daughters of Zelophehad speak. You shall assuredly give them a hereditary holding in the midst of their father's brothers, and you shall transfer their father's inheritance to them. And you shall speak to the Israelites, saying: 'If a person dies and he had no son, then you shall transfer his inheritance to his daughter... And it shall be for the children of Israel a statute of judgment, as the Lord commanded Moses'" (Numbers 27:5–8).

In using the daughters of Zelophehad story in his explication of the verse *lo ta'asun kein l'adonai elohekha* as "You shall not make just (the laws of) the Lord your God," Elimelekh presents an interpenetration of divine commandment and biblical narrative. While the narrative of Zelophehad's daughters serves as the instantiation and affirmation of "You shall not make just (the laws of) the Lord your God," this commandment sanctions and requires actions like those of the daughters of Zelophehad. Moreover, we see the just claim of these women being championed and formalized into law, in their name, by God Himself. God presents the emerging narrative as making for a new "statute of judgment," even as His response to the daughters of Zelophehad is in fulfillment of His law *lo ta'asun kein*, "Do not make just (that which is not just)." God is thus portrayed by Elimelekh as an examplar of employing the integrative engagement of *nomos* and narrative. The established *nomos* must not lie beyond the grasp of a questing narrative so that when infused with its living spirit it gives birth to a new law, which itself becomes generative of that spirit.

The daughters of Zelophehad, as Elimelekh hopes for the *haverim* for whom he has written this book and who attend to the divine voice of Torah, were attuned to a voice of God that could not yet be heard within the prevailing community. Those whose moral sensibilities make for a deeper understanding of the divine moral conscience are God's partners in bringing a new revelation and law into the divine community. In challenging as unjust God's command, which was heretofore perceived and held as just by the community, and in being responsible agents in rectifying it, the daughters of Zelophehad are making the Lord their God just.

The rabbis present Zelophehad's daughters as saying "human beings extend greater mercy to males than they do to females. But, He who spoke and the world (*'olam*) came into being is not so (*kein*). Rather, His mercy

is upon both males and females."[12] One can hear Elimelekh pointedly reading this midrash as God does not say *kein* to, or affirm as just and correct,
those who, in limiting His mercy through law, do not truly express the
divine moral conscience. Rather, *yomar na yisra'el, ki le'olam ḥasdo* (Psalm
118:2)—all "Israel," in exercising His Law, "should say 'His (the Creator's)
lovingkindness is everlasting and to all His world.'"

Speaking to an injustice still practiced today in the name of God's Law,
we might hope that, like that of the daughters of Zelophehad, the plight
of the *'agunah* would evoke within us all Elimelekh's divine command *lo
ta'asun kein.*[13] Cast in the words of a present day activist for the liberation of
"enchained women," even as it might have been expressed upon a protesting
placard of a would-be abolitionist, this rebbe's reading of this verse might be
rendered "Do not give the nod to a narrow God." Justly resolving the plight
and compassionately responding to the protest of the *'agunah* through a
remedying of the Law releases us and our God from the fetters of injustice.

As exemplified by Zelophehad's daughters, disobedience is at times obedience, even as obedience is at times disobedience. Elimelekh asks us to
see that the blessing is sometimes found in following the commandment
not to follow the commandments. Present day research, as expressed here
in the words of Pearl Oliner, the author of *Saving the Forsaken*, finds that
"significantly higher percentages of bystanders, as compared with rescuers,
cited obedience as a primary value."[14] In Elimelekh's view, we are divinely
challenged to have the courage of conscience to speak out for ourselves and
others by rightly declaring His laws unjust.

How, though, can we be certain when disobedience in deeming His laws
unjust constitutes obedience in fulfilling the commandment "Do not make
just (the laws of) the Lord your God"? In opening his exegesis of the verse
lo ta'asun kein, Elimelekh notes that, for some, Jewish living is "religious
behaviorism" (*ḥoq qavu'a lahem*). However, the wise individual (*maskil*)
understands that

> no single day is the same as another, [so that] at times, the
> self-same deed that constitutes a commandment one day

---

[12] Sifrei ba-Midbar, Pinḥas, ed. H.S. Horovitz (Jerusalem: Shalem, 1992), 176 (pisqa 133).
[13] Because the Bible (Deuteronomy 24:1) presents the man (alone) as issuing a writ of divorce, when men are unwilling or unable to do so, women remain chained to their husbands in perpetuity; see "Resolution on Agunot in Israel," Rabbinical Assembly, www.rabbinicalassembly.org/resolution-agunot-Israel?tp=110.
[14] Pearl Oliner, Saving the Forsaken (New Haven, CT: Yale University Press, 2004), 107.

is a transgression the next. And it is impossible to further explain the matter, for the wise one will discern on his own. And it was regarding this that our Torah warns us in saying "do not do *kein* to the Lord your God," [*kein*] meaning [living always] "thus," the same, never changing behavior (Elimelekh, *Agra dekallah*, 320b).

The slippery slope is always present, but one is a deviant in refusing to deviate. If wise, our behavior in observing the law will change when we correctly discern what is required. Although we might not always be correct, there is greater risk in not risking than in risking; that will result in an ossified religion, God and self. For Elimelekh, when righting our ever-evolving Torah, we are God's active partners in further revealing and realizing the divine moral conscience.

Apposite to Elimelekh's remark that the proscriptive and prescriptive may at times interchange is his second interpretation of *lo ta'asun kein*, which we will now consider. The rabbi of Dynov writes:

> An allusion to another [meaning of] *lo ta'asun kein* [is provided] on the basis of what our rabbis, may their memory be for a blessing, said: "Greater is a transgression committed for God's sake (*lishmah*), than a commandment performed not for His sake (*shelo lishmah*)"...as you know from the matter of Ya'el, the wife of Ḥever, the Kenite [whose adulterous action saved her people; see b. Nazir 32b and b. Horayot 10b, cf. Judges 7:17–22]. And this is what the Torah was indicating [by] *lo* [*ta'asun kein*], meaning that against which you are warned by *lo* ("no"), being the negative commandments, you shall make *kein* ("yes") "for the sake of the Lord your God" (Elimelekh, *Agra dekallah*, 321a).

Thus, complementing his first reading of *lo ta'asun kein l'adonai elohekha* as a negative commandment, "Do not make just (the laws of) the Lord your God," Elimelekh here reads this verse as presenting a positive commandment, "Make the "no/*lo*" (negative commandment) into a "yes/*kein*" (prescribed action). In his first exposition of this verse, God's "yes" becomes "no" when proscribing the prescribed, as we challenge rather than perform a morally reprehensible action. In this understanding of the verse, God's "no" becomes "yes" when prescribing the proscribed, as we commit ourselves to the ethically laudable for the sake of God.

It is instructive that, in discussing those whose practice is fixed (*ḥoq qavu'a*) and who are unable to discern that at times proscriptions are to become prescriptions (or the reverse), he later writes:

> This is what is alluded to in the verse "And you shall not erect an [immutable] pillar/stone (*matsevah*) for yourself" (Deuteronomy 16:22). That is, [do not create] a condition (*matsav*) in which your service [of God] is constant without change (Elimelekh, *Agra dekallah*, 327a).[15]

In the verse immediately preceding *lo ta'asun kein* (Deuteronomy 12:4), the Bible, in referring to the idolatrous nations which Israel is to displace, says: "You shall break their pillars, or standing stones (*matsevotam*)" (Deuteronomy 12:3). When we are not discerning and, in our unchanging way, adhere to a proscription that is not for "God's sake" (*lishmah*) rather than seeing it now as a prescription to be fulfilled for the sake of God, we are idolizing the Law rather than serving God.[16]

Elimelekh is reminding us that God, and hopefully our experience of God, is beyond the boundaries of Torah; He is, and hopefully we are, not limited to or by His Torah. This rebbe relates that God Himself, as we sometimes are expected to do, "violates" the Torah for His sake (*lishmah*). Thus, in explaining God's appearance in Egypt (*mitsrayim*), the land of "defilement," he writes:

> "And I will pass (*'avarti*) through the land of *mitsrayim* on that night" (Exodus 12:12). God, may He be praised, Him-

---

[15] The verse "And you shall not erect an [immutable] pillar/stone (matsevah) for yourself" concludes with "which the Lord your God detests." To be sure, Elimelekh is speaking of both inspired and aspiring religious practice. A nonchanging, habitual performance is hollow service to God. So, too, commitment not coupled with critical consciousness can make for unconscionable behavior. As soulful service is sought by God, so a challenging mindfulness, making for a morally progressive practice, is His delight.

[16] Similarly, Elimelekh presents the biblical verse "For these nations, whom you are to dispossess, hearken to soothsayers, and augurs; but you, not likewise (lo kein) does the Lord your God suffer you to do" (Deuteronomy 18:14) as meaning: You (Israel), in contrast to the idolaters, God has granted [to sometimes make] the "no" (lo) "yes" (kein) in fulfillment of the principle "greater is a transgression committed for God's sake." Elimelekh, Agra dekallah, 326a.

self, in His own glory (*beatsmo ubikhvodo*), revealed Himself in *mitsrayim*?! Behold, the rabbis, may their memory be for a blessing, said: "Greater is a transgression committed for God's sake." The Creator, may His name be praised, Who "sanctified us through His commandments" (*kideshanu bemitsvotav*)—that is to say, His commandments for He Himself fulfills the same *mitsvot* [which he commands of us]—said: "And I will pass (*'avarti*) through the land of *Mitsrayim*." He did not say "I will go down" or [use] any other term but "and I will pass (*ve'avarti*)," [meaning] a "transgression (*'aveirah*) committed for God's sake (*lishmah*)" (Elimelekh, *Agra dekallah*, 186a).[17]

This midrash aggadah and the midrash halakhah—through which the commandment *lo ta'asun kein* is a divine prescription for a transgression committed for God's sake ("You shall make the 'no', a transgression, a 'yes'")—are complementary and mutually affirming. Here, too, through an interplay of law and narrative (one speaking to our greatest national myth), Elimelekh provides us with a divine calling that should stir us to redress an injustice that some would continue to perpetuate in the name of God. Should we not feel summoned to ask, if God makes a "no" a "yes", abrogating a proscription in performing it as a prescription, when He enters *mitsrayim* to liberate His people from the realm of impurity not of their own making, lest they themselves be counted as impure, should we not do likewise for the *mamzer*, who, being a product of an illicit union, is cast into a context of impurity through no desire or action on his part? Rather than recording who is or might be a *mamzer* in order to restrict his access into the Jewish community based on the verse "A *mamzer* shall not enter (*lo yavo*) the congregation of the Lord"

---

[17] See also Elimelekh, Agra dekallah, 87b and Maimonides, Sefer haMitsvot (Jerusalem: Mossad Harav Kook, 1971), Lo ta'aseh 46. The rabbis present God as violating His commandments and asking others to do the same in lying (b. Yevamot 65b), over against "Distance yourself from falsehood" (Exodus 23:7), and in erasing His name (Leviticus Rabbah 9:9 and Tosefta Shabbat 14:4), in the face of "You shall not do thus" (Deuteronomy 12:4, the contextual meaning of lo ta'asun kein), which is traditionally understood as "You shall not erase His name as you would that of the idolatrous nations and their gods." In both instances, God and humans, upon the divine behest, violate the Torah for the purpose of shalom ("peace, wholeness"). Significantly, the rabbis recognize God's name as "Shalom"; see Derekh Erets Zuta (Vilna 1870), 130–31 (Pereq ha-shalom); cf. Judges 6:24. Thus the destruction of God's name in its physical form here makes for preservation of the same in its more ultimate form. Indeed, in these instances, preserving the former would serve as idolatry, leading to destruction of the latter.

(Deuteronomy 23:3), should we not make the "no" (*lo*) a "yes" (*kein*) and, committing a transgression for the sake of God rather than performing a precept that does not serve Him, bring the *mamzer* into our community as God brought the Israelites into His.[18]

God asserts, explain the rabbis, that a Jewish community and its legislators that use My law to oppress rather than comfort those in need are not serving Me:

> "But I returned and observed all the oppressions that are done under the sun; and behold the tears of the oppressed, and they have no comforter; but from the hand of their oppressors comes power, but they have no comforter" (Ecclesiastes 4:1). Ḥanina the Tailor interpreted this verse: "All the oppressions" this refers [to what is being done] to the *mamzerim* (those illicitly conceived), "and behold the tears of the oppressed," [for] their mothers transgressed, but it is these humiliated ones that are being marginalized. This one's father had illicit sexual relations, but what did he (the child) do?! Why should it have consequence for him?! "They had no comforter" but "from the hand of the oppressor there comes power"—this refers to the Great Assembly of Israel which comes upon them with the power of the Torah and marginalizes them in the name of "No *mamzer* shall enter the community of the Lord" (Deuteronomy 23:3). But, [since] "they have no comforter," the Holy One Blessed be He says: "It is upon Me to comfort them" (Leviticus Rabbah 32:8).[19]

---

[18] David Weiss Halivni, "Can a Religious Law be Immoral," in Perspectives on Jews and Judaism: Essays in Honor of Wolfe Kelman, ed. Arthur A. Chiel (New York: Rabbinical Assembly, 1978), 165–69, citing this midrash, argues that the "case of mamzerut" is the lone exception in which the rabbis of the Talmud were willing to openly entertain the notion that a conflict existed between the religious law and morality. Consequently, and ironically, this might account, Halivni argues, for why the "problem of mamzerut" has not been "solved," while the morally challenging cases of capital punishment and lex talionis, which "were never presented by the Rabbis of the Talmud as a moral problem," were resolved through rabbinic "alteration" of the law. Presenting this conflict between morality and law precluded any "adjustment" in the case of mamzerut, for "any subsequent change will be interpreted as an admission that initially there was no moral sensitivity, imputing to the Lawgiver a defective moral awareness."

[19] Vayiqra Rabbah, ed. Mordechai Margoliyot (New York: Jewish Theological Seminary of America, 1993), 654–55.

The governing body uses My Law, complains God, to aggravate rather than ameliorate the plight of the *mamzer*. The midrash thereafter concludes that, in a future world (*'atid lavoh*), God will create an inclusiveness of all that the current world (*'olam hazeh*) is incapable of achieving. At the same time that God presents humans as making His law an obstacle in creating a truly divine community, one hears, as well, His persistent hope that it would not be so.[20]

The rabbis, in bringing attention to the profound pain being experienced by the *mamzer*, yet presenting God as the only avenue of redress, might be commenting upon a community that—by sacralizing its "moral integrity" so that it is not violated by countenancing the "stain" of *mamzerut* upon its collective moral fabric, lest it be placed in the precarious position of incurring the wrath of a punitive God—may be blinding rather than binding itself to that God whose will it seeks to fulfill. Returning to the words "Behold, I set before you today a blessing and a curse—the blessing if you heed the commandments of the Lord your God, which I command you this day, and the curse if you do not heed the commandments of the Lord your God but turn away from the path which I command you today to go after other gods" (Deuteronomy 11:26–28), we find the following teaching of Elimelekh:

> And this is the meaning of "Behold, I set before you today a blessing." I place before you and in your hands that which will arouse a blessing for Israel. And "a curse" you will actualize if you do not listen to the commandments of the Lord your God, only insofar as it is in the manner that I command you this day to do this transgression; that is a transgression (*'averah*) committed for God's sake (lishmah), for that is to be included among My commands. By that means (committing a transgression for God's sake) you will actualize "going after other gods"—that is, you will

---

[20] Interestingly, this midrash suggests, through the mouth of God Himself, that the divine law, as refracted through the Torah text, is not to be seen as the final and ultimate word. Indeed, leaving matters as they are would be an affront to God. The Conservative Movement's Committee on Jewish Law and Standards echoed and acted upon the sentiment expressed in this midrash. Adopting Rabbi Kaplan Spitz's position paper, in which he argued that "We need to address mamzerut precisely because it raises the question whether we will enforce a Torah law that strikes us as unconscionable in light of other Torah values," its rabbis concluded that "we render mamzerut inoperative." See Rabbi Elie Kaplan Spitz, "Mamzerut," Rabbinical Assembly, https://www.rabbinicalassembly.org/sites/default/files/2022-09/spitz_mamzerut.pdf.

actualize the curse upon other gods (Benei Yissakhar 82a).[21]

For Elimelekh, we are commanded to both heed and transgress God's commands. Blessing and curse are presented together, but it is our discriminating response to God's commands that determines which we bring upon ourselves and which upon the foreign gods. Contradicting the contextual meaning of the verse, this Hasidic rebbe reads not heeding God's commandments and turning away from the path as that "which I (God) command you to do," in the particular instances constituting transgressions for the sake of God. Thus, in heeding God's command by not heeding "God's" command, we destroy foreign gods who might otherwise blind us.

Indiscriminate adherence to a particular law may undermine the whole of the Law with which it is at variance, thus violating rather than valorizing God's Torah. Indeed, for Elimelekh, moral sensibilities that issue from outside the Law and serve to contravene a law are sometimes most consonant with the Law in which it may find its greatest support. In his midrashic "misreading" of *lo ta'asun kein* as both a positive and negative commandment to do what is right and just, Elimelekh shows how stimulus for change can originate outside the Law and at the same time be sanctioned within the Law. This stimulus, in turn, finds its nurturing within the moral spirit of the Law, as reflected in many of its commandments, and serves to deepen and expand our understanding of the divine moral conscience, which it further concretizes in a renewed revelation of God's Law.

Elimelekh is heir to a rabbinic tradition that reminds us that the Torah begins and ends with an act of lovingkindness on the part of God (b. Sotah 14a). For this Hasidic rabbi, we are enjoined to make the whole of the law an expression of God's lovingkindness. While some rabbis in the time of Elimelekh and beyond argued—as did the second–third century Amora, Samuel—that slaves must not be released lest we violate God's Law, others, looking to a Torah reflective of a caring and loving God, rendered this law inoperative.[22]

In our own time, in an address entitled "Being Frum and Being Good," Rabbi Aharon Lichtenstein writes regarding filicide and genocide when

---

[21] *Benei Yissachar*, 2 vols. (Jerusalem: n.p., 1983), vol. 1. Within this earlier and more widely known work of Elimelekh, this textual analysis of blessing and curse in observing and transgressing God's commands appears in an extended discussion of the verse "And I will pass (*'avarti*) through the land of mitsrayim," which, as we have seen, serves as God's modeling for us a transgression for the sake of God.

[22] Schorsch, *Jews and Blacks* 287–303.

discussing God's command to Abraham to sacrifice his son and the biblical commandment that we eradicate Amalek:

> Wiping out Amalek...killing "from child to suckling babe"...I am not saying, God forbid, it is immoral in our case, where God has specifically commanded the destruction of Amalek...The same holds true of the Akeida...in the context of the divine command, surely it partakes of the goodness and morality of God... When there is a conflict between the *tsav* (Divine command) and the moral order, what do we do about it? For us, the answer is perhaps practically difficult, but surely it is conceptually clear and unequivocal... The message of the Akeida is clear: God's command takes precedence in every respect, over our moral sensibility and our conscientious objections... As those who educate towards *yirat shamayim* (fear of heaven), we must communicate the message of the *akeida* boldly, loudly and clearly.[23]

His contemporary, Rabbi Harold Schulweis, in his book, *Conscience: The Duty to Obey and the Duty to Disobey*, presents a contrasting perspective, one with which Elimelekh would appear to concur.

> What does Judaism have to say to those who, on moral grounds, may challenge commander and commandment, rabbinic and scriptural narratives and laws? ...Legislation and obedience are essential aspects of Judaism, but are controlled by a persistent moral conscience. The deep respect in Judaism for courage of conscience cultivates a sensibility significantly different from [that] of the religious believer who stands passive, acquiescent, and trembling before God and scripture... Contrary to those who split asunder the duty to obey and the duty to disobey, viewing them as contradictory, we Jews regard both duties as complementary.[24]

---

[23] Aharon Lichtenstein, By His Light: Character and Values in the Service of God (New York: Ktav, 2003), 123 and 127.
[24] Harold Schulweis, Conscience: The Duty to Obey and the Duty to Disobey (Woodstock: Jewish Lights, 2008), 3–4.

When God's "Yes" is "No" and God's "No" is "Yes"

When confronted with a Constitution that does not recognize the full humanity of black people or their right to freedom, some abolitionists rejected the former in their commitment to the latter. Elimelekh, reflective of the Jewish tradition, sees that fidelity to those marginalized by the Law requires us to rectify rather than forsake that Law.[25] We advance our shared humanity in more fully realizing a Torah of morality. It is through a "redemptive righting" of our Torah, as found in and promoted by the teachings of this Hasidic rebbe that we make for and are blessed by a renewed revelation of the divine moral conscience.

Rabbi Daniel Z. Siegel has served as Head of Jewish studies and Jewish Life programs in Australia, Canada and the United States. He is a lifelong educator, teacher and student of our Jewish textual tradition.

---

[25] See Robert M. Cover, "Nomos and Narrative," Harvard Law Review 97, no. 1 (1983), 38 (Foreword in The Supreme Court, 1982 Term) for discussion of "Redemptive Constitutionalism" in contrasting the "anti-slavery anti-constitutionalism" of the Garrisonians with the "radical constitutionalism" of Frederick Douglas: "Douglas was the escaped slave. His escape constituted a redemption. Douglas' greatest need was for a vision of law that both validated his freedom and integrated norms with a future redemptive possibility for his people. The radical constitutionalists criticized the Garrisonians precisely for their failure to adopt such a vision. The Garrisonian alternative showed, to the constitutionalists, an abdication: 'Dissolve the Union on this issue..who shall stand up as deliverers, then?'"

Halakhic Possibilities for Patrilineal Descent

Natan Hason

For many progressive Jews whose practice is in dialogue with the halakhic tradition, there has been a tension between the commitment to matrilineal descent and a desire to positively recognize the Jewishness of our patrilineal fellows. In this brief article, I will propose one possibility for the development of a halakhic path toward the recognition of the status of patrilineal Jews. My hope is that this will spark a dialogue among progressive *posqim* on the feasibility of this approach and, if it is unable to be the basis of a possible resolution, that it may inspire the search for other pathways toward what I believe to be full recognition of the dignity of a marginalized segment of our community.

Metahalakhic Framework

Within the Conservative movement and progressive denominations generally there has been a long-held commitment to a wider and more expansive halakhic conversation than a narrow review of technical legal sources. Coming from this place, I feel it is important to begin with sources that speak to the ethical values of our tradition. These should be an integral element in wider halakhic discourse, as well as in the particular case with which this article is concerned—recognizing patrilineal descent. Rabbi Seymour Siegel said the following in an address to the Rabbinical Assembly Convention in 1971, which speaks to the ethos of this paper:

> It is possible to formulate the approach in terms of the relationship between the *aggadah* and the *halakhah*. If we loosely define the *aggadah* as the expression of the ethical and theological values of Judaism, and the *halakhah* as their embodiment, then our thesis is that the *aggadah* should control the *halakhah*—not vice versa...
>
> For us, the *aggadah* is all important, for it is the expression of Jewish values and world-outlook. The *halakhah* is its

embodiment. We do not intend, of course, to diminish the value of the *halakhah* in pressing this formulation. Indeed, it is our view that there is no better way to preserve the integrity and the authority of Jewish law than by revising it when it needs revision. Edmund Burke, perhaps the greatest of all conservative (politics, of course) thinkers, said: A state without the means of changing its laws is without the means of preserving its laws. Menachem Mendel of Kotzk put the idea in a striking saying: Do not make a *pesel* [an idol] of the *asher tsivkha hashem elokekha* [what God has commanded you].[1]

Other articulations of this call to appreciate the legal implications and force of aggadah can be found in the writings of Abraham Joshua Heschel, Neil Gillman, Gordon Tucker, and others. It is within this approach that I offer these first three sources as a metahalakhic framing for this paper. They represent what I believe are the values in our tradition that should be embodied in our halakhic rulings regarding this issue.

The first is taken from the Tur, *Orakh ḥayyim* 199:1:

שמש שאכל כזית מזמנין עליו... תניא עם הארץ אין מזמנין עליו
והאידנא אמר ר"י שמזמנין עם עם הארץ כדי שלא יהא כל אחד
בונה במה לעצמו פי' אם היו פורשין מהם היו גם הם פורשין מן
הציבור לגמרי וכ"כ ר"ח האידנא רגילין לזמן אפי' עם עם הארץ
גמור:

One who eats a *kezayit* of food that would make one obligated to say grace after meals should make a *zimmun*... [the] Mishnah teaches that an '*am ha'arets* does not count towards a *zimmun*. Now Rabbi Yitzhak said that you do form a *zimmun* with an '*am ha'arets* in order that one will not build a division between himself and there will be a separation from them so that they will be separated completely from the community. Rabbeinu Hananel has written that we are now accustomed to making a *zimmun* even with a complete '*am ha'arets*.

---

[1] Seymour Siegel, "Ethics and the Halakha," *Conservative Judaism* 25, no. 3 (1971): 36.

Here, out of an interest in not losing these marginal members of the community, the Tur codifies the *abrogation* of a mishnaic instruction that one does not include an *'am ha'arets* in the counting of a *zimmun*. How many Jews of patrilineal descent have felt a division built between them and the rest of the community by their exclusion from participation in the ritual life of our community? How many, feeling the doors to the synagogue closed to them, have decided to walk away from our communities because of this? This concern for the potential loss of members of our community is taken seriously enough that it is considered justification for the overturning of a mishnaic teaching.

Secondly, we find the following anecdote in b. Kiddushin 70a:

וְכָל הַפּוֹסֵל פָּסוּל וְאֵינוּ מְדַבֵּר בִּשְׁבָחָא לְעוֹלָם וְאָמַר שְׁמוּאֵל בְּמוּמוֹ פּוֹסֵל

> He further said: And anyone who disqualifies others by
> stating that their lineage is flawed, that is a sign that he
> himself is of flawed lineage. Another indication that one's
> lineage is flawed is that he never speaks in praise of others.
> And Shmuel says: If one habitually claims that others are
> flawed, he disqualifies himself with his own flaw. The flaw
> he accuses them of having is in fact the one that he has.[2]

In this text we learn that we should avoid the impulse toward shutting others out based on questions of parentage and are exhorted against it with a *middah keneged middah* isolation of the one who does so. Our disposition in these matters should be toward searching out ways to include others rather than taking a defensive stance toward the status quo.

Lastly, in y. Yevamot 1:6:8 there is recorded the dispute between Beit Hillel and Beit Shammai regarding issues of marriage that could lead to serious transgressions in the area of status and permitted relationships:

רִבִּי יוֹסֵי בֵּירִבִּי בּוּן אָמַר. רַב וּשְׁמוּאֵל. חַד אָמַר. אִילּוּ וְאִילּוּ כַּהֲלָ־ כָה הָיוּ עוֹשִׂין. וְחַד אָמַר. אִילּוּ כְהִילְכָתָן וְאִילּוּ כְהִילְכָתָן. מַמְזֵרֶת בֵּינָתַיים וְאַתְּ אָמַר הָכֵין. הַמָּקוֹם מְשַׁמֵּר וְלֹא אוּרְע מַעֲשֶׂה מֵעוֹלָם.

Rebbi Yose ben Rebbi Abun said, Rav and Samuel, one

[2] Adin Even-Israel Steinsaltz, ed., *The Koren Talmud Bavli Noé* (Jerusalem: Koren, 2016).

said both acted according to valid practice; the other said, each party followed its own practice. Bastardy is between them and you say so? The Omnipresent watched and no case ever happened.[3]

Rather than allow for a deep division within the community to take place, they responded with a deus ex machina solution. Given the mutually exclusive approaches to marriage practices between these two segments of the community, it is impossible to conclude that by marrying with each other no such violations of their own norms took place. Yet the response was to say that God made sure no such violations occurred. When backed into a corner, they gave up legal resolutions and held tightly to the value of Jewish unity.

The Evolution of the Matrilineal Principle

To dive further into the particular question being investigated in this article, we will begin with a brief overview of the matrilineal principle. Works like Rabbi Dr. Shaye Cohen's "The Origins of the Matrilineal Principle in Rabbinic Law"[4] and Rabbi Ethan Tucker's series "Matrilineality and Patrilineality in Jewish Law and Community"[5] have already clearly established the long historical process involved in the development of this halakhic approach. Readers interested in the details of this should read these works which give in-depth analysis of the relevant texts.

In summary, the first attestation of any kind of matrilineal principle in Jewish text is found in Tannaitic material. There is no clear reference to any matrilineal principle in either the Tanakh or the literature of the Second Temple period. On the contrary, as most readers are probably aware, there is instead a clear patrilineal principle. In the Tannaitic period we encounter opinions that accept the status of a child from a Jewish mother and non-Jewish father as Jewish. However, at this earliest stage, the Mishnah accords them the status of a *mamzer*, and it is only in the Amoraic period that this status is overturned. Tucker, in his overview of the complex status of Jews

---

[3] Heinrich Guggenheimer, trans., *The Jerusalem Talmud* (Berlin: de Gruyter, 2005).
[4] Shaye J. D. Cohen, "The Origins of the Matrilineal Principle in Rabbinic Law" *AJS Review* 10, no. 1 (1985): 19–53.
[5] Ethan Tucker, "Matrilineality and Patrilineality in Jewish Law and Community," Hadar Institute (December 2015), https://www.hadar.org/torah-tefillah/resources/matrilineality-and-patrilineality-jewish-law-and-community-part-1.

of matrilineal descent and of patrilineal descent, points out that even some eighteenth- and nineteenth-century rabbinic authorities ruled that Jews of matrilineal descent required conversion. It is clear from the evidence that the matrilineal principle as we practice it today has been more fluid, even within the past two centuries, than is often assumed in popular discussion of the topic.

This is not to claim that these later texts are less authoritative or that the principle of matrilineal descent does not carry weight by virtue of being a later innovation, but simply to recognize the breadth of historical change that has taken place regarding this principle. The matrilineal principle of today is not the same as what is found in earlier literature. It raises the question, "If it has not always been this way in the past, then perhaps it may not always be this way in the future?" When tackling halakhic questions such as this one, which are often perceived as being almost untouchable, it may be helpful to keep in mind Rabbi Yoseph Hayim's description of the halakhic process, as summarized by Professor Zvi Zohar: "a rabbi who makes a halakhic decision is not bound by a majority of relevant precedents...if his own best understanding of the halakha leads him to formulate a decision completely without precedent, he may in good faith rule according to the halakhic truth as he sees it."[6]

The Status of Quasi-Jewish Groups in Rabbinic Texts

Professor Christine Hayes makes the following argument about rabbinic constructions of identity:

> Yet the rabbis resist simple dichotomies and locate many gentiles along a spectrum of proximity, as seen in rabbinic discussions of the righteous gentile, the venerator of heaven and the convert. Some others—non-rabbinic Jews of various types—are, by birth and culture, heirs to the text but have neglected, distorted, or abandoned it in some way.[7]

Identity creation and maintenance is a complex process; it is fluid and hard-

---

[6] Zvi Zohar, *Rabbinic Creativity in the Modern Middle East* (New York: Bloomsbury Academic, 2013), 68.
[7] Christine Hayes, "The Other in Rabbinic Literature," in *The Cambridge Companion to the Talmud and Rabbinic Literature*, ed. Charlotte Elisheva Fonrobert and Martin S. Jaffee (Cambridge: Cambridge University Press, 2007), 263.

ly a clear-cut matter. We can find the rabbis negotiating this "spectrum of proximity," as Hayes refers to it, in their opinions on the status of the Samaritans and later regarding the Karaites. Both communities have a claim to an identity as Israelite/Jewish, and the rabbis accept that claim at various points and to varying degrees. Further, this recognition of Jewish status carries over into areas of ritual practice and is not simply a validation of genealogy. The Samaritans and Karaites are communities that have a principle of patrilineal descent for determining group identity.[8] Recognizing and validating the status of Samaritans and Karaites implies acceptance of the validity of their practice of following the father's line in determining status.

Lawrence Schiffman wrote an in-depth review of the early rabbinic literature regarding the status of Samaritans, and he concludes:

> Up to a certain point the Samaritans were accepted as Jews. From that point on, the trend began to change, and this is reflected in both explicit statements and redactional tendencies which classify the Samaritans with non-Jews. This change of attitude can be traced even further, starting with the view of R. Judah the Prince that they are non-Jews, through the various negative statements of the Amoraim, and culminating in the ruling that the Samaritans are unquestionably considered as Gentiles.[9]

His review of the sources is compelling, and, while it may be that rabbinic tradition eventually develops in another direction, it is clear that, the Tannaim by and large accepted Samaritans as Jews.

There are a few sources from Tannaitic material that demonstrate this point. We find in m. Berakhot 7:1 that the *tanna' kama'* states: שלשה שאכלו כאחד, חיבין לזמן... והכותי, מזמנין עליהם, "When three persons eat together they are obligated in *zimmun*... [if there are two] and a Samaritan, then they make a *zimmun*." We also find the following disagreement in t. Terumot 4:13, והכותי כנכרי דברי ר׳ רשב״ג אומר כותי כישראל, "the Samaritan is like a

---

[8] On the Samaritans, see Monika Schreiber, *The Comfort of Kin: Samaritan Community, Kinship, and Marriage* (Leiden: Brill, 2009), 28–29, 149. On the Karaites, see Bernard Revel, "Inquiry into the Sources of Karaite Halakha," *Jewish Quarterly Review* 3, no. 3 (1913), 376–77 n. 100. See also "Marriage and the Laws of Matrimony," Universal Karaite Judaism, http://www.karaite.org.il/karaite/Nisuaim_veisut (Hebrew).

[9] L. H. Schiffman, "The Samaritans in Tannaitic Halakha," *Jewish Quarterly Review* 75, no. 4 (1985): 349.

non-Israelite. R' Shimon ben Gamliel says, 'A Samaritan is like an Israelite.'"
Finally, Rabbi Shimon ben Gamliel again takes the stance of upholding the
status of Samaritans in t. Pesahim 2:2

מצה של כותים מותרת ואדם יוצא בה ידי חובתו בפסח ורבי אלי־
עזר אוסר לפי שאין בקיאין בדקדוקי מצוה רשב״ג אומר כל מצוה
שהחזיקו בה [כותים] הרבה מדקדקין בה יותר מישראל.

Samaritan matzah is permitted and the one who [eats it]
has fulfilled his obligation on Passover. Rabbi Eliezer rules
it forbidden since [the Samaritans] are not exact in the laws
[of matzah]. Rabbi Shimon ben Gamliel says, "any mitzvah
which the Samaritans have taken on, they are more exacting in its observance than an Israelite."

It is the case, as noted in the quote from Schiffman above, that the rabbis
eventually pushed the Samaritans further out on that "spectrum of proximity," culminating in their being treated as outsiders. Equally true is the
reality that we have authoritative precedent within the halakhic tradition,
represented in the sources above, for recognizing the status of groups prac-
ticing patrilineal descent.

The Karaite community has also had a history of acceptance, although
contested, from rabbinic authorities down to the modern day. Documents
from the Cairo Geniza testify to the practice of marriages between Karaites
and rabbinic Jews, with marriage documents in some cases enshrining the
Karaites' right to practice their own customs. While controversial to some,
this practice was accepted by many rabbinic authorities in Egypt.[10] More
recently than this medieval practice, the Committee on Jewish Law and
Standards accepted a *teshuvah* in 1984 affirming the status of Karaites as
Jews.[11] In this *teshuvah*, Rabbi David H. Lincoln provides a brief review
of some relevant responsa, which he points out are primarily concerned
with the question of marriage between the two groups. He explains that
the major concern in these responsa is *safeq mamzerut*. This is the fear

---

[10] Ariel Stone, "Marriage with Sectarians: The Case of the Karaites," in *Marriage and Its Obstacles in Jewish Law: Essays and Responsa*, ed. Walter Jacob and Moshe Zemer (Pittsburgh: Rodef
Shalom, 1999), 141–75. See also Zohar, *Rabbinic Creativity*, 319–51.

[11] David H. Lincoln, "Acceptisng Egyptian Karaites into Our Communities," in *Proceedings of
the Committee on Jewish Law and Standards of the Conservative Movement, 1980–1985*, ed.
Rabbinical Assembly (New York: Rabbinical Assembly, 1988), 263–66.

that valid marriages may be taking place between Karaites but not valid divorce, leading to bastardy cases and therefore preventing the children of Karaite communities from marrying another Jew. The issue of marriage and potential *mamzerut* are not the primary issues for our question in this paper; rather, the crucial point is, as Lincoln says, "their 'Jewish descent' is not really in question (indeed, that is our problem)."[12] In other words, the foundational assumption of much of the halakhic literature surrounding Karaites is that they are, in fact, Jews. If this were not the case then there would be no concern of *safeq mamzerut*, the validity of their marriages, their ability to be valid witnesses, or other such issues.

The late chief Sephardic rabbi of Israel, Rabbi Ovadiah Yosef also per-mitted marriages between Karaites and rabbinic Jews, therefore recognizing the Jewish status of the Karaite community. His response on this issue can be found in *Yabia' omer* EH 8:12. There he relies primarily on the rulings of Rabbis David ben Solomon ibn Abi Zimra (the Radbaz) and Yaakov de Castro, from the fifteenth and sixteenth centuries, who both held that it is permissible to intermarry with Karaites. In these sources the issue that is dealt with is *safeq mamzerut*, which, as already mentioned, is a relevant con-cern only in cases of marriage between Jews. The Radbaz makes this explicit in his writing on the issue of Karaites, intermarriage, and *safeq mamzerut* in Radbaz, *Teshuvot* 4:219, where he says: עוד יש טעם כללי לכלל הקראין שהרי ישראל הם, "Furthermore, there is a general argument concerning the Karaites as a whole, since they are Jews."

As with the case of the Samaritans, we have halakhic precedent that ac-knowledges the validity of the Karaite claim to Jewish status. As this group holds to a standard of patrilineal descent, it is difficult to argue that these rulings have not already granted a recognition of the Jewishness of individ-uals whose proximity to this identity is through their father's line. In our hands are sources both modern and ancient that provide at least the implicit recognition of this practice.

Conclusion

As progressive Jews we value a halakhic discourse that is not limited to legalistic sources. The metahalakhic framing offered above in sources that speak to our values of inclusion and unity, even in matters of lineage, should be considered in our discourse on par with *teshuvot* and legal codes. How-

---

[12] Lincoln, "Accepting," 264.

ever, we do not need to rely on this metahalakhic argumentation alone. The sources reviewed in this article contain halakhic precedent—both classical rabbinic sources and modern responsa literature—for accepting the status of communities en masse that hold to a principle of patrilineal descent. From here it appears that the same may be offered to individual Jews of patrilineal descent, since functionally this has already been done in the recognition of Samaritan and Karaite claims to Jewishness. It is my hope that this article can play some role in deepening and widening the conversation around this sensitive and pressing issue.

Natan Hason is a graduate of the Pardes Educators Program and received his master's degree in Jewish Education from Hebrew College. Since 2018 he has been a member of the Jewish Studies Department at Rochelle Zell Jewish High School.

Lenegdi: Being in Relation

Mitchell M. Frank

"Best friend in childhood." That is how my patient referred to God during one session early in psychotherapy. It was part of his narrative about losing his religious faith during adolescence, when he came of age to discover that the world was far worse than promised. Losing his best friend involved genuine feelings of loss, which might explain why he never abandoned his interest in spirituality altogether. In adulthood, that interest mostly took the form of an intellectual pursuit.

The spirituality of which my patient spoke consisted primarily of eastern religious ideas and an on-again, off-again practice of meditation. God, if anywhere, was inside. It had to be so, because the loving Protector my patient's Jewish upbringing had billed God to be could not be running a world so full of suffering. Besides, he knowledgeably pointed out, kabbalah itself provides a model for finding an immanent God inside.

My patient's musings reminded me of my own. Nevertheless, my religious thinking had evolved to resemble what my patient left behind in childhood. God, as I had come to see it, has to be a relational partner—a comfort, not only a concept. And we can have a relational partner only when God is outside us. If we look for God exclusively inside, on what basis do we cry out, "From the end of the earth I call to You when my heart is faint… for You are my refuge (Psalm 61:3–4)?

In that cry for a relational partner, it is possible to detect Naḥman of Bratslav's voice while in solitude with God, and Martin Buber's theology of God in relation. This essay elaborates on the ideas of these two figures, along with theory and research in psychology, in order to develop the theme that the source of spiritual experience is not initially within ourselves but in the dyad of self and God, and to discuss the change and growth that occur in us when we approach spiritual engagement in that way.

Zero, One, and Two

In his *The Varieties of the Meditative Experience*, Daniel Goleman cites his mentor, Joseph Goldstein: "All meditation systems either aim for One or Zero," One being union with God and Zero involving insight into self-lessness.[1] Goldstein is referring to meditation across religions, theistic and nontheistic, and describing the ultimate insights of meditation, where attainments such as mindfulness and equanimity are intermediate goals potentially leading to One and Zero.

Both of these aims are known to Jewish mysticism. In *devequt*, or cleaving to God, we have Judaism's One.[2] In the Hasidic doctrine of *bitul hayeish*, or nullifying personal ego, we find Judaism's Zero.[3] In both, an omnipresent God is made accessible inside by clearing the way, either by focusing (One) or emptying ourselves of ego distraction (Zero). But what can we say about Two—God and I—as a path of insight? Two directs our attention outward toward the other, not inward. Can that be a path of spiritual experience and growth?

Two not only poses a question about spiritual practice, it also refracts a conceptual issue. There is a premise that underlies One and Zero—namely, that all being is one, or at least part of God's oneness. That premise is what allows for God to be simultaneously outside and inside of us and thus accessible by way of meditation. The sixteenth-century Safed kabbalist, Moshe Cordovero, put it this way: "Do not say, 'This is a stone and not God.' Rather, all existence is God, and the stone is a thing pervaded by divinity."[4]

This concept has a psychological corollary. The idea, proposed by prominent mid-twentieth century psychoanalytic theorists, that in infancy we exist in a state of symbiotic oneness with mother only to individuate in the course of development suggests that we have access to a universal oneness because we ourselves emerged from it.[5] The problem with this theory is that it runs contrary to the findings of the late-twentieth-century empirical research on infancy. Extensive study has demonstrated that from the earliest stages of life we are psychologically differentiated (that is, not merged, or

---

[1] Daniel Goleman, *The Varieties of the Meditative Experience* (London: Rider & Company, 1978), xix.
[2] Norman Lamm, *The Religious Thought of Hasidism, Text and Commentary*, (Hoboken, NJ: Yeshiva University Press, 1999), 133–72.
[3] Jacob Immanuel Schochet, *Bitul Hayesh, Total Self Negation* (Kehot Publication Society), https://www.chabad.org/library/article_cdo/aid/115045/jewish/Bitul-Hayesh-Total-self-negation.htm.
[4] Daniel C. Matt, *The Essential Kabbalah, The Heart of Jewish Mysticism* (San Francisco, CA: Harper Collins, 1996), 24.
[5] This idea is most clearly represented in Margaret Mahler, Fred Pine, and Anni Bergman, *The Psychological Birth of the Human Infant, Symbiosis and Individuation* (New York: Basic Books, 1975), esp. 44–46.

one, with mother) and relational.[6] Two—our experience as a member of a dyad with mother—not One, is our psychological foundation.

Does not Two aspire to One, as in love? Could Two be merely derivative of a deeper oneness? The kabbalah articulates this possibility by way of the descending levels of the *sefirot*, or emanations, in which the highest, *Keter*, is associated with *'Ein Sof*, God as infinite and encompassing all reality, while the *Shekhinah* (or the emanation of *Malkhut*) at the lowest rung represents God manifest in the world, an Other with whom we can enter into relation.

Yet even if we can conceive of One and Two as coexistent or somehow continuous on a deeper spiritual plane, Two remains our psychological reality from birth, and the ramifications of this are far-reaching. In Two we have the potential for experiences profound enough to be called spiritual, starting from the sense of connection we feel in touching other minds. Two provides a context for our sense of existential awe, dread, and reverence, all of which demand an object separate from ourselves. And Two provides the ground for relationship—"covenant," in religious terms. Surely Two must involve a path to spiritual growth no less than Zero and One.

A quote from Psalm 16:8 adorns the ark of many a synagogue: "I shall set God before me—*lenegdi*—always." In contrast to modern Hebrew, in which *neged* means simply "across from" or "against," the biblical term also connotes something more mutual: a counterpart.[7] To say that I set God before me always is to describe a dyadic relation involving God's abiding presence and our receptive awareness. As a term for that relation, *lenegdi* is pregnant with potential pathways and meaning.

Being in Relation

In most life situations, observes Buber in *I and Thou*, the other, be it a person or any living thing, is "It" to us—an object of our expedient needs, a projection of our desires and fears, inevitably limited by what we know.[8] To the extent that we can be truly present, we penetrate this "itness" and discover "You." Relating subject to subject, not subject to object, we perceive the other as whole, as opposed to a function that is of interest to us, and as

---

[6] Daniel N. Stern, *The Interpersonal World of the Infant, A View from Psychoanalysis and Developmental Psychology* (New York: Basic Books, 1985), esp. 10 and 37–47. In the same book, Stern cites a private communication between Mahler and himself in which she acknowledges the then new research and adapts her theory to some extent in accordance with it (234–35).

[7] See, e.g., Genesis 2:18 and Psalm 18:23.

[8] Martin Buber, *I and Thou*, trans. Walter Kaufmann (Edinburgh: T &T Clark, 1970).

particular, as opposed to a character type or representative of a category. The effect is almost revelatory: "Every actual relationship to another being in the world is exclusive. Its You is freed and steps forth to confront us in its uniqueness. It fills the firmament—not as if there were nothing else, but everything else lives in *its* light."[9]

Buber's prose is evocative and at times elusive. But there is no mistaking the sense in which he uses his basic terms. He writes: "I require a You to become; becoming I, I say You."[10] Others have made a point that seems similar. For example, George Herbert Mead proposes that the sense of self is formed in childhood through contact with others.[11] But Buber's language signifies something different—namely, that we become transformed by the encounter with the other. In the I-You meeting we engage the other authentically (having escaped the inauthenticity of relating to another as "It"), and we experience a taste of freedom.[12] That transformation is what makes possible our "becoming I," and it is in that state that we can, in truth, "say You." Elsewhere Buber expresses a simpler version of the same idea when he says: "Egos appear by setting themselves apart from other egos. Persons appear by entering into relation to other persons."[13]

In part, Buber's *I and Thou* is an ethical model for how people should ideally regard one another. More essentially, though, it is a treatise on mysticism that guides us to discover God in the everyday world.[14] "In every sphere, in every relational act, through everything that becomes present to us, we gaze toward the train of the eternal You; in each we perceive a breath of it; in every You we address the eternal You."[15]

The encounter with "You" is mystical in the sense that the self-transcendence that comes from being truly present with the other is the same self-transcendence we bring to the I-You encounter with God. Buber fully acknowledges the unknowability of this realm but regards the I-You relation as the portal through which we can approach. "Of course, God is

---

[9] Buber, *I and Thou*, 126.

[10] Buber, *I and Thou*, 62.

[11] Israel Scheffler, *Four Pragmatists, A Critical Introduction to Peirce, James, Mead, and Dewey* (London: Routledge & Kegan Paul, 1974), 161–66.

[12] For Buber's assertion that the causality of the "It world" is suspended in the I-You encounter, allowing for the experience of freedom, see Buber, *I and Thou*, 100–102.

[13] Buber, *I and Thou*, 112.

[14] Samuel Hugo Bergmann, *Faith and Reason, Modern Jewish Thought*, trans. Alfred Jospe (New York: Schocken, 1963), 84–85 makes the point that, in finding the spiritual in the everyday, Buber was influenced by the Hasidic principle that all manner of profane existence can be raised up to holiness.

[15] Buber, *I and Thou*, 150.

the wholly other; but He is also the wholly same: the wholly present. Of course, He is the *mysterium tremendum* that appears and overwhelms; but He is also the mystery of the obvious that is closer to me than my own I."[16] Buber acknowledges that it is impossible to sustain the I-You relation for very long. Our lives demand of us to be "It." But the I-You relation is our spiritual center. It lives in us as a kind of latent knowledge, primordial and waiting, very much in the sense of keeping God always *lenegdi*.

It is perhaps surprising that Buber takes little interest in the psychological aspect of what we might call the I-You experience, what we undergo internally as a byproduct of the I-You encounter. He does discuss the passivity with which we initially encounter You and the activity we undertake to enter into the relation.[17] Aside from that, his focus is entirely on the spiritual dimension. But what if we set our sights on the personal experience of the I-You encounter and ask, in keeping with the analogy to the Zero and One meditative states: What does this expression of Two consist of as an internal state, and where does it lead?

Being Cognition

In his *Toward a Psychology of Being*, Abraham Maslow provides a summary of research findings concerning "peak experiences" – unique moments when we are overtaken by beauty in music, art, or nature; by the process of our own artistic creating; and by feelings of love.[18] What Maslow discovered was a set of characteristic perceptions that belong to what he terms "Being Cognition." They bear a remarkable similarity to Buber's I-You encounter.

The foremost similarity is that the object of interest tends to be seen as whole, detached from all expediency and purpose. The object is perceived with complete absorption, becoming all figure without ground. Repeated encounters result in the object of perception becoming richer rather than merely familiar. The object evokes fascination and caring. It is perceived as unique, as opposed to a member of a class; its worth seems intrinsic.[19]

The consequences of Being Cognition are profound. Perception heightens the observer's own sense of being even as it intensifies that of the observed object. It brings about a sense of wholeness. The value of the peak experience seems built in and need not be assigned to it. It may even elicit

---

[16] Buber, *I and Thou*, 127.
[17] Buber, *I and Thou*, 124–25.
[18] Abraham Maslow, *Toward a Psychology of Being* (New York: D. Van Nostrand, 1968).
[19] Maslow, *Toward a Psychology of Being*, 74–96.

feelings such as "I can die now," as an expression of our sense of complete fulfillment.

The parallels between Buber's I-You encounter and Maslow's being cognition are striking. Standing out is the concept of wholeness, applied both to how the object is perceived and how we, as subjects, experience ourselves; related to this is the complete absorption in the other. Another characteristic that Being Cognition shares with the I-You encounter is that volition has little part in it. Maslow's phrase "to be overtaken," whether by beauty or feelings of love, fits well with the passive nature of the initial encounter with You that Buber cites. We can prepare for it by letting go of our expectations, by being interested and in the moment—in short, being present. But we cannot make the moment happen.

There are notable elements in Maslow's findings on Being Cognition that diverge from Buber's I-You. One of these is that peak experiences include being overtaken by the beauty of a poem or painting; this stands in contrast to Buber's concept, which involves an encounter with an actual other. The divergence is more seeming than real, however, given what art accomplishes: to be overtaken by the effect of a work of art is to intuit the You of the artist and be moved. Indeed, the term "empathy" (*Einfühlung* in the original German) was minted in the nineteenth century to describe the process of feeling one's way into a work of art and thereby understanding it more deeply.[20]

A second divergent element between Buber and Maslow is more significant. Among the kinds of peak experiences that can lead to Being Cognition according to Maslow is creating, and not merely responding to, an other's artistic creation. This is a meaningful departure from Buber and does not have a counterpart in *I and Thou*. However, Maslow's research finding opens the door to a different aspect of the dyad, including the spiritual dyad. Implicit in I-You is not only what occurs when we connect with another but also the possibility of our being You to another's I. We want to have someone else connect to *us*. Whether in the creative act or in a loving relationship, as well as in our spiritual longings, we long to be heard and understood.

[20] Empathy, or *Einfühlung* in German, was a new term at the time, minted by the nineteenth-century German philosophers of aesthetics, Robert Vischer and Theodor Lipps, to describe the process of feeling oneself into a work of art. See Timothy Burns, "Theodor Lipps on the Concept of Einfühlung," in *Theodor Lipps (1851–1914). Psychologie, philosophie, esthétique*, edited by David Romand and Serge Tchougounnikov (Lausanne: Sdvig Academic Press, 2021). The term was translated and coined as an English word at the turn of the twentieth century by British psychologist Edward Titchener and first employed as a clinical term by psychiatrist Harry Stack Sullivan.

The surprising problem is that, much as we usually relate to others as It, so do we ourselves usually strive to be It instead of You to others. We manipulate our image to earn what we think will be the other's approval. We make of ourselves a commodity in other ways as well. After all, we are material beings, and material needs are satisfied in the "It world," as Buber called it.

Fragmentation and Wholeness

A key term that crops up in both Buber's description of the I-You encounter and Maslow's research on Being Cognition is the sense of wholeness. This is an ambiguous term that is best defined by contrast with its opposite: our usual state of fragmentation. We give expression to our fragmentation in everyday discourse when we say that "a part of me" feels such and such, and another part of me otherwise. Psychoanalysis began with Sigmund Freud's investigation into the ways that body and mind are set against each other, while later psychoanalytic theory has largely focused on the fragmentation arising from interpersonal relations, including the false selves we adopt for relational benefit. Pervasive guilt and shame are inherently fragmenting in that they make us objects of our own loathing. We feel our very sense of agency abandon us when, despite our intentions, we procrastinate and in other ways self-sabotage, or obsess over and doubt our own feelings and desires. And then of course there is trauma, which shatters our inner sense of continuity and cohesion. Our fragmentation is what makes change so hard. We resolve to alter some habit or to live up to a standard in line with our values, but the state we are in when we try to execute our resolution is not the same as the state we were in when we initially made the resolution. Maimonides teaches in *Hilkhot teshuvah*, the *Laws of Repentance*, that, in atoning for sin, the penitent is effectively committing to abstain from it going forward.[21] That would be an easy matter if we were whole beings. Our fragmented nature is what makes *teshuvah*, or penitence, such a profound and difficult process.

Psychological fragmentation is a byproduct of our usual I-It relational state. While it is a natural human condition, it is a painful one. The desire to be made whole is an aspiration to be released from suffering of our own inevitable making. In wholeness, we aspire to be truly You, not a fragmented It, to an other's I. In our everyday lives, we become You to an other's I by

---

[21] Maimonides, *Mishneh Torah, Sefer Madda* chs.1–2 (*Hilkhot teshuva*). Text can be found online at sefaria.org.

being genuinely ourselves with someone we trust. That person's acceptance and understanding can make our fragmented selves feel more whole.

There is another way to experience being You to an other's I. It may seem paradoxical at first, but it is through solitude. In contrast to loneliness, in solitude we feel the presence of an Other—the remembered voice of an old friend, the long-ago sense of our childhood home, the smell of the living forest. In solitude we can feel comforted, because we experience the subliminal effect of a comforting Other. The acute awareness of being alive and the feeling of gratitude that accompanies it are enhanced by solitude. It was in solitude that Moses first encountered God "at the end of the wilderness" (Exodus 3:1). And it is in solitude that we reach out to God much as the first Adam, our relationship unique and primal, even as we are one of billions.

Hitbodedut

Naḥman of Bratslav, a great grandson of the founder of Hasidism and one of its leading innovators, encouraged disciples to spend an hour each day talking to God in a state of *hitbodedut* ("solitude"), preferably in the midst of nature. In Reb Naḥman's case, this was the mountainous wood country that surrounded him in Ukraine at the turn of the nineteenth century. Such talk was to be formless; Reb Naḥman employed the Hebrew word *siḥah* with echoes of Genesis 24:63, where the patriarch Isaac is pictured alone in the fields engaging in silent speech. What distinguishes this *siḥah* from fixed communal prayer is that in *hitbodedut* the person speaks in the singular, not in the plural of typical Jewish prayer, and expresses personal, spontaneous, content. In turn, that personal aspect of *hitbodedut* is what furthers its purpose—to come "close to Him, to His worship in truth."[22]

Being our authentic, vulnerable, selves is of the essence in *hitbodedut*. Without it, we are It (not You), to God's I. Toward that end, Reb Naḥman emphasized that our talk should be in our mother tongue (as opposed to Hebrew, when Hebrew is not one's everyday language). The heart, explained Reb Naḥman, is "easily broken" in our native language. During *hitbodedut,* the person should express "all that is in his [or her] heart to say and speak before Him, blessed be He, both regret and repentance concerning the past, and beseeching." Reb Naḥman's focus on brokenness and regret, on the one hand, and penitence and coming near to God, on the other, involves a

---

[22] Nachman of Bratslav, *Likutei Moharan*, Part 2, Torah 25. Text can be found online at sefaria.org.

progression from fragmentation toward wholeness.

Reb Naḥman made no assumption that talking to God should come easy. The very prospect of seeking an intimate partner in the remote universe seems almost a paradox. Certainly, people who are afflicted often find it difficult to speak to anyone, let alone to God. Reb Naḥman knew well the challenge that grief and unjust suffering place on faith; the precariousness of Jewish existence was all too plain to him. Understanding such struggles, he wrote:

> And even if, on occasion, one's speech is blocked and the person cannot open his [or her] mouth to speak to Him, may He be blessed, nevertheless, this [effort] is itself very good. That is, the preparation in standing before Him, may He be blessed, and the person's desire and yearning to speak, even if unsuccessful, is very good. Such person might even attempt to speak about that itself—to cry out and beg before Him, may He be blessed, who has come to seem so distant that it is hard to speak, and to ask Him for compassion and mercy so that he [or she] may be able to open their mouth before Him.[23]

As moderns, addressing God in solitude rarely comes naturally, as it might have to great grandparents who poured out their hearts to "Gottenyu" (intimate and loving God), or to ancients who beseeched God to "heed the sound of my cry" (Psalm 5:3). On the other hand, a broad stream of clinical theory and research in psychology demonstrates that the sense of self is formed and maintained in dyadic relationships, both actual and internalized. It is our nature as humans to form internal representations and to experience the subliminal presence of an other. We are built for just the sort of dyadic relation that occurs in *hitbodedut*.

Two as our Psychological Foundation: Kohut and Stern

For Heinz Kohut, one of the twentieth century's foremost psychoanalytic theorists, the core drama at the heart of the psyche is not so much internal conflict but the integration and disintegration of the self.[24] He considered

---

[23] Nachman of Bratslav, *Likutei Moharan*, Part 2, Torah 25.
[24] Kohut's theoretical writings are notoriously abstruse. A good introduction to his thought is

the self per se to be beyond definition but knowable through its attributes—the subjective sense a person has of being continuous from an early age to the present, of being cohesive in spite of changing emotions and states, and being volitional. These manifestations of selfhood exist in nascent form from birth, Kohut theorized, but require a unique other, beginning with a parent, to transform them from potential to actual. The dyadic relation with that other evolves over the course of development and comes to include not only an actual person but also an internalization of the functions that such person provides. These functions, in turn, are the main subject of Kohut's investigations.

The most central of these functions is the mirror. For the infant, what the parent is mirroring is not only its feelings, but also its budding sense of joyful being, which Kohut thought of as healthy narcissism. With adequate mirroring, or encouraging, in infancy and early childhood, healthy narcissism becomes shaped into ordinary self-esteem, and the primitive mirroring needed by the infant graduates into the empathic responsiveness we require throughout our lifespan. That lifelong empathic function is supplied in part by actual empathic partners, but also by an internalized or subliminal empathic listener. It is an internalization that does not always go well. In light of that, Kohut summarized the essence of psychotherapeutic treatment as "the opening of a path of empathy" between the self and the self's internalized listener.[25]

Extensive empirical research into the precursors of subjective experience in infancy and early childhood, summarized in Daniel Stern's landmark 1985 *The Interpersonal World of the Child*, details the dyadic origins of the sense of self. In the 1970s and 1980s, when the research leading to Stern's book was conducted, the technology of frame-by-frame video analysis as a research tool was new—and eye opening. Exquisitely synchronized escalations and deescalations of affect exchanged between mother and infant were observed in multiple studies; their analysis led to a myriad of discoveries, which Stern systematized developmentally.[26] These research findings documented the way the infant uses and gradually adopts for itself the regulating effect of the parent's soothing. As the child matures, this regulation evolves from being biologically based to encompassing the regulation of mood that

---

Ernest S. Wolf, *Treating the Self, Elements of Clinical Self Psychology* (New York: Guilford, 1988).
[25] Heinz Kohut, *How Does Analysis Cure*, ed. Arnold Goldberg (Chicago: University of Chicago Press, 1984), 66.
[26] Stern, *Interpersonal World*, esp. 37–182.

comes from feeling understood. In a most essential way, much as Kohut had posited, our psychological life is formed as part of such a dyad, both actual and internalized, consisting of a subject expressing feeling and an other who empathizes (or falls short of doing so). The product of this dyadic function—the subliminal experience of feeling understood—continues to sustain us psychologically throughout life.

Lenegdi

The very same dyadic relation—of one who expresses feeling and an other who understands—lies at the heart of *hitbodedut* and is a key aspect of the I-You encounter. To keep God *lenegdi*, as our counterpart, is to grow that relation. When we do this, certain changes occur in our consciousness. Comparable to the equanimity and mindfulness brought about by meditation, in the I-You encounter we grow to be more present, and in both the I-You encounter and *hitbodedut* we feel more whole. Moreover, just as meditation may lead to goals of personal growth and spiritual insight, so, too, can keeping God *lenegdi* lead to such goals. Springing up from our empathy and sense of presence in the I-You encounter, and from feeling understood in *hitbodedut*, is compassion. In turn, expressing compassion for others increases our own sense of well-being and happiness.[27] But it also does more. Our tradition of sacred text teaches that living our lives with compassion brings us into harmony with God because the compassion we feel is rooted in God.

That tradition stems from the central theme that we are created in God's image (Genesis 1:27). Likewise, the biblical instruction, "be holy for I am holy" (Leviticus 19:2) conveys the idea that humankind is capable of emulating God's spiritual character. These verses do not specifically state anything about compassion, however. Conversely, there are biblical texts in which God is identified with compassion, but nothing is said about endowing humankind with this attribute. For example, there is the set of God's attributes made known to Moses: "The Lord, compassionate and gracious, long-suffering, abounding in love and truth" (Exodus 34:6 and Numbers 14:18; restated in Jonah 4:2 and Psalm 103:8). And there are verses stating that God expects our compassion, such as "Love your fellow as yourself" (Leviticus 19:18) and the repeated commandment to love the foreigner be-

---

[27] Emma Sepala, "The Compassionate Mind," *Association for Psychological Science* (April 30, 2013), https://www.psychologicalscience.org/observer/the-compassionate-mind.

cause of our experience being foreigners in Egypt (Exodus 22:30; Leviticus 19:34; Deuteronomy, 10:19). Yet, again, these texts do not directly link our compassion to God's. We come closer to that in Rashi's gloss on Deuteronomy 11:22, which interprets "walking in all His ways" to mean "just as He is compassionate, so, too, should you be compassionate."

In Hasidism we encounter a further elucidation of the link between God's compassion and our human compassion. According to the Hasidic reenvisioning of kabbalah, the Creator's emanations became immanent in human beings after the cataclysm of creation, forming an inner template that aligns, in human dimension, with that of God. This template includes a balance between the traits of compassion and judgment. As an extension of this concept, the compassion (as well as the exacting element of judgment) that is built into the psyche is first built into the universe. Rashi's interpretation, "just as He is compassionate, so, too, should you be compassionate," may be understood in this light as being founded on a potential in human nature that goes back to creation.

While Reb Naḥman included beseeching God in *hitbodedut*, he said nothing about expecting our prayers to be answered. Whether one's theology is that God's will determines all and that our prayers may be granted, or that events in the world are random, speaking to God comes naturally if we let it because the need to feel heard and understood is at our emotional center. We do not need to ask God for favors in order to engage God as our compassionate other. We are fragmented and call out "from the depths" (Psalm 130:1). In the process of feeling more whole, we also grow our own compassion.

The Spiritual as Two

The spiritual has always been understood, at least in part, as a bridging of the divide between self and other. From telepathy to empathy, from healing touch to prayer, the spiritual moment has been imagined as a form of making contact. In *I and Thou*, Buber put it this way:

> Spirit is not in the I, but between I and You. It is not like the blood that circulates in you, but like the air in which you breathe. Man lives in the spirit when he is able to respond to his You. He is able to do that when he enters into this relation with his whole being. It is solely by virtue of his

power to relate that man is able to live in the spirit.[28]

The idea that the spiritual bridges the divide between self and other raises a fundamental question about the access we have to other minds. How do we know we have made contact with the other, as opposed to merely imagining we have? It is an age-old question, but we cannot conceive of an I-You encounter, or of intuiting God on the basis of that encounter, without addressing it. We begin with the principle of René Descartes that body and mind are thoroughly distinct realms. A consequence of this principle is that other people's minds and feelings can only be inferred. The agency of knowing belongs to the mind, which has only indirect access to tangible knowledge and no direct access to other minds.

As recently as the first half of the twentieth century this Cartesian principle held such sway that it colored psychoanalysis at its origin. Freud viewed the psyche as beginning life in an insular state of hallucinatory wish-fulfillment, protected by a stimulus barrier, and only gradually forming an ego that achieves contact with social reality. Other people are "objects" of drives or of interest, and are "cathected" (invested with psychic energy) by the self-contained psyche.

A similar outlook was shared by the philosopher Edith Stein, who titled her 1916 doctoral thesis for Edmund Husserl, "On the Problem of Empathy."[29] The phenomenon of empathy, then a new concept, was considered problematic because, as Stein put the question: "Have the barriers separating one 'I' from another broken down, has the 'I' been freed from its monadic character?" Her conclusion: "Not entirely, I feel my joy and empathically comprehend the other's and see it as the same."[30] In other words, even such a seeming boundary breach as empathy does not violate the principle that different beings are separate and utterly secluded from each other. At the other extreme, philosophical monists such as Baruch Spinoza and Henri Bergson or the kabbalist Moshe Cordovero would probably not have been troubled by the phenomenon of empathy since they viewed all of life to be undivided.

---

[28] Buber, *I and Thou*, 89.
[29] Edith Stein, *On the Problem of Empathy*, trans. Waltraud Stein (Washington, D.C.: ICS Publications, 1989 [1916]). Stein is perhaps best known in Jewish circles as a German Jewish intellectual and proto-feminist who converted to Catholicism and became a nun, only to be considered a Jew by the Nazis and killed at Auschwitz. She was beatified and declared a saint by Pope John Paul II in 1987.
[30] Stein, *On the Problem of Empathy*, 17.

In between the self as insular and the self as continuous with all other selves is the term "connectedness," as used by Stern in discussing the infancy research literature. If we replace monism's term, "oneness," with "connectedness," we arrive at many of the same meanings. Connectedness implies contiguity, like oneness. On the other hand, it also implies that there are individual nodes—differentiated selves capable of connection. In "connectedness," as opposed to "oneness," there is still individuality and, hence, the consequences of individuality, including responsibility and ethics. Practically speaking, connectedness exists on a continuum, both as state and trait. As a state, we may feel in sync with an other, as if we were one; in contrast, we might feel detached. As a trait, we know people we consider empaths as well as people who are characterologically aloof.

What makes us connected? The answer brings us back to the empirical research on infancy. One of the key findings of this research is that the affectively attuned responses between mother and infant are "amodal"—that is, they do not rely on one sense modality; mother and infant are not merely mimicking one an other's facial expressions.[31] If that were the case, then empathy would be little more than a feedback loop between facial muscles and brain. On the contrary, various modes of expression are interchangeable. The infant's excited motor act might be matched by the mother's tone of voice, facial expression, or touch and responded to in turn by the infant in yet a different mode. Amodal perception demonstrates that what parent and infant respond to is meaning or intention. Of course, this does not refer to meaning in its mature, cognitive, sense. On the other hand, from earliest life, the infant is discerning variation in features such as intensity and rhythm that cross between modes of voice, facial expression, and body language. These features are precursors to feelings. To the adult interacting with the infant they are meaningful and form the basis of their response to the baby. From the earliest stage of life, the contact points of our connectedness are feelings, intentions, and meanings. Connectedness is all about understanding and being understood.

British pediatrician and psychoanalyst D. W. Winnicott posed the allusive question: Where is "the place we live" when we play or create? It is not inside us, in thought or dreaming, nor purely outside, in sheer behavior. We live, he posited, in an "intermediate zone" of meaning, language, and culture.[32] Infants find their way naturally enough to the intermediate zone, where

---

[31] Stern, *Interpersonal World*, 47–68 and 146–61.
[32] D. W. Winnicott, *Playing and Reality* (London: Tavistock, 1971), 95–110.

they learn their first words and play. But being able to continually function in an intermediate area using the cultural tools of the social group while feeling authentically oneself is not a given. In the extreme, in schizophrenia, inside and outside are confounded, and societal conventions can become incomprehensible. Winnicott theorized that transitional objects such as the infant's blanket or teddy bear are discovered by the baby as real objects in the world, yet simultaneously created, or endowed with the inner, affective sense of "mine." They serve as a bridge to that "place where we live"—between inside and outside, as cultural beings in an intermediate area.

Analogous to Winnicott's question about the place we live, we might ask the question: Where is the place from which we speak to God? We cannot hope to reach God in an impossibly remote, celestial abode, yet neither are we encountering God if our search is solely for a divine spark inside ourselves. The place from which we speak to God must, like Winnicott's intermediate area, be somehow in between—a "cleft in the rock" (Exodus 33:22), as it were—from which we address God as other using a shared language of meanings. In part, that shared language is the symbolism of religion, which acts like transitional objects endowed with both private and communal meanings. But it is also the everyday language of conversation. Throughout history, including the biblical era, people have addressed God with the same words they use to express themselves to their fellow human beings. Reb Naḥman could have framed *hitbodedut* as a mystical practice; instead he depicted it as talk from the heart in which any person can engage. Our connection to God is all about feeling heard and understood.

For spirit to be, as Buber put it, "not in the I, but between I and You" is to say that it is found in an intermediate zone of meaning, language, and culture, which are the contact points of our connectedness, and in the modes of gaze, voice, and touch through which we transmit meaning preverbally. Knowing other minds is not mysterious, but it does involve discovery. The "ah-ha!" of authentic encounter, the intuiting of another mind, is an experience of self-transcendence. That is when, in Buber's words, we "gaze towards the train of the Eternal You."

Lenegdi: Conclusions

To keep God *lenegdi*, as a counterpart, is to participate in a dyadic relationship. One component of that relationship is the intuition of God that stems from the I-You encounter, as described by Buber. A second component is

Mitchell M. Frank

the sense of closeness to God that comes from being You to God's I, as in Naḥman of Bratslav's discourse on *hitbodedut*, or solitude with God. In both the I-You encounter and *hitbodedut*, the essence of the dyad is the complementary relation between one who understands and another who is understood. That same complementary relation is at the heart of Kohut's psychoanalytic theory. Mental health throughout the lifespan, in his view, is built upon the subliminal sense of feeling understood, which is an internalized representation of early parent-child empathy.

Our psychological foundation is the dyad. The infancy research clarifies that we are never in a state of oneness or symbiotic merger with our mother or any early caregiver. The mystical goal of achieving oneness with God through meditation or states of ecstasy may fit a higher mystical concept, but it does not conform to any psychological reality we can actually know. On the other hand, the dyadic relationships known to us in infancy and childhood, out of which our sense of self is formed, serve as internal models for knowing another. To know another person (or an animal), we must bridge the gap between separate centers of awareness. From the gaze that is met to the metaphor that is created, we make contact. In doing so, we are Two, not One—in dyadic relation, not merged.

Applying Buber's terminology, we can be Two in an I-It relation, in which we regard the other as an object of our needs, or we can be Two in an I-You relation, in which we regard the other as a subject, not an object. When perceived as You, the other is a whole, unique, being, not a fragment. Similarly, when we are the other to our partner's I, we can present ourselves as It, and we often do. This is what occurs, for example, when we create a false self, an image that we convey to others and come to believe ourselves. Alternatively, we can be You—our authentic selves, vulnerabilities and all.

One of Buber's key messages in *I and Thou* is that the spiritual is not primarily inside us or remotely beyond us but between us. Winnicott described this sphere as "the place where we live," an "intermediate zone" that is neither inside, in thought or dreaming, nor outside, in sheer behavior. It is the zone in which the private and unformed finds expression, whether in poetry, prayer, or simply the careful listening of a friend. This place where we live, in which we understand and feel understood, is the space in which we grow as spiritual beings.

The I-You encounter and the experience of closeness to God in *hitbodedut* are not easy to come by. Our needs and desires naturally guide us to I-It relations. We tend to resist the vulnerability that contributes to a sense of intimacy with God in solitude. We are blocked by ego. Learning to hold God *lenegdi* often constitutes a breakthrough. In a way, it is a life project, with ebbs and flows. Expressed in it is the striving for self-integration and personal authenticity. Paradoxically, to the extent that we achieve these mature manifestations of selfhood, we grow not in self-centeredness but in compassion.

For the psalmist, God's compassion was a given. Less discernible was the human's merit in being its recipient: "I look at Your heavens, the work of Your fingers, the moon and stars which you have established—what then is man that You remember him, and humankind that You are mindful of?" (Psalm 8:4–5). The psalm answers its own question: "You have made him slightly less than the angels" (Psalm 8:6). Buber and Reb Naḥman would answer the question differently. The reason we matter stems not from some noble faculty with which people are endowed, but from the capacity humans possess for dyadic relation, for understanding and feeling understood. What is transcendent is the connection with another living being that we establish in the I-You moment. It is the intimacy with God that we feel, mere speck in the universe though we may be, in the solitude of the anonymous forest.

Dr. Mitchell M. Frank is a clinical psychologist. He lives with his family in Queens, New York, where he has a private practice in psychotherapy.

Yashan Noshan

From the Archives of Conservative Judaism

Letter from Jerusalem: The Yom Kippur War

Conservative Judaism 28:2, Winter 1974

Theodore Friedman

This letter, written a few months after the Yom Kippur War, is the modest contribution of one eye-witness to the recording of a moment in Jewish history fraught with the gravest implications for the future of Israel—the State and the people. On that unforgettable Yom Kippur, none of us could possibly have surmised that our collective fate hung in the balance.

None, except of course, the high command was aware of the depth of the Egyptian-Syrian penetration and the imminent perils it posed. During those first three days, Israeli military censorship saw to it that as soothing a face as possible be put on a desperate situation by our media. Once more, it was a case of *eyn baal haness makir benisso*. This time, the inexplicable saving wonder was that the Egyptians and Syrians, having once broken through the thinly-manned Israeli defenses, did not maintain their momentum. Instead of plunging ahead towards the heartland of Israel, they halted their advance long enough for Israeli forces to mobilize and rush to the front.

But of all this, we on the home front, were happily unaware. For us, Yom Kippur day dawned with skies as unclouded as our hearts and minds. True, there had been a newspaper item on the previous Thursday to the effect that Egyptian and Syrian troops had been noted massing on the borders. Such notices, however, were fairly regular occurrences and had heretofore proved nothing more than false alarms. That Yom Kippur morning, on my way to shul in Netanyah (where I was conducting services for the local Conservative congregation), the sight of three Phantoms flying north failed to recall the relatively small item in Thursday's paper. The sight merely evoked some astonishment that the Israeli Air Force would dispatch a routine flight on Yom Kippur. Those planes were just about the only machines in motion one could see that Yom Kippur morning in Netanyah or, for that matter, anywhere in Israel. From my seat in the synagogue which looked out upon one of Netanyah's main thoroughfares, not a car or taxi was to be seen all morning. The total quiet of Yom Kippur had descended on the town, as it had over all Israel.

At two in the afternoon—the fateful hour—as previously announced, our *musaf* service ended. There would be a three-quarter of an hour recess before *Minḥah*. As I left the synagogue with a few friends for a brief stroll, I noticed, to my amazement, clusters of people huddled around transistor radios as well as a sudden movement of traffic. (I knew, of course, that Israel's radio broadcasting goes off the air on Yom Kippur.) To my incredulous question about what had happened, I got the answer that at ten minutes of two, the Egyptians and Syrians had attacked in force.

Within minutes, a police patrol car went through the streets with its loudspeaker blaring, calling on the populace to turn on their radios. Taxis were soon racing through the town with hastily drawn signs in their windshields: *besheyrut tzevai*, in Army service. Their drivers were handing out mobilization orders. I saw several men receive them on the street. As they did, they went back into their homes, reappearing in a few minutes garbed in their army uniforms and carrying their guns. With a hasty farewell to their families, they were on their way to the predesignated assembly points to await the trucks or buses that would take them to their units at the front. One noticed a growing number of men in uniform going to the assembly points, most of them accompanied by a mother, a wife and, in some instances, their children. (Some wag remarked that it was the first time in history that Jewish women sent their menfolk off to war on an empty stomach.) To judge from the remarks I overheard, the mood was one of grim seriousness spiced by a supreme confidence as to the outcome of the war: "We'll finish them off in three days." That mood was to be echoed by both Dayan and Elazar in their speeches that evening on television.

A much diminished congregation reassembled for *Minḥah*. People were glued to their radios to catch the news, which was now being broadcast every fifteen minutes. (For the duration of the war, Kol Yisrael was to be on the air twenty-four hours a day, broadcasting news every hour on the hour.) By the beginning of *neilah*, the synagogue began to fill up. During the service, I noticed several women enter and whisper something to their respective husbands. The latter, thereupon, removed their *talleitim* and left. Obviously, their wives had brought the message that their husbands had received a call-up notice.

At 5:00 p.m., the *gabbai* informed me that we would have to vacate the building and remove all our paraphernalia by 6:00 p.m. The building—the local headquarters of the Gahal Party—would be taken over by the army at that time. I had planned to conclude *neilah* at 5:42 p.m. (strange, how such details remain starkly sketched in one's memory, as if the events of the afternoon were things one would never forget); however, the service was not destined to continue to that time. Precisely at 5:30 p.m., we had our first air raid alarm. I instructed the Cantor to proceed immediately to the *Shema*. We rose, blew the Shofar and with a lusty cry—*leshanah habaah beYerushalayim habenuyah*—the entire congregation, the men still wrapped in their *talleitim*, proceeded to the adjacent shelter. The tension was palpable. I asked the cantor to lead us in singing *kadsheynu*. The *kavanah* in the shelter, I suspect, was even more genuine than it had been in the synagogue. In about twenty minutes, the all clear sounded and we emerged to face the blackout that was to last for eighteen nights.

Sunday morning, after an 8:00 a.m. air raid alarm, I was driving back to my home in Jerusalem. The road was lined with soldiers on their way to army bases. Every ten or fifteen kilometers, I was stopping to pick them up or drop them off. Ordinarily, the parting greeting to a soldier to whom you have given a "tremp" is "kol tuv." Under the circumstances, I felt it singularly inappropriate. In a few hours, these boys would be under fire. So, as they left, I called after them, *shetachzor beshalom.*

My car radio informed me that the hospitals in Jerusalem were calling for drivers with cars. I made straight for Shaare Zedek. Yes, they could use me to transport hospital personnel to and from the hospital. Overnight, public transportation, including most taxis, had all but disappeared. The army had mobilized thousands of buses and drivers.

For the next two weeks, I lined up with my car at the tiny transportation office of the hospital and conveyed doctors, nurses and patients. I learned that at the outbreak of the war, the hospital had been cleared of all but critically sick patients in order to make room for the expected war casualties. The latter were not slow in arriving. In the courtyard that fronts the hospital, a squad of white-coated teenagers wearing kippot—volunteers from a Jerusalem yeshivah—awaited their arrival, ready to serve as stretcher bearers. Late Sunday afternoon, the first contingent arrived. To transport them from the Jerusalem airport, where they had been brought from the front by helicopter, commercial panel trucks had been pressed into service to supplement the few ambulances available.

Letter from Jerusalem: The Yom Kippur War

The casualties brought to Shaare Zedek were the relatively lightly wounded. Most of them were discharged after a week or so. According to Zahal regulations, they were entitled to some days of relaxation at the army rest home in Netanyah. Most of them refused to go and insisted instead on returning to their *chevrah* at the front line. One fellow—the story made the newspapers—had some surgery and in a few days was ambulatory. Anxious to return to the line, he put on a coat over his pajamas and walked out of the hospital. He had been wounded on the Golan and by hitchhiking managed to get back to where he had been stationed. To his dismay, he discovered that his unit had in the meantime been transferred to Sinai. Undaunted, he hitchhiked to Sinai and rejoined his unit.

Perhaps the following small incident reflects the spirit of Israel's essentially civilian soldiery. On the day after Yom Kippur, the police were suddenly flooded with reports of stolen cars. Investigation revealed that the cars had not been stolen but merely borrowed by men anxious to get to the front. The cars were found on the Golan and in Sinai, some of them with notes reading: "Excuse me, but there was no other means of transportation. Thanks for the use of your car."

With such spirit animating the army, it was no wonder that our civilian population responded in kind with an avalanche of volunteers. Within a few days, one could see the following sign on the main entrance to Hadassah: "Sorry, we can not use any more volunteers. Thanks." The story going the rounds was that one needed "protekziya" to get a volunteer job.

It was not, however, in service alone that the Yishuv responded with a tremendous outpouring. On the third day of the war, the government announced a Compulsory War Loan, beginning with seven per cent of one's monthly salary. Two days later, a Voluntary War Loan was launched. In my bank, I found that I had to stand in line to buy war bonds. I could not help but overhear the transactions of the two women ahead of me. One had come to buy a war bond for a hundred lirot; the other made a purchase for two hundred lirot. These people, and thousands like them, were obviously scraping the bottom of the barrel. As of this writing, upwards of five hundred million lirot has been raised by the Voluntary War Loan; this is in addition to the Compulsory Loan.

Life in blacked-out Jerusalem was far from normal. Virtually all men between the ages of eighteen and forty-five had disappeared from the streets. Suddenly, there was plenty of parking space in downtown Jerusalem. At nightfall, the streets were deserted. The few bus lines still operating stopped running shortly after dark. Restaurants, movies, concert and lecture halls were closed. If one had to go out at night, one walked with a searchlight in hand. Most of us stayed home in the evening to listen to the radio and watch television.

Between the hourly broadcast of the news, the radio treated us to a twenty-four hour flow of music. I now know the words of every Israeli hit song of the past ten years. If they had read Tanakh instead of playing popular music, I might conceivably know the Bible by heart, for like most Israelis, I became a radio addict and would jump out of bed at three or four in the morning to catch the news. Aside from remarkable reportage from the front, the television also treated us to impromptu entertainment.

For two hours every night, the radio served as the means of communication for many families to their menfolk at the front. The messages ran something like this: "Chayim X: Your mother has returned from the hospital and is recuperating nicely after her operation." "Yosef Y: Your wife had a baby boy. Weight three kilos. Mother and child doing well. Mazal Tov." "David Z: Where did you leave the keys to the car?"

Communication between the front lines and the home front was two-way. Within forty-eight hours of the outbreak of war, mobile phones were installed at the front and soldiers were telephoning home to inform their families that all was well. However, thousands of Israeli families have yet to acquire telephones. Spontaneously, business firms and organizations inserted ads in the newspapers giving their phone numbers and informing the soldiers at the front that they could call any hour of the day or night and their message would be relayed to their families by messenger. In this bizarre fashion, the old irrefragable Jewish value of strong family ties surfaced and found expression. The war transformed us from a people notorious for its lack of civility into one *mishpachah*, deeply concerned for one another and touchingly eager to help one another.

The early days of the war found Jerusalem rife with rumors as to the number of casualties. The first official announcement, on the eighth day of the war, came as a thunderclap. Anxiety and tension gave way to collective grief as we learned whose son or husband would not be coming back. In the States, the government informs families of fallen soldiers by telegram: "The Secretary of Defense deeply regrets," etc. In Israel, the fearful news is brought by volunteer committees of at least three people. Usually, the committee includes a doctor or psychologist who, of course, tries to cushion the blow. The committee does more than inform the family. It stays as long as necessary. Later, some member of the committee returns for the *shivah*.

The mood at this moment? Concern, anxiety, depression. But there is something else. And on that something else our whole future may hinge. Nothing expresses it better than a small item in the paper. The senior classes of the high schools of the *kibbutzim* have presented an appeal and a petition to the Minister of Education requesting that their studies be accelerated so that the current school year be terminated by this coming Pesach. "In the present situation," the students write in their appeal, "we cannot go on with business as usual as if nothing has happened or is happening. We are all anxious to enter the army as soon as possible or perform some other service in these days of national emergency."

Can such a people be defeated?

Rabbi Theodore Friedman (1908-1992) was a congregational rabbi from 1931 to 1954 and Rabbi Emeritus of Congregation Beth El of South Orange, New Jersey from 1954-1971. He served as president of the Rabbinical Assembly (1962-1964), Chairman of the Committee on Jewish Law and Standards (1951-1954), and, after making Aliyah, as first chairman of the Israel RA's Va'ad Halakhah. Rabbi Friedman held a Ph.D. from Columbia University and taught on the faculties of the Jewish Theological Seminary, The Schechter Institute of Jewish Studies, and the Seminario rabinico latinoamericano named for his son-in-law, Marshall T. Meyer. Rabbi Friedman served on the editorial board of this journal's precursor, Conservative Judaism.

Weaving Prayer: An Analytical and Spiritual Commentary on the Siddur, by Jeffrey Hoffman. Ben Yehuda Press, 2024

Reviewed by Sam Levine

The *siddur*, the Jewish prayerbook, has inspired Jews for as long as it has existed. The prayers of the *siddur* express the yearnings, aspirations, and tribulations of the Jewish people and articulate our relationship to God through words of praise, gratitude, faith, supplication, and confession.

In our age, however—particularly, but not exclusively, in the liberal denominations—two impediments exist that challenge the modern contemplative reader's ability to appreciate and derive meaning from the words of the *siddur*. The first is a conception of God as a binary choice, what Arthur Green in his new commentary on the *siddur*, *Well of Living Insight: Comments on the Siddur* (2023), calls "the simplistic either/or of personified theism versus atheism ('do you believe in God, the old fellow in the sky, or not?')." The second is the difficulty that the modern reader has in relating to the prayers of the *siddur* and the concept of God they express. The vast majority of the material in the traditional *siddur* is centuries, if not millenia, old, and as such expresses ideas and beliefs about God that can feel antiquated. As a consequence,

many people simply turn off to organized prayer and avoid statutory communal prayer experiences, thereby robbing themselves of the profound rewards that can be gained by engaging with the *siddur*.

Enter Jeffrey Hoffman's invaluable new book, *Weaving Prayer: An Analytical and Spiritual Commentary on the Siddur*. This companion to the prayerbook addresses both of these impediments and brings an entirely fresh and much-needed evaluation of the *siddur* that speaks to the modern worshipper and would-be worshipper. The book systematically goes through the *siddur*, offering scholarly analyses of the daily, Shabbat, and festival prayers that draw on Hoffman's extensive knowledge and research as a liturgist. His analytical commentaries, while academically rigorous, are accessible, and they reflect the masterful teaching and communicating skills that I experienced as Hoffman's student. Utilizing a vast array of sources, both traditional and academic, he situates the *tefillot* (prayers) in their historical context, offering innovative, well-reasoned insights into their origins and development. Additionally, he provides thorough literary analyses of the prayers, treating them as the poetic formulations that they are. The extensive notes (helpfully presented at the bottom of each page) will appeal to those wanting to go even deeper.

The analytical commentary alone would make *Weaving Prayer* a valuable addition to any library. But what makes it *invaluable* are the spiritual commentaries. In these, Hoffman unpretentiously faces the impediments mentioned above with intellectual honesty and a profound respect for the reader. For each *tefillah*, Hoffman suggests at least one alternative reading that speaks to a modern spiritual sensibility, opening up new understandings of prayers that never resonated or had grown stale. In the first blessing of the *Amidah*, to cite but one example, Hoffman suggests that invoking our patriarchs, Abraham, Isaac, and Jacob—our fellow clan members—creates "a personal and direct connection with God at the very beginning of this central prayer" by reminding worshippers that their own family has "worshipped this God for hundreds of generations."

The spiritual commentaries guide the reader to new approaches to the prayers. But, in a larger sense, they demand that readers reconsider their own relationship to *tefillah* in general. In the spiritual commentary on *Pesuqei dezimra*, Hoffman lays out this spiritual thesis: "We all benefit when we try to attune ourselves to the simplest, most direct question to be asked of any prayer or prayer service; in what way does this, or could this, connect me to God, to the transcendent? And to the extent

that it does not serve this goal, we can ask ourselves what we can do to improve our spiritual experience with this prayer or prayer service."

To this end, Hoffman is unafraid to confront controversial aspects of our liturgy. In discussing "the Chosen People idea" as expressed in the festival prayer *Attah veḥartanu*, Hoffman writes, "scholarly integrity...requires that I express what the blessing actually says as opposed to what we might wish it to say." Rather than sanitizing or offering apologias for difficult passages like those that express hostility or vilify "the non-Jewish Other," he faces them head-on, unapologetically, confessing his own discomfort with them and at times offering helpful takeaways. As Hoffman himself says in his commentary to *Birkat haminim* ("Blessing of the Sectarians") in the *Amidah*, "the only way to progress toward religious pluralism is to forthrightly identify those portions of our own tradition that expressed intolerance toward other religious outlooks. Only then can Jews request with integrity that other religions honestly come to grips with teachings in their own traditions that vilify Judaism." Offering an alternative, divergent (and lovely) understanding of that particular blessing (based on a Hasidic teaching) in an attempt to grapple with his discomfort, Hoffman boldly asserts that "channeling the words of this blessing...may be a step toward repairing and healing [it]."

The book's pluralistic approach, which Hoffman also discusses in the introduction, is another unique feature. Hoffman draws upon *siddurim* (prayerbooks) from all the major denominations, commenting on innovations from those movements that expand our understanding and appreciation of the liturgy.

Hoffman ends the book in an unexpected manner with a short story that he composed. "A Medieval Kabbalist on the Upper West Side" creatively and charmingly fleshes out the concept of God that he articulated in his introduction to the book. The story presents the reader with an image of God that is *not* "the old fellow in the sky" as it unlocks much of the spiritual commentary in the book and highlights the overall courageousness of *Weaving Prayer*.

The overriding aim and intent of this brave and inspiring book is to offer the worshipper ways to *experience* the prayer and the prayer service in a deep, engaged, and meaningful manner. If, at times, this comes at the expense of normative performance, then so be it. The object is connection and communion with the divine through prayer. This willingness to stray from a strictly traditional presentation of the liturgy and lay out a much broader vision of Jewish prayer is what makes *Weaving Prayer* such a refreshing

and essential contribution to the library of books on Jewish liturgy.

Sam Levine serves as rabbi and cantor of the East Midwood Jewish Center in Brooklyn, New York. He is a graduate of the Academy for Jewish Religion rabbinical program and of the H. L. Miller Cantorial School at the Jewish Theological Seminary.

The Accusation: Blood Libel in an American Town, by Edward Berenson. W. W. Norton, 2019.

Reviewed by Jeff Wechselblatt

On Saturday, September 22, 1928, the chief of police in Massena, New York sounded the town's fire horn. Barbara Griffiths, the four-year-old daughter of Dave and Marion Griffiths, had disappeared into the woods of Massena, a town of ten thousand residents that borders Canada. Within hours, a search party of hundreds began surveying the woods, looking for the little girl. As the search for Barbara continued, an unknown "someone" started a rumor that the town's Jews kidnapped and murdered Barbara to harvest her blood for ritual use on the Yom Kippur holiday that was to begin at sundown the next day. Massena was home to approximately twenty Jewish families, including the family of Edward Berenson.

The horrible accusation quickly took hold and was adopted even by Massena's mayor, W. Gilbert Hawes, who authorized Corporal H. M. (Mickey) McCann, the New York state trooper leading the effort to find Barbara, to begin an investigation into ritual murder. With Hawes's blessing, McCann interviewed two Jewish residents and even summoned Rabbi Berel Berenglass, Massena's rabbi, to the town hall for questioning, where, after wading through a menacing crowd of some three to four hundred people, he was asked if "[his] people are offering human sacrifices on a holiday" or if they use human blood (33–34). The rabbi, expressing what the reader is likely feeling as the book unfolds, replied that he was "dreadfully surprised to hear such a foolish, ridiculous and contemptible question from an officer in the United States of America."

The Jews of Massena began to gather for Yom Kippur services that afternoon, fearing the worst. What would happen if Barbara never returned? Would they be accused of murder? Would there be a pogrom in New York? This threat of violence motivated the president of the local synagogue to phone prominent Jewish leaders in New York City for assistance.

And then it was over. At 4:30 on Sunday afternoon, Just twenty-four hours after her disappearance, Barbara emerged from the woods unharmed, spotted by two teenage girls in a field a mile from home. She had lost her way and fell asleep in the tall grass. She was reunited with her overjoyed parents. Dorothy took Barbara and her sister to New York City to escape the charged atmosphere in Massena. A short story about Barbara's disappearance and return was written in the local *Massena Observer*, with no mention of the blood libel. If the Massena press felt the affair resolved, the national media did not; the national press gave "elaborate" coverage to the story. "By early October 1928, the Massena blood libel had been transformed from a strange local event to a huge national scandal."

In *The Accusation: Blood Libel in an American Town*, Berenson masterfully retells this story. A professor of history at New York University and a son of Massena, he first heard of this story from his grandparents, one of Massena's twenty resident Jewish families in 1928. The book is engaging and interesting, and I found it difficult to stop reading once I started.

Berenson not only tells the events of that fall in 1928, he also travels far beyond this local story, linking the Massena incident to larger historical forces. He traces the history of the blood libel from medieval England to modern Europe, showing how this ancient slander reappears in different historical contexts, almost as part of the collective unconscious of gentile Europeans. Berenson provides a history of antisemitism and its development from religious persecution into racial hatred. I found it horrifying to read this pre-Holocaust history, as we know the unspeakable conclusion of this evolution.

His account of Henry Ford's antisemitism and the nativism that surrounded the 1928 election sadly resonated. Describing Ford and his demagoguery, Berenson writes: "[h]e distrusted elites, urbanites, and intellectuals and claimed to value folk wisdom over book learning, his own hunches over what passed for scientific truth" (144). These words can be written about any number of today's politicians. Berenson quotes a Democratic politician who claimed that the greatest threat to the republic is "'the threatened and complete control of government and society by the body of ignorance, prejudice and superstition' embedded in [Herbert] Hoover's Republican Party."

My experience of Berenson's book would have been different had I closed the pages for a final time on October 6, 2023. Reading it after the events of October 7 had particular resonance. I am neither a historian, a sociologist, or an anthropologist, so I can only speak of my personal experience, but the book made me realize my own fear of violence against Jews and the precariousness of our sense of acceptance in the broader culture. I have never knowingly experienced antisemitism, yet, like the Jews of Massena (who were much closer in time to the pogroms they feared), I felt that violence was a real and present danger. I was surprised by my own feeling of vulnerability.

The blood libel also seems alive in some of the dialogue and protest around the war in Gaza. Hamas's false accusation that Israeli forces killed hundreds of Palestinian civilians while bombing a Gazan hospital was instantly reported as fact by the international media, including the *New York Times* and the *Wall Street Journal*. These false accusations of intentional killing of innocents by Jews had real consequences. I have seen placards showing Bibi, wearing a Hitler mustache, devouring a Palestinian child. The world seems all too eager to accept that the IDF is prosecuting this war with a bloodlust. Berenson's description of the blood libel and its reappearance in different contexts felt all too relevant.

Jeff Wechselblatt is a lawyer in private practice who lives in the Bronx with his wife and their four children. He has studied at Yeshivat Hakotel and at the Pardes Institute of Jewish Studies. Jeff is an active member of the Conservative Synagogue Adath Israel Riverdale (CSAIR) in the Bronx.

Recent books from *Ben Yehuda Press*

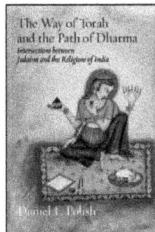

The Way of Torah and the Path of Dharma: Intersections between Judaism and the Religions of India by Rabbi Daniel Polish. "A whirlwind religious tourist visit to the diversity of Indian religions: Sikh, Jain, Buddhist, and Hindu, led by an experienced congregational rabbi with much experience in interfaith and in teaching world religions." —Rabbi Alan Brill, author of *Rabbi on the Ganges: A Jewish Hindu-Encounter*

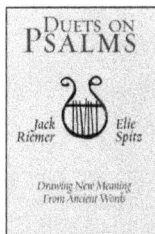

Duets on Psalms: Drawing New Meaning from Ancient Words by Rabbis Elie Spitz & Jack Riemer. "Two of Judaism's most inspirational teachers offer a lifetime of insights on the Bible's most inspired book." — Rabbi Joseph Telushkin, author of *Jewish Literacy*. "This illuminating work is a literary journey filled with faith, wisdom, hope, healing, meaning and inspiration." —Rabbi Naomi Levy, author of *Einstein and the Rabbi*

Weaving Prayer: An Analytical and Spiritual Commentary on the Jewish Prayer Book by Rabbi Jeffrey Hoffman. "This engaging and erudite volume transforms the prayer experience. Not only is it of considerable intellectual interest to learn the history of prayers—how, when, and why they were composed—but this new knowledge will significantly help a person pray with intention (*kavvanah*). I plan to keep this volume right next to my siddur." —Rabbi Judith Hauptman, author of *Rereading the Rabbis: A Woman's Voice*

Renew Our Hearts: A Siddur for Shabbat Day edited by Rabbi Rachel Barenblat. From the creator of *The Velveteen Rabbi's Haggadah*, a new siddur for the day of Shabbat. *Renew Our Hearts* balances tradition with innovation, featuring liturgy for morning (*Shacharit* and a renewing approach to *Musaf*), the afternoon (*Mincha*), and evening (*Ma'ariv* and *Havdalah*), along with curated works of poetry, art and new liturgies from across the breadth of Jewish spiritual life. Every word of Hebrew is paired with transliteration and with clear, pray-able English translation.

Forty Arguments for the Sake of Heaven: Why the Most Vital Controversies in Jewish Intellectual History Still Matter by Rabbi Shmuly Yanklowitz. Hillel vs. Shammai, Ayn Rand vs. Karl Marx, Tamar Ross vs. Judith Plaskow... but also Abraham vs. God, and God vs. the angels! Movements debate each other: Reform versus Orthodoxy, one- two- and zero-state solutions to the Israeli-Palestinian conflict, gun rights versus gun control in the United States. Rabbi Yanklowitz presents difficult and often heated disagreements with fairness and empathy, helping us consider our own truths in a pluralistic Jewish landscape.

Put Your Money Where Your Soul Is: Jewish Wisdom to Transform Your Investments for Good by Rabbi Jacob Siegel. "An intellectual delight. It offers a cornucopia of good ideas, institutions, and advisers. These can ease the transition for institutions and individuals from pure profit nature investing to deploying one's capital to repair the world, lift up the poor, and aid the needy and vulnerable. The sources alone—ranging from the Bible, Talmud, and codes to contemporary economics and sophisticated financial reporting—are worth the price of admission." —Rabbi Irving "Yitz" Greenberg

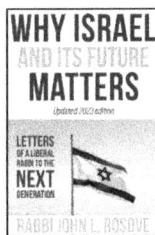

Why Israel (and its Future) Matters: Letters of a Liberal Rabbi to the Next Generation by Rabbi John Rosove. Presented in the form of a series of letters to his children, Rabbi Rosove makes the case for Israel — and for liberal American Jewish engagement with the Jewish state. "A must-read!" —Isaac Herzog, President of Israel.

www.ingramcontent.com/pod-product-compliance
Lightning Source LLC
Chambersburg PA
CBHW062108080426
42734CB00012B/2794